IELTS PREP
ORANGE **BOOK**

雅思橙皮密卷

真题解密+机考模拟

雅思哥学术研发中心 / 编著

机械工业出版社
CHINA MACHINE PRESS

本书是雅思官方 IDP 战略合作伙伴"雅思哥"重磅推出的七彩密卷系列之一，由雅思哥学术研发中心与雅思前考官及资深外教精心编写，结合了数百万雅思考生的考试经验，高度符合近年雅思考试的出题趋势。全书包含 4 套完整的全真雅思模拟试题、参考答案和详细解析，内容具有以下特点：

- 精准还原雅思考试：所有题目均根据近年高复考率的雅思考试真题研发，在考点、题型、编排上与真实的雅思考试完全一致。

- 紧跟考试新趋势：在难度和题型等方面紧跟出题趋势，合理增加相应题型的内容比例。

- 配有详细解析辅导：阅读部分解析以题型为单位进行归类，清晰呈现了审题、定位、分析、判断并得出答案的全过程；写作部分提供了可参考的写作思路，帮助考生触类旁通；口语部分配有参考答案、亮点词汇、固定搭配和俗语，考生可以在积累口语素材的同时，学到高分表达。

- 配有专业听力录音：听力音频均由英国、美国以及澳大利亚专业人士录制，语速和口音严格依照最新雅思考试听力音频执行标准。

相信通过对本书的学习，考生一定能取得理想成绩！

图书在版编目（CIP）数据

雅思橙皮密卷：真题解密＋机考模拟／雅思哥学术
研发中心编著. —北京：机械工业出版社，2020.8
　ISBN 978 - 7 - 111 - 66407 - 9

　Ⅰ.①雅…　Ⅱ.①雅…　Ⅲ.①IELTS -习题集
Ⅳ.①H310.41-44

中国版本图书馆 CIP 数据核字（2020）第 160673 号

机械工业出版社（北京市百万庄大街 22 号　邮政编码100037）
策划编辑：孟玉琴　田　旭　于　雷　　责任编辑：孟玉琴　田　旭　于　雷　徐春涛
版式设计：张文贵　　　　　　　　　　责任校对：裴春明
责任印制：孙　炜
保定市中画美凯印刷有限公司印刷
2020 年 9 月第 1 版·第 1 次印刷
184mm×260mm·15.75 印张·387 千字
00 001 - 10 000 册
标准书号：ISBN 978 - 7 - 111 - 66407 - 9
定价：42.00 元

电话服务　　　　　　　　　　网络服务
客服电话：010 - 88361066　　机 工 官 网：www.cmpbook.com
　　　　　010 - 88379833　　机 工 官 博：weibo.com/cmp1952
　　　　　010 - 68326294　　金 书 网：www.golden-book.com
封底无防伪标均为盗版　　机工教育服务网：www.cmpedu.com

前言
Preface

　　本书是雅思官方 IDP 战略合作伙伴 "雅思哥" 重磅推出的七彩密卷系列新作，由雅思哥学术研发中心与雅思前考官及资深外教精心编写，结合了数百万雅思考生的考试经验，高度符合近年雅思考试的出题趋势。本书包含 4 套完整的全真雅思模拟试题、参考答案和详细解析，内容具有以下特点：

精准还原雅思考试

　　本书中试题部分的所有题目均根据近年高复考率的雅思考试真题研发，在考点、题型、编排上与真实的雅思考试完全一致。

紧跟考试新趋势

　　难度方面，本书试题的整体难度符合近年雅思考试难度变化的趋势；题型方面，以阅读为例，本书结合雅思阅读中选择题和配对题比例增加的趋势，合理增加了相应的内容比例，紧跟出题趋势。通过使用本书，考生可以对目前雅思考试的出题难度和题型有更深刻的理解，从而更高效地备考。另外，对雅思考试的基本结构和特点有一定了解并想进一步提升能力的考生，本书将是进阶必备书籍。

配有详细解析辅导

　　本书的另一大亮点在于详细的试题解析。在阅读部分，答案解析以题型为单位进行归类，每个小题的思路解析清晰地呈现了如何审题、定位、分析、判断并得出答案的过程，以帮助考生全方位理解出题点并掌握解题技巧；在写作部分，除了雅思前考官对范文的评分，还突出了范文中考生可以借鉴的优秀表达，并针对每个题目提供了可参考的写作思路，帮助考生触类旁通，学会写作中如何快速形成写作思路；在口语部分，参考答案配有高分表达，如亮点词汇、固定搭配和俗语，并对这些表达进行了释义，考生可以在积累口语素材的同时，学到高分表达。

配有专业听力录音

　　4 套题目的听力音频均由英国、美国以及澳大利亚专业人士录制，语速和口音严格依照最新雅思考试听力音频执行的标准。考生通过练习，可提高对于主流英语口音的辨识度，并适应考试中的听力音频语速。

　　相信通过对本书的学习，考生一定能取得理想成绩！

雅思哥学术研发中心

目 录
Contents

前言

第一部分　试　卷

Test 1 ·········· 003　　Test 3 ·········· 055

Test 2 ·········· 029　　Test 4 ·········· 076

第二部分　解　析

Test 1　　// 103

Listening ·········· 104

Reading ·········· 116

Writing ·········· 129

Speaking ·········· 133

Test 3　　// 173

Listening ·········· 174

Reading ·········· 187

Writing ·········· 199

Speaking ·········· 203

Test 2　　// 139

Listening ·········· 140

Reading ·········· 152

Writing ·········· 164

Speaking ·········· 168

Test 4　　// 208

Listening ·········· 209

Reading ·········· 223

Writing ·········· 237

Speaking ·········· 240

附录　Sample answer sheets ·········· 245

IELTS PREP
ORANGE
BOOK

第一部分
试　卷

第一部分

基础

Test 1

PART 1   *Questions 1–10*

Questions 1–5

Complete the notes below.

Write **ONE WORD AND/OR A NUMBER** *for each answer.*

ECO-FARM

The farm is a member of the Northern Hotel Group.

Personal information:

- Name: Helen **1** ....

- E-mail address (work): helen123@ **2** .... com

- Home address: **3** .... Road, Sheffield

Source of information: **4** ....

Membership number: **5** ....

Questions 6–10

Complete the table below.

*Write **ONE WORD ONLY** for each answer.*

	Recommendations	**Customer preferences**
Accommodation type	lodges	a **6**.............................
Accommodation location	lakeside	near the farm or in the **7**.............................
Food	a wide range of food	meat, seafood and **8**............................. food
Transport	train or **9**.............................	ferry and van
Courses	flower planting course	active courses (e. g. a **10**............................. course)

PART 2   *Questions 11–20*

Questions 11–15

*Choose the correct letter, **A, B** or **C**.*

UK Driving Licence

11   What is the basic requirement for applying for a UK driving licence?

   A   a medical report

   B   a valid licence from another country

   C   current residency in the UK

12   What is true about the translation of original licences?

   A   Applicants need to go to a recognised organisation.

   B   It is not always necessary for foreigners when applying for a UK licence.

   C   Applicants need to pay an extra fee for translation services.

13   When applying for a UK licence, which type of photos will NOT be approved?

   A   photos in which the applicant is wearing glasses

   B   photos with a cream background

   C   photos that are undersized

14   What does the speaker think of the licence checking service?

   A   The process is too slow.

   B   The application form is confusing.

   C   Some of the steps are unnecessary.

15   What does the speaker recommend about making an application?

   A   choosing a quiet location

   B   visiting the nearest branch

   C   completing the forms online

Questions 16–20

What is the current feature of traffic management in each of the following cities?

*Choose **FIVE** answers from the box and write the correct letter, **A–H**, next to Questions 16–20.*

Features

A   good signage

B   multiple access roads

C   police control points

D   ring roads

E   one-way streets

F   effective traffic lights

G   additional lanes

H   pedestrianised areas

Cities

16   London   ....

17   Edinburgh   ....

18   Cardiff   ....

19   Manchester   ....

20   Oxford   ....

PART 3   *Questions 21–30*

Questions 21–25

*Choose the correct letter, **A**, **B** or **C**.*

Project on Classroom Management

21 Joy wants to finish this assignment soon because

  A there is a lot to do and the assignment will affect her final grade.

  B they have another assignment to do and there isn't much time.

  C they have to put their findings into practice before the semester ends.

22 Why does Tim want to ignore the theory chapter in their textbook?

  A The theory is too complex to be of practical help.

  B The focus of their project differs from the topic in the book.

  C There is insufficient time to read the entire chapter.

23 Joy thinks that on the discussion board students should post

  A responses to materials they have studied.

  B suggestions on what books they think would be useful.

  C new areas of research that need to be investigated.

24   What does Tim want to discuss?

  A the function of a teacher

  B the role of individual learner

  C teacher-student dynamics

25 Joy and Tim decide not to interview the teachers because

  A the teachers are too busy.

  B the result will be marked by the teachers.

  C interviewing students would be more productive.

Questions 26–30

What comment do Tim and Joy make about each of the following factors involved in successful learning outcomes?

*Choose **FIVE** answers from the box and write the correct letter, **A–G**, next to Questions 26–30.*

Comments

A   It needs funding.

B   It is necessary for progress.

C   It needs better supervision.

D   It is a basic requirement.

E   It should be optional.

F   It saves time.

G   It is the key to success.

Factors

26   classroom management   ....

27   feedback   ....

28   lesson planning   ....

29   individual tutoring   ....

30   access to technology   ....

PART 4   Questions 31–40

Complete the notes below.

Write ONE WORD AND/OR A NUMBER for each answer.

Fairy Terns

Conditions:

* Nests are built alongside coastlines and **31** .... where they can be camouflaged.
* Populations are now rising, but in 1983 there were only **32** .... breeding pairs.
* Low numbers and unstable habitats make it difficult to **33** .... population.

Reasons for declining tern populations:

* **Human activity:** Housing developments mean beaches are used more often. Increased coastal **34** .... means that more animals trample nests.
* **Wildlife:** Adult birds are rarely at risk, but predators target the **35** ....
* **Environment:** Nests are in vulnerable locations and are at risk of destruction by **36** ....

Protection measures include:

* securing individual nests with a **37** .... caring for them all day.
* introducing **38** .... to prevent humans from entering nesting areas.
* tagging individual chicks with **39** .... bands to monitor activity.
* hand-rearing abandoned chicks until they can be released.
* captive breeding programs, although these need more research.
* raising awareness through the **40** ....

READING PASSAGE 1

You should spend about 20 minutes on **Questions 1–13**, *which are based on Reading Passage 1 below.*

World Ecotourism in Developing Countries

A   According to the Ecotourism Society, ecotourism can be defined as traveling through nature in a manner that promotes environmental conservation and enhances the livelihoods of the citizens. Ecotourism is regarded as a favorable way of improving and enriching tourism standards, as this style of tourism honours the locals and their natural heritage. Ecotourism also conforms to the population thresholds each heritage and natural site can handle.

B   It is palpable that Cuba is an ecotourism destination. It has breathtaking ecological water bodies, reserves, beaches, and landscapes in rural areas. In addition to this, the enhanced road infrastructure and communication networks promote ecotourism. Among the Caribbean Nations, Cuba comes second as a popular destination for tourists.

Ecotourism enhances the ability of the local and foreign tourists to learn in awareness concerning the environment. Even better ecotourism inspires the willingness of people to act on environmental conservation. Furthermore, ecotourism is closely associated with the advancement of peace, which is achieved by increasing cultural exchange and educational opportunities. The health and safety of tourists are assured.

Former Cuban President and Fidel Castro's brother, Raul Castro, introduced an initiative aimed at salvaging an important Cuban practice. He reinvigorated the use of herbal medicines in the healthcare system. An ecotourism community school in Las Terrazas imparts herbal healthcare knowledge to the students by teaching them the application and the cultivation of herbal medicine which is used in creams, tinctures, teas, and ointments.

Ecotourism has become a useful tool in the elimination of poverty in Cuba. It injects economic wealth and creates jobs for the locals. The efforts by Raul Castro have increased job opportunities for the residents in the ecotourism communities as well as Cuban ecotourism in general.

C   South America is most probably the region that demonstrates the negative aspects of ecotourism. Histoplasma Capsulatum happens to be a type of dimorphic fungus associated with the most prevalent endemic fungal infection in the United States. The dimorphic fungus is linked with exposure to bird or bat dung. In recent times, epidemics have become a common health occurrence for travellers returning from South and Central America. Travellers who engage in adventure tourism, spelunking, ecotourism, and other recreational activities are most vulnerable. It is a common phenomenon for them to ignore proper sanitation during travel. After participating in risky activities, it is advisable to hose off boots and place clothes in airtight bags pending laundry after wearing them. Travellers with cardiovascular diseases should keep off risky environments and behaviours like cave voyaging.

With the biodiversity, adventures into the far-flung areas that have wildlife wealth provide for ecotourism opportunities as opposed to nature exploration. Sustainable tours promote ecotourism and they allow communities and nature to grow together simultaneously in a privileged environment. Travellers usually find pleasure in all the stages that advance their experience in the journey towards sustainability. Some of the most potent threats to tropical forests in South America are deforestation emanating from the desire to expand cultivation land, unlawful coca farming, mining, oil spills and extraction, logging, colonisation activities, cattle ranching, etc. Due to deforestation, indigenous people lost their territory and saw their population diminish significantly. More people are embracing ecotourism and also trying to perpetuate efficient use of all resources for sustainable tourism development.

D   To enhance ecotourism and boost economic benefits, East Africa should be more focused on alleviating unlawful hunting. This will rejuvenate the wildlife population, hence allowing an opportunity for trophy hunting. Peter Lindsey, who authors the 'New Study', said that illegal wildlife hunting has robbed wildlife resources more so because the activity diminishes wildlife value. This value can be realised through alternatives like ecotourism and trophy hunting. Many East Africa residents believe that ecotourism has the potential to offer solutions. They favor community empowerment. Peter Lindsey praised the conservation efforts happening locally, saying that it promotes ecotourism and cultivates environmental awareness.

E   In the year 1995, ecotourism was starting to become a fundamental concept in Indonesia. To enhance domestic tourism, the government has to target the appropriate markets, which will facilitate ecotourism. Market segments for ecotourism in Indonesia include the following: a) 55—64 age bracket or 'Silent generation'. These are people with enough wealth, a good education and no children depending on them. They can travel for a month. b) 35—54 age bracket or 'Baby Boom generation'. These are the well-off junior managers who will most probably travel in the company of their children and family. They can travel for two to three weeks. To them, traveling helps alleviate stress. c) 18—29 age bracket or 'X generation'. This generation loves to tour the world backpacking. Often their travel can be anywhere between three to twelve months. They can spend anywhere between USD $300 to USD $500 per month. Different ecotourism packages in Indonesia should be designed to target different cohorts. The country attracts diverse tourist categories.

F   There are as many services offered by ecotourism as there are in traditional tourism. Belize is a country cushioned between the Caribbean Sea, Mexico, and Guatemala. It is a favourite destination for Hamanasi honeymoons. Tourists receive champagne after arriving, private services on their first night, three daily meals, and an adventure of their choice. Hamanasi also has 6 & 7 nights' honeymoon options on offer. Lovers will receive several custom tours that include trips to Brimstone Hill Fortress and a neighbouring island. Some of the guided tours may also include plantation, volcano, and rainforest tours.

Gregory Pereira is an outgoing and very knowledgeable tour guide and hiker. He says that ecotourism adventures incorporate transport from specially designed Land Rovers, wholesome tropical juices, island pastry picnics, knowledgeable island guides, and comprehensive insurance coverage for the participants.

G   Kodai is an ultimate splendor spot for those who love being close to mother nature. The tourists who want a tonic for their mind and body will find Kodai magnificent. It is said that every bird has to sing its throat. The same is true for the tourists because they should map out their path through the motley and raw nature of steep mountains and deep valleys. The Kodai cheese factory which is situated inside the forest is known to export droves of cheese globally. The cheese is a delicacy for tourists and the distinct eating experience is a famous form of ecotourism.

Questions 1–4

Look at the following statements (Questions 1–4) and the list of regions below.

Match each statement with the correct region, A–E.

Write the correct letter, A–E, in boxes 1–4 on your answer sheet.

List of Regions

A Cuba

B South America

C East Africa

D Indonesia

E Belize

---

1 It is a favourite destination for newlyweds.

2 It has not yet addressed many of the health concerns that threaten travellers.

3 It aims at attracting different demographics.

4 It offers courses designed to promote traditional medicine.

Questions 5–9

Reading Passage 1 has seven sections, **A–G**.

Which section contains the following information?

*Write the correct letter, **A–G**, in boxes 5–9 on your answer sheet.*

5   a suggestion that ecotourism may reduce the loss of wild species

6   an example of a product as a tour highlight for eco-tourists

7   mention of several safety precautions for particular activities

8   an example of a series of considerate services for typical guests

9   a reference to the conservation of a cultural heritage

Questions 10–13

Complete the summary below.

*Choose **NO MORE THAN TWO WORDS** from the passage for each answer.*

Write your answers in boxes 10–13 on your answer sheet.

Ecotourism is an approach to tourism that allows tourists to empower local communities and support **10** .... A Cuban institution, for instance, introduces the value of **11** .... to learners fromdifferent angles, while some African nations are using ecotourism to **12** .... animal populations. Ecotourism has become a **13** .... and its further development motivates some governments to target all segments of tourists from young backpackers to older tourists.

READING PASSAGE 2

You should spend about 20 minutes on **Questions 14–26***, which are based on Reading Passage 2 below.*

Book review on *Musicophilia*

A review of Oliver Sacks's latest offering on music

A Being a neuroscientist with expertise in auditory learning and memory, I think the brain and music are both enthralling subjects, and the duo seems especially fascinating. Consequently, I had high hopes from Oliver's latest work, *Musicophilia*. But with a sense of guilt, I admit that my reactions to the book are rather ambivalent.

B Sacks himself is a neurologist and prolific author. He has sumptuously chronicled his life in the book and unveiled a number of highly personal events. The cover of the book features him wearing headphones, with eyes shut and deeply submerged while Alfred Brendel performs Beethoven's *Pathetique Sonata*. This cover aptly summarises the contents of the book, or I can say, that it is borne out of it. Throughout the book, his language is lucid and erudite, but at no point does he sound pompous, self-promoting or bigoted.

C Sacks has beautifully explained the insights that he gathered from the wide and fast-growing body of work of neural quintessence of musical perception and imagery, in addition to the intricate and eccentric disorders that these are prone to. He also accentuates the value of the art of observation as well as the human context and looks to blend the two with the latest diagnostic method in the tech world, in order to penetrate into the experiences of his patients and subjects. Besides, if you read his *Musicophilia*, you will realise that though he has been practicing neurology for one-third of a century, he is torn between the age-old method of observation and the contemporary high-tech approach; he is aware that the modern version is more apt, yet, his heart lies with the traditional one.

D The book has comprehensive accounts of cases concerning the patients that Sacks had seen during his practice. Multiple contemporary neuroscientific reports have been generously sprinkled in the form of brief discussions in the book. In the first part, the 'Haunted by Music' part, one particular case of

Tony Cicoria is especially fascinating, as he is a middle-aged surgeon who is completely nonmusical, but one incident of being struck by lightning produced a deep passion for music in his heart. He began having a sudden urge to listen to piano music, which he had never even bothered about before. His love for music gradually culminated into playing piano and composing music, which came naturally to him, in a deluge of notes.

E But what could be the reason behind this sudden interest or musical skills? It might be psychological, as he had had a near-death encounter when the lightning struck him. Or perhaps, there might have been some direct impact of the incident on his auditory regions of the cerebral cortex. The initial Electroencephalography (EEG), conducted immediately after the incident and when his love for music became apparent, declared that his brain waves were completely normal. Though more sensitive tests could have dug deeper into the mystery, Cicoria refused to undergo them.

F In part two of the book, Sacks covers an array of topics, but regrettably, most of the chapters have little to nothing remarkable or nothing we do not already know. For instance, the thirteenth chapter simply reflects on the knowledge that the blind have a better sense of music than the rest. Certainly, the strangest cases capture maximum attention. The eighth chapter pertains to 'amusia,' an inability to hear sounds like music, and another specific impairment that eliminates the ability to hear harmony while the subject still retains the ability to understand melody, which Sacks termed as 'dysharmonia'. There are several more cases from his experiences that you will find throughout his *Musicophilia*.

G The third part 'Memory, Movement, and Music' is all about the unrewarded field of music therapy. He has explicitly mentioned how 'melodic intonation therapy' comes to the aid of those suffering from Expressive Aphasia (a condition that inhibits a person from expressing their thoughts verbally generally as an aftermath of a stroke or other cerebral incident), to regain their fluency in speech. In another chapter, Sacks illustrates how music can bring life and movement into patients with severe Parkinson's disease or other body movement disorders that confine them to specific postures. This extraordinary power of music has so far not been rationalised in terms of any scientific phenomenon.

H However, for those who are not familiar with the concepts of neuroscience and music behaviour, *Musicophilia* is full of mesmerising information. Nevertheless, it fails to satiate the taste buds of those hungry for the cause and implications of the phenomenon, as Sacks mentions. Moreover, Sacks appears to be more comfortable with discussing patients than discussing experiments, in addition to being somewhat imprudent in trusting scientific findings and theories.

I   While the reasons behind music brain oddities have not been precisely understood, Sacks could have done a little more to outline all the successful treatments that he and other neurologists have performed and the implications of their careful observations. For instance, Sacks could have divulged on the many specific dissociations among components of music perception, as in the case of losing the ability to comprehend harmony but not melody, signifying that the music centre in the brain is missing. And since many readers of the book will assume that all mental functions are located in specific parts of the brain, i. e. brain localisation, he probably missed a great opportunity to educate the masses.

J   One may also conclude that there is no cure for neurological problems that involve music. One drug may have some effects on one patient and different effects on another; it might relieve the pain of one and worsen in another, or perhaps it may have a set of positives and negatives in the same patient. Most treatments mentioned by Sacks are exclusively antiepileptic medications, which slightly axe down the excitability of one's brain in general, though their efficacy varies extensively.

K   Lastly, in *Musicophilia*, in most of the cases, patients have been reported to have a normal EEG result, irrespective of the variations in their music brain symptoms. Though Sacks is well aware of many new technologies that are much more meticulous than the neurological EEG tests to study the brain waves of a patient, he does not call for their use. In fact, despite conveying a clear passion for the patients, he does not display or call for any urgency to pursue innovative avenues in the diagnosis and treatment of music brain disorders. This is somewhat visible in the very beginning of the book, in Preface, where he voices his concern that 'the simple art of observation may be lost' if we lean on the modern technology a bit too much. However, he vouches for both mechanisms, and we can trust the neurological community to respond.

Questions 14–17

Choose the correct letter, **A, B, C** or **D**.

Write the correct letter in boxes 14–17 on your answer sheet.

14   What is the writer's opinion of *Musicophilia* in paragraph A?

    A   He has mixed feelings.

    B   He feels shameful.

    C   He dislikes it on the whole.

    D   He is enamoured with it.

15   As well as exploring the connection between music and neuroscience, Sacks's book is also

    A   a manual for neuroscientists.

    B   an assessment of the field of psychiatry.

    C   a philosophical work.

    D   partly autobiographical.

16   When working with his patients, Sacks prefers

    A   to improve the effectiveness of observation in a technical way.

    B   to treat technology equally with observation.

    C   to carefully examine the medical history of each patient.

    D   to apply traditional methods for better outcomes.

17   The writer feels that the second part of the book

    A   presents the reader with a number of fascinating studies.

    B   does not provide novel or unique insights.

    C   should have increased the variety of topics.

    D   includes previously unknown research.

Questions 18–23

Do the following statements agree with the claims of the writer in Reading Passage 2?

In boxes 18–23 on your answer sheet, write

> **YES**   *If the statement agrees with the claims of the writer*
>
> **NO**   *If the statement contradicts the claims of the writer*
>
> **NOT GIVEN**   *If it is impossible to say what the writer thinks about this*

18   Sacks needed to spend more time discussing his home life.

19   The front cover is an inadequate metaphor for the content of the book.

20   The book needs more complete descriptions of Sacks's patients.

21   The exact cause of Cicoria's condition is unknown.

22   Sacks should have expanded on effective remedies for music-specific disorders.

23   Sacks's methods of treating neurological problems show consistent and predictable results.

Questions 24–26

*Complete each sentence with the correct ending, **A–E**, below.*

*Write the correct letter, **A–E**, in boxes 24–26 on your answer sheet.*

24   The ability to orally state opinions clearly will deteriorate

25   People will have difficulty in moving around flexibly

26   People may fail to fathom harmony even if they understand melody

---

A   after they recover from a lightning strike.

B   because parts of their brain are unable to associate with these.

C   as a consequence of frequent EEG tests.

D   when they suffer from Parkinson's disease.

E   as a result of cerebral damages like having a stroke.

READING PASSAGE 3

*You should spend about 20 minutes on **Questions 27–40**, which are based on Reading Passage 3 below.*

Communication in Science

A   Science is the cornerstone of life — it is the essence of better understanding what we think we know and developing new knowledge. Despite the important role science plays in the advancement of humanity, communicating scientific findings is more difficult than ever. Miscommunications and distortion lead to unnecessary confusion and misunderstandings.

B   Perhaps the biggest challenge in advancing scientific knowledge starts with scientists themselves. Scientists tend to use complicated language which at times can be difficult for the intended audience to understand.

Moreover, many people wrongfully assume that the esoteric nature of new scientific research implies that the findings are erroneous. Rather, it should be viewed as a tribute to the success of human ingenuity in solving some of the more pressing issues.

Some of the more notable examples include pressing global issues currently dominating media headlines. Solving the global warming crisis certainly comes to mind as well as improving the lives of people suffering from cancer. Of course, science can extend to other topics that are not necessarily life and death, such as understanding how a diet affects weight loss.

C   Ambiguous language by definition can have more than one interpretation which leads to misunderstanding and crafts further debates among the scientific community. Scientists sometimes feel guilty of using colloquial language, including slang and jargon that may be easy for some to understand, but an incomprehensible concept for others.

One such example is the term 'relativity' which is by definition intrinsically misleading. Some would say it implies everything is relative, and there are no absolutes, considering for example Einstein's 'theory of relativity' which focuses on finding an intra variant description of physical phenomena.

D The 'uncertainty principle' is another term that is frequently misused in the scientific community. Some people take a look at the term and conclude it refers to a limitation on observers and the ability to make measurements.

E One can also make the argument that the word 'theory' is problematic. Many people define 'theory' as a yet to be proven idea that requires further evaluation. The process varies across the scientific community as physicists, for example, look at a definite physical framework within a set of fundamental assumptions about the world that could yield a set of predictions.

Theories by definition never represent truth and they are never completely correct, especially in the early stages of the scientific process. One of the more notable examples is Einstein's nearly decade long quest to perfect his research on the theory of relativity. Even today it remains a theory in the sense that it cannot be proven correct.

F Global warming continues to dominate media headlines but even the name itself is problematic. Climate scientists are tasked with modeling potential fluctuations in temperatures and should not be considered predicting weather trends for the upcoming months.

However, many people fail to understand the science behind climate research. Instead, many are quick to brush off the scientific community and question their credibility if an upcoming winter proves to be colder than usual.

Therefore, there is a controversy within the scientific community of this field about whether it is necessary to have a name change from global warming to climate change, though such change will not generate any benefit to the research itself.

G Harvard University was ground-zero for useless and meaningless debates exploring if gender determines the ability of a scientist to generate results. The data could not be any clearer: some social factors may account for small differences between men and women, but as a whole, there is no correlation between gender and scientific ability.

A perfect analogy would be information gathered from an unmanned space mission is no more or no less legitimate if the same data was compiled by astronauts.

H It would be a mistake to assume that questioning the data compiled by a scientist is a direct attack on the scientist themselves. This may be even more of an important topic for scientists working in fields that have urgent implications.

Also, if a scientist acknowledges it is nearly impossible or completely impossible to come to a conclusion, it would be an error to assume the project was a complete failure. More specifically, there may be some mathematical significance in the study, although the public tends to treat maths with skepticism.

I At the end of the day, one of the biggest takeaways is to recognise that science is complex. Accepting only the simple findings that are easy to understand may make us feel good, but the world will not progress.

Scientists can also play a role in helping the world understand important topics. They may want to consider taking time out of their busy schedule and offer an easy-to-understand explanation of their work. The public should embrace scientists who go the extra mile and be more patient to comprehend how scientists process their studies.

Nevertheless, avoiding every conflict, misunderstanding, or difficulty is simply impossible. Science is a never-ending experiment that has no deadline and no one knows the big picture — at least not yet.

Questions 27–31

*Choose the correct letter, **A**, **B**, **C** or **D**.*

Write your answers in boxes 27–31 on your answer sheet.

27 According to section A, the writer points out that science
   A broadens our horizons for further discoveries.
   B expands our knowledge in humanity solely.
   C reduces miscommunications and misunderstandings.
   D grows to be more difficult for common people.

28 In section C, the writer states the opinion that
   A the exploration of new ideas should be recorded in comprehensible language.
   B scientific theories are generally filled with misleading terms.
   C imprecise language leads to unnecessary confusion among scientists.
   D the popularity of using colloquial language is rising in the scientific community.

29 When referring to the change of a climate terminology, the writer emphasises that
   A it will help the public understand climate scientists.
   B it will not help scientists in any meaningful way.
   C it will increase the credibility of relative research results.
   D it cannot reverse climate change.

30 What does the writer imply in section H?
   A A project can still be valuable even if there is no outcome.
   B More accurate research is needed.
   C Research must be goal driven.
   D Arguments made earlier are wrong.

31 What point does the write emphasise in section I?
   A Full explanations should be left out of the public sphere.
   B Simple findings make no contribution to scientific development.
   C It is easy for scientists to explain what they have achieved in research.
   D In the field of science, we will always encounter miscommunication.

Questions 32–35

Do the following statements agree with the information given in Reading Passage 3?

In boxes 32–35 on your answer sheet, write

> **TRUE**   *If the statement agrees with the information*
>
> **FALSE**   *If the statement contradicts the information*
>
> **NOT GIVEN** *If there is no information on this*

32   Scientists always believe it is reasonable to use informal terms.

33   The uncertainty principle means we can never have absolute confidence in our measurements.

34   Theories are true when they are based on scientific experiments.

35   The gender of scientists does not influence the outcome of research.

Questions 36–40

Complete the summary below.

Choose **NO MORE THAN TWO WORDS** *from the passage for each answer.*
Write your answers in boxes 36–40 on your answer sheet.

The language used to discuss science can often lead to confusion. Some people think the **36** .... nature of current scientific studies is a relevant reason. The author identifies a few examples of misleading terms. The term **37** ...., for instance, is commonly referred to as an idea that has not been proven. Even within scientific communities, there is a debate; for example, some scientists question the necessity of using the term **38** .... to redefine their field of research. It is necessary to realise that science, as a field, is **39** ....and that scientists need to avoid overusing technical terms when conveying their ideas to others. At the same time, **40** ....should take more time to understand how the scientific process works.

WRITING

WRITING TASK 1

You should spend about 20 minutes on this task.

> **The table below shows the primary funding sources of international students in the US during the year 2003 and 2013.**
>
> **Summarise the information by selecting and reporting the main features, and make comparisons where relevant.**

Write at least 150 words.

Change of primary funding sources of international students in the U. S.				
Primary sources of funding	2003		2013	
	Number of students	% of total	Number of students	% of total
Personal and family	383, 600	67%	574, 129	65%
U. S. college or university	132, 015	23%	171, 218	19%
Foreign government or university	11, 699	2%	66, 147	7%
Current employer	16, 054	3%	49, 503	6%
Other sources	29, 141	5%	25, 055	3%
Total	572, 509	100%	886, 052	100%

WRITING TASK 2

You should spend about 40 minutes on this task.

Write about the following topic:

> *In many countries today, people in big cities prefer to live alone or in small family units rather than large, extended family groups.*
>
> *Is this a positive or negative trend?*

Give reasons for your answer and include any relevant examples from your own knowledge or experience.

Write at least 250 words.

SPEAKING

PART 1

The examiner asks the candidate about him/herself, his/her home, work or studies and other family topics.

EXAMPLE

Cake & Dessert

- Do you like dessert?
- Do you like eating cakes?
- What desserts do Chinese people like?
- Have you ever made cakes?

PART 2

> **Describe a person who taught you something.**
>
> **You should say:**
> who this person is
> what he/she was like
> what he/she taught you
>
> **and how you felt about him/her.**

You will have to talk about the topic for one to two minutes. You have one minute to think about what you are going to say. You can make some notes to help you if you wish.

PART 3

Discussion topics:

Teachers and learning

Example questions:

What qualities do you think a good teacher should have?

Who do you think can learn better, old people or youngsters?

What do you think is the best age for children to go to school?

Do you prefer to study by yourself or with your friends?

Test 2

PART 1   Questions 1–10

Complete the notes below.

Write **ONE WORD AND/OR A NUMBER** for each answer.

Medical Consultation

Patient Information

- Name: Anu **1**...........................
- Post code: **2**...........................
- Current address: **3**........................... Avenue
- Birthday: October 1st **4**...........................
- Phone number: 875934

Health Condition

- Background: Illness has lasted for **5**........................... days
- Symptom: see **6**........................... lights
- Possible cause: the room was too **7**...........................
- Previous hospital: **8**........................... Hospital

Suggestions

- Have a good rest after staring at a **9**........................... for a long time
- Use some medicine to ease eye **10**...........................

PART 2   *Questions 11–20*

Questions 11–14

Complete the notes below.

*Write **ONE WORD AND/OR A NUMBER** for each answer.*

Student Union

Basic information:

- There is no requirement for **11**............................ fees.
- A yearly **12**............................ is adopted for selecting candidates running the student union.
- On-campus location: next to the **13**............................

Available clubs:

- 30 clubs related to sports
- **14**............................ clubs offer non-athletic activities.

Questions 15–17

*Choose **THREE** letters, **A–G**.*

Which **THREE** areas does the student union itself offer help on?

    A academics

    B communication

    C dental health

    D finance

    E student conflicts

    F legal issues

    G mental well-being

Questions 18–20

What is the feature of each of the three clubs in the student union?

*Choose **THREE** answers from the box and write the correct letter, **A–E**, next to*

Questions 18–20.

A large size
B good reputation
C fun people
D low price
E free trips

18 The Movie Makers   ....

19 Team Travel   ....

20 Campus Radio, 94.7 FM   ....

PART 3   *Questions 21–30*

Questions 21–25

*Choose the correct letter, **A**, **B** or **C**.*

Maori Greenstone Tiki Carvings

21 Amy and Mike agree that the greenstone tikis

    A take great skill to produce.

    B are fascinating curved shapes.

    C have interesting stories behind them.

22 According to Amy, why are so few genuine old tikis found on archaeological dig sites?

    A Not many people know about them.

    B They tend to be stolen by treasure hunters.

    C The majority become inherited items.

23 The Maori people considered tikis to be

    A decorative items.

    B religious objects.

    C tribal symbols.

24 Tikis are classified into one type or the other by

    A where they originated.

    B the materials used.

    C the position of the body.

25 How can modern reproductions be easily distinguished from genuine Maori carvings?

    A The materials differ.

    B They are too regular in shape.

    C They are of different sizes.

Questions 26–30

What tool did Maoris use to carry out each of the following tasks?

*Write the correct letter, **A–E**, next to Questions 26–30.*

Traditional Tools and Materials

A Sandstone block

B Plant glue

C Stone scoring tool

D Bone point

E Stick drill

---

26 creating a blank ....

27 smoothing the surface ....

28 carving details ....

29 making holes ....

30 fixing coloured decorations ....

PART4   *Questions 31–40*

Questions 31–36

Complete the notes below.

Write **ONE WORD ONLY** *for each answer.*

Green Mountain Fossil Park

Types of fossils:

- transitional fossils: rare, show evidence of evolutionary change
- **31** .... fossils: more common, actual fossilised remains
- **32** .... fossils: indirect evidence of animals, such as footprints or tunnels

Fossilisation processes:

- Organism trapped in volcanic ash
- Petrifaction
  - An animal is **33** .... in the mud after death.
  - Mud dries and hardens.
  - **34** .... replace the bones leaving a stone shape.

Purchasing fossils:

- Site: Shop outside the park or from the park's **35** ....
- Prices: generally **36** ....

Questions 37–40

Complete the table below.

Write **NO MORE THAN TWO WORDS** *for each answer.*

Tools	Function or purpose
A tape measure	Record the **37**........................ of each fossil
A notebook	Record the types of **38**........................
A camera	Get some **39**........................ of the fossils
A compass	Detect **40**........................ to locate the fossils

READING PASSAGE 1

*You should spend about 20 minutes on **Questions 1–13**, which are based on Reading Passage 1 below.*

Museum Blockbuster

A   Blockbuster is a trendy term that has been used since 1980. The term represents the art gallery, science, or stunning museum displays. Elsen in 1984 stated that a blockbuster is a large-scaled display that attracts crowds that would otherwise not visit museums. These people wait for long hours to view the objects. James Rosenfield wrote in 1993 in *Direct Marketing* that blockbuster exhibition success is the success of marketing and curatorial prowess. A blockbuster can be understood as a famous and prominent exhibition that is only displayed for limited time. The blockbuster definitions by Rosenfield and Elsen overlook the fact that crowds are ready to part with money for a chance to view the blockbuster. Their definitions also ignore the fact that a blockbuster applies to movie exhibition.

B   Giving a movie or an exhibition the name blockbuster does not mean that they indeed are. The term blockbuster can only be validly used if the item had tremendous response and success from people. Literature items from the USA and UK apply the word blockbuster for non-elitist, less scholarly, and popularist purposes. The argument by critics is that the design of blockbusters aims to attract the public. Some blockbusters attempt to inspire project cooperation from scholars and offer displays that cover a wide spectrum of society, instead of the limited privileged sector.

C   New museology is a means implemented to sustain and grow the number of visitors. This can only be achieved through continuous product growth. The growth must not be limited to the formation or contracting of blockbuster displays but rather regular changes in innovations and exhibitions. Blockbuster visitors are becoming customers instead of normal visitors. The skills applied in museums, galleries and science centres to attract more customers are changing. Entrepreneurial qualities, marketing and business skills top the requirements list. Curators have become managers. To become an art gallery director today a degree in art is not necessary. The 1994 *Economist* summarised it best by stating that skills in public relations and business intellect, and their capacity to contend with rival museums to offer traveling displays that attract multitudes, were fundamental requirements for the director.

D   As a result of new museology, museum tours, cultural industry, pleasure-giving, and profit-making have received wide coverage. This has created great debate concerning the suitability of acclimatising institutional activities to closely demonstrate marketplace priorities and understanding of whether it is okay to view museums as principally tourist attractions. While commentators think science centre, art galleries, and museum managers globally seek clever avenues to merge commerce and culture, blockbuster displays are still leading the way. Although blockbusters are components of new museology, you do not require an art gallery, science centre, or museum to gain blockbuster power or present a blockbuster.

E   The question is whether blockbusters staged in an institution can generate the surplus needed to finance other initiatives. If the goal is to make a profit, then numerous major galleries and museums have demonstrated that ability. Some museums may need money to restore some of their collections or repair the buildings. Some Australian museums and galleries seek the chance to demonstrate their attempt to recover some of the costs of operation, or finance other initiatives with the revenue that was not budgeted for. This will make economic rationalists merry. Some exhibitions acclaimed as blockbusters are really not. Some fail to generate revenue. Most accounting systems in institutions will most likely not acknowledge the actual costs of contracting or creating a blockbuster.

F   Huge capital expense is required for blockbusters as they require resources from all organisational branches. There are more costs involved. Apart from the huge capital investment, the cost of managing the human resource adds to the actual costs. Touring exhibitions entail huge expenses. They also require resources from various structures of management in the style of project management. Every person, including the service unit, general laborer, education, technical, administrative and front house personnel is expected to do more errands. As Australian institutions seek to grow their visitors and members for better revenue through blockbuster displays, there are fewer chances that a surplus will continue for subsidising other initiatives owing to the level of competition in the market. The resources from customers are limited and blockbuster visitors will have to choose between products from various blockbusters.

G   The unfortunate thing is that when bottom lines become the fundamental objective of blockbuster displays, it becomes very difficult to sustain the results. Institutional personnel are getting exhausted in the process of hiring and creating blockbusters and the actual costs in the entire institution are hard to calculate. On the other hand, the hiring or creation of blockbusters can have many positives. For instance, a famous blockbuster can raise an institution's profile, making the perception of the museum more favorable. Blockbusters boost the economy by adding employment opportunities for restaurants, hotels, retailers, transport industry, and shops although they subject staff to stress and the unpredictability of the market. Blockbuster achievements or failures are likely to demonstrate the requirement for policy-makers and managers to reconsider their approach. Nevertheless, the trend in favor of blockbusters and new museology will probably make art galleries, museums, and especially science centres be perceived as components of the tourism and the entertainment industry instead of as icons of culture that merit philanthropic and government support.

H   Maybe the best route is to offset regular exhibitions and blockbusters. The middle ground is only likely to work if there are ample space and alternative funding sources to further the support of less thrilling exhibitions. To ensure exhibitions and regular initiatives are more inviting, it is essential to seek what locals want more from an exhibition. Most people seek to visit overseas venues (science centres and museums) that are cost-effective.

Questions 1–4

Reading Passage 1 has eight paragraphs, **A–H**.

Which paragraph contains the following information?

*Write the correct letter, **A–H**, in boxes 1–4 on your answer sheet.*

1 a summary of the outlays required to run a blockbuster

2 a description of the qualifications required to run a gallery today

3 a contrast between the benefits and drawbacks of blockbusters

4 mention of the fact that artistic and cultural venues are unnecessary for displaying blockbusters

Questions 5–8

Complete the summary below.

*Choose **NO MORE THAN THREE WORDS** from the passage for each answer.*

Write your answers in boxes 5–8 on your answer sheet.

A blockbuster is a show or an event run by a gallery and generally lasts for
5 .... With the adoption of **6** .... as a key to increase visitors,
there is an increased focus on blockbusters. One possible benefit is that these
events may provide a financial **7** .... , which can fund less profitable
aspects of their organisation. However, presenting blockbusters and promoting new
museology can change certain sites from being **8** .... to mere
entertainment venues, thus cutting the support from charity organisations and the
government.

Questions 9 and 10

*Choose **TWO** letters, **A–E** .*

Write the correct letters in boxes 9 and 10 on your answer sheet.

Which **TWO** factors mentioned in this passage motivate museums and institutions in Australia to run blockbusters?

    A They may offset the spending on day-to-day maintenance and administration.

    B They help museums to expand collections.

    C They promote the advancement of science among the public.

    D They encourage investors to create partnerships with them.

    E They can aid in achieving further profit targets.

Questions 11–13

*Choose **THREE** letters, **A–F** .*

Write the correct letters in boxes 11–13 on your answer sheet.

Which **THREE** of the following statements are criticisms against blockbusters in this passage?

    A Attendees are now treated as customers rather than as visitors.

    B Cultural centres now belong to the entertainment industry.

    C Blockbuster events are not academic enough and generally appeal to the majori

    D Managers must readdress their approach to running a public space.

    E Blockbuster events add considerable pressure on employees.

    F The cost of running a blockbuster event is high.

READING PASSAGE 2

*You should spend about 20 minutes on **Questions 14–26**, which are based on Reading Passage 2 below.*

Ancient Storytelling

A　The first stories were probably narrated to people crouching around a bonfire. These included tales of mighty adventures, like near-death encounters, hunting excursions, or an escape from mortal peril, or perhaps a mystery or divine anecdotes. However, irrespective of the subject, there was one principal objective behind all these tales: to keep the listener intrigued and engaged, to make them overlook their worries or fatigue, and only one query must prevail in their mind — what happens next?

B　Finding the initial stories ever told in human history is like herding cats, as these were preserved in the minds of the storytellers. This kind of storage or memorisation, however, shall not be deemed as ineffective. Several documented oral traditions of Australia, Balkans, and other parts of the world apprise us of master storytellers and poets of the time that could recite thousands of verses and proses from their memory, word to word! However, while such memorisation seems like art or sorcery, the essential idea of creating symbols is to have a system of reminders or mnemonics that helps one recall specific information in one's mind.

C　In a few Polynesian societies, the storytellers used a notched memory stick for assistance in successive stages of recitation. However, among many other global communities, the art of storytelling led to the invention or development of writing systems. For instance, the onset of literacy in ancient Greece is attributed to the fact that the epic tales of the Trojan War and the Voyage of Odysseus were so captivating that there was a need to preserve them. Thus, the Greeks, in 750 B. C. — 700 B. C. borrowed the alphabet system from their east Mediterranean neighbours, the Phoenicians.

D　The pristine practice of documenting stories on parchment and other materials can be traced to many ancient civilisations. The priestly papyrus archives of ancient Egypt and the birch-bark scrolls used by North American Ojibway Indians are excellent examples. It has emerged as a tried and tested practice, thanks to which stories are today synonymous with words on paper. Even the practice of oral storytelling is believed to have been taken over by journals, novels, comic strips, etc. However, written texts are not the primary source for humans to access stories. But then, what is it?

E Each year, over seven billion people head towards the silver screens to watch the latest offerings of national and international cinema. Yes, the chief storyteller of the day is none other than the Cinema! The movies encompass storytelling in the form of motion pictures, which is a contemporary phenomenon in comparison to reading information on paper or still photography. It is more so an illusion that was originally accepted by the method of sequencing images in a particular order. Even so, it is imperative to acknowledge that the art of visual storytelling must hold a profoundly atavistic vibe to it. In spite of the advantage, the conventional patterns of storyline and characterisation that have been instilled in storytelling for ages are indispensable for a good story.

F While thousands of scripts land dust on the desks of major film studios, all an aspiring screenwriter needs to look up to is the fourth-century Greek philosopher, Aristotle. In his incomplete work, *The Poetics*, he left several lecture notes describing the art of storytelling in multiple literary and dramatic mediums. Though it is highly unlikely that he envisaged the popcorn-fuelled atmosphere of today's multiplexes, he had ample perception of how to gather and retain large crowds to such creative centres. Aristotle examined the process with impressive rationalism. He states that when a story fascinates us, we lose the sense of where we are, our fears, and accept fiction. This is one of Aristotle's principles of theatre, which he calls — 'the suspension of disbelief.'

G The audience know the feeling! They might have experienced episodes of horror, grief, astonishment or ecstasy, sitting on the theatre seats or even days after the show, knowing that it is all fiction yet letting it impact their state of mind. They seldom think through why they are caught in the web of the storyteller.

H Aristotle taught at Athens, the city where theatre emerged as a prime mode of public's leisure and entertainment. So it is evident that he might have observed suspended disbelief in action. Two theatrical storytelling types, tragedy and comedy, made Athenians immerse themselves in gloom and glee, respectively. Of which, Aristotle explicitly acknowledged tragedy as a potent weapon to trigger the most heartfelt emotions of the spectators, so he explored over the factors in the storyteller's art that brought about such a subconscious commotion. For this, he studied the masterpieces of classical Greek tragedies by Euripides, Aeschylus, Sophocles, and even that of Homer. Even at that time, Homer's stories commanded the same awe as today. His *Iliad* and *the Odyssey* were considered literary landmarks and used as a scale to measure all other stories.

I So what is the mystery behind Homer's captivating narratives? Homer conceived credible heroes that were powerful and majestic but did not turn into fantasy figures in the end. He made them sulk, quarrel, cheat, and whine. They were the characteristics that an audience could relate to, or wish to follow. This naturally intrigued them to know what happens next. As Aristotle observed, the heroes with a human side, a mix of flaws and vulnerability to which humans are inclined, are aptly dramatic.

Questions 14–18

Reading Passage 2 has nine paragraphs, **A–I**.

Which paragraph contains the following information?

*Write the correct letter, **A–I**, in boxes 14–18 on your answer sheet.*

14   an example of the importance of writing systems to a civilisation

15   a reference to the popularity of a modern form of storytelling

16   mention of a concept that can take audience's breath away

17   mention of oral storytelling losing its popularity due to other forms of recording stories

18   a reference to two distinct types of stories

Questions 19–22

*Choose the correct letter, **A**, **B**, **C** or **D**.*

Write your answers in boxes 19–22 on your answer sheet.

19 In paragraph B, the writer uses the analogy of herding cats in order to exemplify

    A the difficulty of researching original tales.

    B the range of stories available around the world.

    C the originality of ancient storytellers.

    D the reason for discussing writing systems.

20 Some believe that the Greeks created their writing system

    A because the Phoenicians had already invented one.

    B because of difficulty in recalling various stories.

    C to document important stories that they liked.

    D to make the art of storytelling more complex.

21 The writer refers to modern cinema in order to

    A analyse how the fundamentals of storytelling have changed.

    B prove how important stories are to billions of people.

    C demonstrate how the principles of storytelling remain.

    D suggest reasons for why past forms of storytelling failed.

22 The writer encourages screenwriters to read Aristotle

    A to draw inspiration from fourth-century literature on rationalism.

    B to learn how to keep the audience interested.

    C to investigate how storytelling has changed.

    D to examine various elements of storytelling.

Questions 23–26

Complete each sentence with the correct ending, **A–E**, *below.*

Write the correct letter, **A–E**, *in boxes 23–26 on your answer sheet.*

23   Storytellers in the past created

24   A good story triggers

25   Athenians were particularly interested in

26   Homer made engaging stories by using

A   dramas containing either sorrowful events or stories with cheerful ending.

B   strong emotions like long-lasting excitement in one's mind.

C   certain memory devices to retain large pieces of information.

D   scenes that scare the audience to the degree that they could not think rationally.

E   characters who may display controversial behaviour despite their admirable qualities.

READING PASSAGE 3

You should spend about 20 minutes on **Questions 27–40**, which are based on Reading Passage 3 below.

Questions 27–34

Reading Passage 3 has eight paragraphs, **A–H**.

Choose the correct heading for each paragraph from the list of headings below.

Write the correct number, **i-xi**, in boxes 27–33 on your answer sheet.

```
                    List of Headings

   i     Mapping the universe to understand the past

   ii    Indication of an ancient research site

   iii   Declined population due to the lack of food

   iv    The cultural significance of statues

   v     A mystery that attracted early explorers

   vi    A loss of habitat

   vii   The stone-made giants

   viii  Trapped on an island

   ix    Modern assumptions about a coincidence

   x     The early days of the island's thriving environment

   xi    A persuasive explanation for the collapse of Easter Island
```

27   Paragraph **A**

28   Paragraph **B**

29   Paragraph **C**

30   Paragraph **D**

31   Paragraph **E**

32   Paragraph **F**

33   Paragraph **G**

34   Paragraph **H**

The Mystery of the Easter Island

A Easter Island, a small, hilly, treeless volcano, is one of the world's most celebrated archaeological sites. However, it is rarely visited and not inhabited. The island was named Easter Island by Jacob Roggeveen, a Dutch Captain, who visited the island on 5th April 1722 and was the first European to set foot on the island. Following the mystery of its inhabitants, a Norwegian explorer called Thor Heyerdahl visited the island in the early 1950s. Heyerdahl suggested that the original inhabitants of the island were Indian societies that had originated from the Southern coast of America. However, after a broad ethnographic, linguistic and archaeological research, this theory was found to be inaccurate.

B According to research and DNA extracts from the exhumed skeletons on the island, the original inhabitants of the island were from the Marquesas Islands in Polynesia. According to the carbon dating of reeds collected from the graves, these people arrived on the island in 318 AD. It is believed that at that time, the island had lots of trees, swarming with both land and sea birds and there were abundant food sources from fish, plants, and birds that made the human population grow rapidly, giving rise to a rich artistic and religious culture.

C Among some of the most famous features of the culture of the inhabitants are the moai, which are gigantic stone statues. It is believed that there were at least 288 of these moai statues that were erected on about 250 stone plateaus known as ahu and each of the ahu is approximately 1.5 miles from another one, forming a continuous line around the island. In addition to the moai statues that sit on the ahu plateaus, there are other unfinished moai statues that spread across the island. Some of them are found in quarries, and others along ancient roads and coastal areas. On average, the moai statues are 14.5 feet tall with a weight of 14 tones and they are mostly carved from Rono Raraku, a type of volcanic stone, which is tough. There are other larger moai statues that weigh 80 tones with a height of about 33 feet. Going by the enormous size of these statues, it is assumed that it took about 50 to 150 people to move them across the island on rollers and sleds made from trees.

D It has been difficult to conclusively explicate the purpose of the moai statues.

However, it is believed that the idea originated from a similar practice back in Polynesia though it was done differently in the Easter Island. The statues had some human characteristics. According to iconographic and archaeological analysis, the cult of carving the statues was founded on a male philosophy, based on the authority of a certain lineage. Therefore, the statues were symbols of both political and religious authority and power. To the people that used them, they were sources of sacred spirits. In Polynesian religions, when wood objects and carved stones were ritualistically prepared, people believed that some magical spiritual power referred to as mana changed them. Therefore, the ahu platforms on the Easter Islands were sanctuaries while the moai statues were the sacred objects.

E   The island also has other names like the Mata-Ki-Te-Rani, which means 'Eyes Looking at Heaven', and Te-Pito-O-Te-Henua, which means 'The Navel of the World'. These two names, though ignored by most archaeologists, show that there is a possibility that the island could have been used as an astronomical observatory site and a geodetic sign respectively. Graham Hancock, in his book *Heaven's Mirror*, suggests that the island may have been an important scientific outpost of the antediluvian civilisation. Other scholars like Robert Lomas and Christopher Knight have studied the ancient geodetic signs and suggested that they were used for forecasting and preparing for future disasters in their book called *Uriel's Machine*.

F   At the end of the 20th century and the beginning of the 21st century, scientists and writers came up with a number of theories as to why civilisation on Easter Island declined just about the time the first European made contact with the island. One of the theories, which has been rendered inaccurate, was formulated by Jared Diamond in his book known as *Collapse: How Societies Choose to Fail or Survive*.

G   Basically, most of these theories state that the island was unable to replenish itself ecologically following the demand for lots of resources for the growing population after colonisation. As a result, the forests on the island had been depleted by 1400s. The ground cover had been removed. Springs had dried up and the swarms of birds had vanished. Since there were no trees to cut logs for building canoes that could have been used for offshore fishing, and the birds and wildlife had been depleted, people lacked enough food. The crop yield had also declined and the consequent famine struck resulting in cannibalism. And since there was no food to feed the population on the island including the priests and administrators, there was a social and cultural collapse. According to the theories, the population had dropped to a tenth of its original number and most of the moai statues were destroyed during clan wars in the 1600s and 1700s.

H   These theories presented defective ideas starting with the racialist's assumptions by Thor Heyerdahl. These ideas were then propagated by writers like Jared Diamond who had no historical archaeological knowledge of the actual events that took place on Easter Island. The most convincing hypothesis is that the devastation of Easter Island was as a result of the cold-hearted European visitors, especially the slavers. They introduced diseases like smallpox on the island and murdered natives on Easter Island and transported them to South America as slaves.

Questions 35–37

Do the following statements agree with the information given in Reading Passage 3?

In boxes 35–37 on your answer sheet, write

> **TRUE**   *If the statement agrees with the information*
> **FALSE**   *If the statement contradicts the information*
> **NOT GIVEN** *If there is no information on this*

35   There are no permanent residents living on Easter Island.

36   After arriving on Easter Island, Polynesians planted lots of trees there.

37   The writer largely agrees with the conclusions drawn by Jared Diamond.

Questions 38–40

Complete the summary below.

*Choose **NO MORE THAN THREE WORDS** from the passage for each answer.*

Write your answers in boxes 38–40 on your answer sheet.

Easter Island is famous for the seemingly unexplained disappearance of its inhabitants, and its infamous giant statues, the moai. These statues are generally found on the island's plateaus but some statues located in other parts of the island are **38** .... The giant statues were formed out of a kind of **39** .... , and while a definitive explanation of the moai is still unknown, current theories suggest that they served a **40** .... function. Many theories on the islanders' disappearance have been proposed.

WRITING

WRITING TASK 1

You should spend about 20 minutes on this task.

> *The diagram below shows the life cycle of a ladybird and its anatomy.*
>
> *Summarise the information by selecting and reporting the main features, and make comparisons where relevant.*

Write at least 150 words.

Life cycle of a ladybird

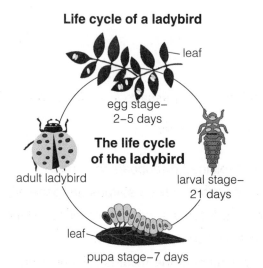

Anatomy of a ladybird

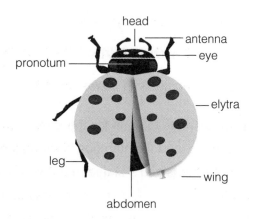

WRITING TASK 2

You should spend about 40 minutes on this task.

Write about the following topic:

> **Once children start school, teachers have more influence on their intellectual and social development than parents do.**
>
> **To what extent do you agree or disagree with this statement?**

Give reasons for your answer and include any relevant examples from your own knowledge or experience.

Write at least 250 words.

SPEAKING

PART 1

The examiner asks the candidate about him/herself, his/her home, work or studies and other family topics.

EXAMPLE

Pen & Pencil

- Do you usually use a pen or pencil?
- Which do you use more often? Pen or pencil?
- When was the last time you bought a pen or pencil?
- What do you think of giving a pen or pencil as a present?

PART 2

Describe an ideal house or apartment where you want to live.
You should say:
where it is
what it is like
who you would like to live with
and explain why you think it is ideal.

You will have to talk about the topic for one to two minutes. You have one minute to think about what you are going to say. You can make some notes to help you if you wish.

PART 3

Discussion topics:

Places for living

Example questions:

Where do people in China like to live, in a house or an apartment?

What are the benefits of living in a house?

Why do many people like to live in the city?

Where do people like to live, in the city centre or the suburbs?

Test 3

LISTENING

PART 1   Questions 1–10

Complete the notes below.

Write **ONE WORD AND/OR A NUMBER** for each answer.

Job Enquiry
Phone call from Amy at: Harvey Entertainment Agency

Job information

- Work location: **1**.................... Island
- Start date: **2**....................
- Job position: **3**....................

Qualifications & skills required

- 2 years' experience
- Can get along with **4**....................
- Can **5**.................... well
- Can drive（have a **6**....................）

Employee benefits

- Offer free accommodation and **7**....................
- Provide cheap lunch

Interview details

- Appointment: on **8**....................
- Bring an updated **9**.................... and a **10**.................... photo

PART 2   *Questions 11–20*

Questions 11–15

Label the map below.

*Write the correct letter, **A–H**, next to Questions 11–15.*

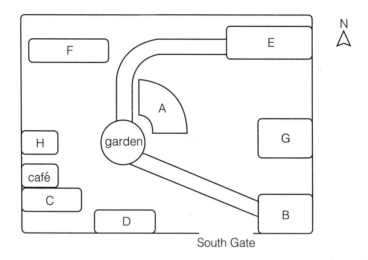

11   Student service office   ....

12   Stadium   ....

13   Health centre   ....

14   International student office   ....

15   Accommodation office   ....

Questions 16–20

Complete the notes below.

Write **NO MORE THAN TWO WORDS AND/OR A NUMBER** for each answer.

On-campus Accommodation

- Each student has his or her own **16** ....

- Laundry facilities situate in the **17** .... of each dormitory.

- Most **18** .... are named.

- An **19** .... is needed to go into the dormitory.

- Electric appliances should be turned off after **20** ....

PART 3   *Questions 21–30*

Questions 21–23

*Choose the correct letter, **A**, **B** or **C**.*

The Project Proposal

21 The project proposal will

A be assessed by professional editors.

B contribute to the final grade.

C be returned with feedback.

22 What should the proposal focus on?

A the topic

B the approach

C the outcome

23 For the proposal, Mr. Brown suggests that

A Linda should follow the instruction.

B the minimum length should be 6,000 words.

C the word limit can be optional.

Questions 24–30

Complete the notes below.

Write **ONE WORD AND/OR A NUMBER** *of each answer.*

Women as business leaders project

Work required for the proposal:

- Conduct an **24** ....

- Make a few workplace observations

Presenting the proposal:

- Text: should be in the correct **25**...........................

- Submission: **26**........................... hard copies of the assignment in addition to a soft copy

- Due date: by **27**...........................

- Changes to proposal:

  — can apply to make changes to the **28**........................... if there is time

  — need to make change requests through **29** .... applications

Content of the proposal:

After stating a hypothesis, focus on the **30**........................... that will be used to gather data.

PART 4   *Questions 31–40*

Complete the notes below.

Write **ONE WORD ONLY** for each answer.

Social Importance of Sports

Reasons behind the popularity of sports:

- It engages a large proportion of a country's **31** ....
- It involves big industries such as **32** ....
- It drives technology like the invention of new **33** ....

Playing sports has health benefits:

- Governments encourage **34** .... in sports.
- Incentives include promotions, such as free entry to **35** ....
- Competing in sports can foster a sense of achievement which positively contributes to **36** .... health.

The media has a huge influence on sports:

- Satellite TV introduces **37** .... sports to a wider public.
- Digital TV allows in-depth analysis of sporting events and better presentation of athletes' skills because details are captured from different **38** ....
- TV and the internet are better at conveying sporting information than books because books contain **39** .... knowledge of sports.
- Newspapers are most often used to check results but sometimes they fail to respect the **40** .... of sporting celebrities.

READING PASSAGE 1

*You should spend about 20 minutes on **Questions 1–13**, which are based on Reading Passage 1 below.*

Ancient societies classification

A   Sociologists and anthropologists classify societal groups based on their access to resources, prestige, or power. There are typically four classifications of society and this has been true throughout history. At the bottom end of the societal scale are clans, followed by tribes, chiefdoms — and at the highest are the states.

B   Clans consist of a small group of people who are typically hunters or gatherers. People in a group tend to number less than 100 and hold no specific home, which allows for flexibility in exploiting the wild and gathering food resources. Members of the clans are typically related to each other through marriage or descent and the group as a whole does not have any formal ranks of leadership. As such, the economic disparity is non-existent between different members due to the vast similarities.

Today there are few societal groups that fit the profile, and most are relegated to areas like the Hadza of Tanzania. They are considered to be one of the last hunter-gatherer tribes within the African region and their population numbers 1,300. Experts consider the small group to be very important as they best represent how humans existed and survived in the past. In fact, the Hadza hunters use many of the same methods that were used thousands of years ago. They hunt animals with bows and arrows that are hand-made and create their own shelter with dried grass and branches. As was the case centuries ago, they own very few possessions, especially compared to their modern day counterparts in Western societies.

Clans are also very mobile and their short-term homes tend to be composed of seasonally occupied camps and other smaller or more specialised pieces of land. One thing that remains consistent is that clans seek out areas where large mammals can be killed and butchered. Equally as important for clans is access to make tools or perform other sensitive activities.

C Tribes are mostly larger than the mobile hunter-gatherer clan groups and it would be usual for a group to include a population above a few thousand. They tend to nourish mostly on cultivated plants and domesticated animals. People belonging to the tribe societal group are mostly farmers, but could also be nomadic with a mobile economy based on the exploitation of livestock. Tribes are generally multi-community societies, with the individual communities integrated into the large society through kinship ties.

Some of the recovered evidence of tribes across the world includes the first farms of the Danube valley in Europe. Others include the Pueblos of the American Southwest, or the early farming village of Catalhoyuk which makes up part of modern Turkey. Although some tribes have officials and even a 'capital' or seat of government, such officials lack the economic base necessary for effective use of power.

D Chiefs are graded on a scale of prestige with senior members holding more power. The more senior chiefs are also tasked with governing the society. Prestige and rank are determined by how closely a person is related to a senior chief but there is no true stratification into classes.

Chiefs also benefit from living in a centre of power with luxuries others barely have access to, in particular temples and residences. Chiefs obviously benefit the most from their power and prestige through surplus local craft products and food which are paid as a tribute. A chief could then keep the tribute to satisfy workers or redistribute them to his subjects. Chiefdoms typically vary greatly in size from one society to another, but a typical range is between 5,000 and 20,000 people.

E Statesmen share many of the characteristics of a chief but with one key difference. Statesmen tend to have absolute power as a king or a queen, which grants them explicit authority to create laws and enforce them through an armed force. The ruling lineage is viewed as the ultimate owner of the land and their luxuries extend beyond the temples enjoyed by chiefs. This is made possible by lower-ranked people who have an obligation to pay taxes to the statesmen.

Statesmen are typically not far removed from capital houses where the bureaucratic administration enforces the collection of revenue and key responsibilities. A centralised location also allows for easier distribution of the revenue to other government members, armed forces, and craft specialists. Early states tend to have developed redistribution systems to best support the essential services and proper functioning of the government.

F Elman Service, William Sanders, and Joseph Marino are experts in the field of societal hierarchy and credited in part with discovering this knowledge. Service provides a good framework to help organise our thoughts on the topic through various papers and books. He, in particular, is credited with developing a 'managerial benefits' theory of society which hypothesises that societies with four levels of hierarchy including a centralised leadership were beneficial to all. At the top of the command, the statesmen or leaders offered benefits to the followers and over time these benefits grew in complexity and improved the whole society.

Service's research also led him to conclude that class war was not present in ancient civilisation. In fact, those on the lower-end of the societal scale were eager to volunteer and perform tasks instead of being forced to do so by the leadership. He also found that arguments or struggles took place among the political elite.

Questions 1–7

Do the following statements agree with the information given in Reading Passage 1?

In boxes 1–7 on your answer sheet, write

> **TRUE**   If the statement agrees with the information
> **FALSE**   If the statement contradicts the information
> **NOT GIVEN** If there is no information on this

1   There is a hierarchy of economic power within clans.

2   Only clans are considered nomadic.

3   Tribes are supported by communities of people who are mostly connected through family relationships.

4   In chiefdoms, residents offer items and foodstuffs to the chief.

5   In a state, citizens are considered as owners of the land.

6   Citizens have to pay taxes to their statesmen before they get benefits from their leaders.

7   Early states benefit from their ability to easily redistribute capital.

Questions 8–13

Answer the questions below.

Choose **NO MORE THAN THREE WORDS** from the passage for each answer.

Write your answers in boxes 8–13 on your answer sheet.

8   In clans, what makes a group of people connected with each other?

9   What do the Hadza use to catch their prey?

10   Where in Europe have archaeologists found examples of early farms?

11   Which two items do chiefs have available to them that other members of society do not?

12   What do statesmen possess that differentiates them from chiefs?

13   What did Service discover to be missing in ancient civilisations?

READING PASSAGE 2

You should spend about 20 minutes on **Questions 14–27**, *which are based on Reading Passage 2 below.*

Aqua product: New Zealand's Algae Biodiesel

A New Zealand's Aquaflow Bionomic Corporation has produced the world's first wild algae biodiesel. It was successfully test-driven in Wellington by David Parker, Minister for Energy and Climate Change Issues. The Minister himself filled the tank of a diesel-powered Land Rover with Aquaflow B5 blend biodiesel. He then drove the vehicle around the Parliament Building's forecourt with a gathering of guests, media, public, and even his Green party co-leader Jeanette Fitzsimons, in attendance. Aquaflow is a Marlborough-based company which first announced the production of the world's first biodiesel fuel from microalgae derived from local sewage pond in May 2006.

B Barrie Leay, the spokesperson in Aquaflow, said, "we believe we are the first-ever company in the world to drive a vehicle powered by wild algae-based biofuel. Besides, this test will surprise others in the industry who predicted this breakthrough to take place in the distant future." He also stated that the company took almost a year to come up with this fuel which will eventually turn out to be an excellent opportunity for the Kiwis and the team who believe in the potential of this eco-friendly technology.

C Algae-based Biodiesel is anticipated to become an economical, and cleaner fuel alternative for New Zealand's automobiles. However, apart from cars, boats, and buses, it can also be used for heating and power generation. Without a doubt, there is a global demand for these eco-friendly fuels, and in billions of litres per year. The best part is that Algae are available in abundance, as they are naturally produced in nutrient-rich wastewater, like in the settling ponds of Effluent Management Systems (EMS). They are both indigenous and renewable, and can generate many beneficial byproducts.

D It all began with Aquaflow's agreement to commence a pilot project with Marlborough District Council last year, to extract algae from their Blenheim based EMS ponds. By using the primary contaminant of these ponds as a fuel feedstock, Aquaflow is also aiding the Council's bioremediation process of cleaning up water discharge. Even dairy farmers and food processing units can adopt the same methodology to reap significant benefits from their wastewaters.

E The biofuels are blended with mineral diesel and not used in raw form. They also help in meeting the government's B5 target of 5% blending. Eventually, this percentage is expected to scale with the increase in the generation of biofuels. In line with this, Aquaflow plans to augment its production capacity to one million litres in the coming year. The company will also launch a prospectus for potential investors before Christmas. And this test drive at Massey University's Wellington campus on December 11th might be the main highlight to woo more investors.

F Apart from biofuels, algae are already used as fertiliser, livestock feed, and soil conditioners. Both aquatic and microscopic species can be cultivated in ponds and clear tanks to treat effluents in ponds. This process is known as Algaculture, and when practiced on a large scale, it becomes a prominent part of aquaculture.

G More so, the production of Aquaflow is subject to a provisional patent which prevents other companies from using their invention illegally. Algae are the simplest plant organisms that can produce and store energy by the process of photosynthesis. They are rich in lipids and combustible elements, which Aquaflow is striving to extract economically. Besides, while algae are good at catching all the nutrients in sewage, too much algae may cause issues like unbearable stench and tinting of water. So an arrangement with Aquaflow is an excellent alternative to algae disposal and cleaning up for the Council.

H Natural seaweeds are also an essential source of food, as they are rich sources of Vitamin B2 (riboflavin), B6 (pyridoxine), B3 (niacin), and C, in addition to iodine, iron, potassium, magnesium, calcium, etc. The commercially produced Algae and cyanobacteria are also marketed as health supplements, Spirulina, Chlorella and Dunaliella (a Vitamin-C supplement), being prominent examples. Besides, it might surprise you to know that algae are ethnic foods in many countries. While the Japanese consume over 20 species of algae, people in China consume over 70. Algae's natural pigments are also used as an eco-friendly alternative to chemical dyes.

I The most noticeable part about cultivating algae is that they neither require any specific care nor compete with food crops for resources like land, chemicals, and fertilisers. All that is necessary for the growth of algae exists naturally and in abundance. From wastewater to free solar energy, the inputs and processes are sustainable, and so is their usage.

Questions 14–19

Reading Passage 2 has nine paragraphs, **A–I**.

Which paragraph contains the following information?

*Write the correct letter, **A–I**, in boxes 14–19 on your answer sheet.*

14 mention of different ways of utilising algae biodiesel

15 an announcement declaring the pioneering role of a firm

16 mention of how algae are consumed as food

17 a description of a real-life experiment

18 the use of algae as food for domestic animals

19 the fact that growing algae does not require a lot of resources

Questions 20–27

Complete the sentences below.

*Choose **ONE WORD ONLY** from the passage for each answer.*

Write your answers in boxes 20–27 on your answer sheet.

20 The biofuel is created by collecting algae which can be found in nutrient-rich.............................

21 Besides being sustainable, algae are also............................. to many places.

22 While extracting algae from particular EMS ponds, Aquaflow contributes to the............................. process which removes harmful substances from polluted water.

23 By combining biofuels with............................. diesel, Aquaflow can produce an environmentally friendly fuel that complies with the requirement of the authority.

24 Algae have already been widely applied in agriculture, such as being processed as............................. for soil.

25 Growing algae in places like ponds for the purpose of addressing water contaminants is known as.............................

26 In order to protect its intellectual property rights on the algae biodiesel, a............................. is essential for Aquaflow.

27 .... enables algae to create and reserve energy for its own sake.

READING PASSAGE 3

*You should spend about 20 minutes on **Questions 28–40**, which are based on Reading Passage 3 below.*

Psychology of New Product Adoption

The corporate universe is very competitive, with companies forced to either innovate or fall behind their competitors. Even when businesses spend billions of dollars investing in new products, the odds are still stacked against them. For example, a recent study found between 40% and 90% of new products fail. Companies looking to sell packaged goods in the U.S. introduced to consumers 30, 000 new items each year and the failure rate was at least 70%. Most products fail to stay on the shelves in stores for more than 12 months. The failure rate has remained consistent for more than two decades. According to another study, even companies who gained a first-mover advantage were eventually pushed out of the category.

The question that experts continue to examine is why good products fail to see success. After all, a product that offers a superior benefit to the end-user should be embraced by consumers who are willing to spend money. The answer to this question could be found in psychology. New products may be at a disadvantage as they require consumers to change some forms of behaviour and that comes with a cost. Consider for example a new smartphone that is more advanced and something a consumer wants but requires the consumer to pay a penalty when switching from one service provider to another. A cost can also come in the form of time if a consumer needs to educate themselves and learn how to use new technologies.

It may be easy for a company to quantify any of these costs, but it is difficult, if not impossible, to quantify the psychological cost associated with switching a cell phone provider or learning a new technology. Consumers are guilty of psychologically acting irrationally because they overvalue the benefits of a product they currently use. Companies also assume that consumers will by default embrace new products that offer incremental value and this alone is reasonable enough for them to buy a product. Communications scholar Everett Rogers hypothesised this theory in the 1960s and called it the concept of 'relative advantage' which argued it was the most important driver of consumers buying new products. The theory behind the concept has a major flaw as it, once again, ignores psychological biases that affect decision making.

In 2002, psychologist Daniel Kahneman explored why and when consumers distance themselves from rational economic behaviour. Kahneman and fellow psychologist Amos Tversky found that humans respond to alternatives in four different ways. First, people tend to value how attractive a new item is based on its subjective or perceived value. Second, consumers consider a new product relative to one they already own or are familiar with. Third, consumers look at improvements in a product relative to a similar product they already own. Finally, and most importantly, deteriorating features have a much larger impact on people compared to a similar-sized improvement.

These traits have been for the most part validated in multiple surveys and studies. One study consisted of people being told they can accept a wager in which there is a 50% chance of winning $100 and an equal chance of losing the same amount of money. Needless to say that few would want to partake in an offer which amounts to a coin toss as they need to be at an advantage. The study then changed the parameters by giving the participants a slight edge in winning $100 over losing $100. It was not until the likelihood of winning $100 was two to three times better than losing $100 before the majority of participants felt comfortable enough to enter a wager.

This loss aversion prompts people to value products they already own more than those they do not. Behaviour economist Richard Thaler referred to this as the 'endowment effect'. Thaler conducted an experiment by giving a group of people coffee mugs and asking what amount of money (from 25 cents to $9.25) they would sell their mugs for. Another group was asked if they would rather receive the coffee mug or cash. The 'Sellers' of the mugs valued their cups at $7.12 on average in the first trial while the 'Buyers' were willing to pay on average just $3.12. In a follow-up trial the 'Sellers' valued their cups at $7.00 while 'Buyers' increased their willingness to buy the mugs on average at $3.50.

Thaler's findings were consistent with a similar study from economist Jack Knetsch who found 90% of participants considered giving up what they already had as a painful loss. The data was compiled from a study consisting of three groups of students. Group one participants were given a choice of receiving a coffee mug or a chocolate bar which had a similar price point in stores. The choices were nearly split evenly, with 56% of students opting for a mug and 44% for a chocolate bar.

Group two had no choice in the matter and were given a coffee mug, and the third group were similarly given just a chocolate bar. At that point, group two participants were asked if they want to trade their coffee mug for a chocolate bar and group three were given a similar option of trading their chocolate bar for a coffee mug. Surprisingly, only 11% of group two participants wanted to trade for a chocolate bar and only 10% of group three participants wanted a coffee mug instead. The researchers of the study felt the outcomes were compelling enough to conclude that a consumer feels a painful loss when they are giving up a product they have in their hands. The most notable takeaway from the psychological experiments is how oblivious most people are to their behaviours. Even when presented with evidence of irrationality, people acted not only shocked but slightly defensive. These behaviour traits have proven to be consistent across all experiments.

Questions 28–31

Look at the following statements (Questions 28–31) and the list of people below.

Match each statement or deed with the correct person or people, **A–C.**

Write the correct letter, **A–C,** *in boxes 28–31 on your answer sheet.*

NB *You may use any letter more than once.*

28 Companies treat all new products with improvements as more likely to be adopted by consumers than older ones.

29 Worsened properties of products will influence customers more than equivalent enhanced ones.

30 Used a special term for people valuing things they possess more than things they may receive.

31 Created an experiment to measure the different value people ascribed to items they owned versus ones they did not.

List of People

A Richard Thaler

B Everett Rogers

C Kahneman and Tversky

Questions 32–36

Do the following statements agree with the information given in Reading Passage 3?

In boxes 32–36 on your answer sheet, write

TRUE	*If the statement agrees with the information*
FALSE	*If the statement contradicts the information*
NOT GIVEN	*If there is no information on this*

32 According to Kahneman and Tversky, the value of an item is objective to the consumers.

33 According to Kahneman and Tversky, people tend to compare a new item to the ones they know well.

34 The coffee cup and chocolate bar had a small difference in value to the participants in the first group of Knetsch's study.

35 Participants in the second group of Knetsch's experiment would be offered chocolate after the experiment.

36 According to the author, the majority of people are aware of their purchasing biases.

Questions 37–40

*Choose the correct letter, **A**, **B**, **C** or **D**.*

Write your answers in boxes 37–40 on your answer sheet.

37 Even if a new product is an improvement on what is currently offered,

   A it will still only be used by customers if necessary.

   B it is still highly unlikely to be accepted by consumers.

   C it may not provide the benefits that customers want.

   D it will only succeed through aggressive advertising.

38 The key weakness of a new product, from a consumer's perspective, may relate to

   A the failure in packaging to suit common people.

   B the fluctuation of prices.

   C the pain triggered by the demand in behavioural change.

   D the unknown running costs.

39 What view does the writer express from Thaler's experiment?

   A The prices offered by consumers are closer to the objective market value of a product.

   B Most people would place a greater value on products of their own.

   C It takes time for sellers to readjust their pricing strategy.

   D People would rather keep what they own than give it away.

40 What can we know from the results of Knetsch's experiment?

   A Products that are similarly priced tend to attract the same type of consumers.

   B It is better to sell an object for a profit than to buy it at a loss.

   C Few people are willing to surrender their ownership of a product.

   D People are less likely to struggle when they choose from products of the same value.

WRITING

WRITING TASK 1

You should spend about 20 minutes on this task.

> **The bar chart below shows the percentage of boys and girls aged 5-14 in Australia who participate in various activities during a two-week period.**
>
> **Summarise the information by selecting and reporting the main features, and make comparisons where relevant.**

Write at least 150 words.

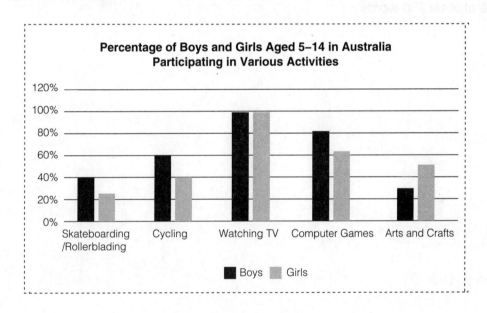

WRITING TASK 2

You should spend about 40 minutes on this task.

Write about the following topic:

> **More and more people are using computers and electric devices to access information, therefore printed books, magazines and newspapers are no longer needed.**
>
> **To what extent do you agree or disagree with this statement?**

Give reasons for your answer and include any relevant examples from your own knowledge or experience.

Write at least 250 words.

SPEAKING

PART 1

The examiner asks the candidate about him/herself, his/her home, work or studies and other family topics.

EXAMPLE

Break

- Do you prefer a long break or several short breaks?
- What do you usually do during a break?
- Why do you need to take a break?
- How often do you take a break?

PART 2

Describe an occasion when you could not use your mobile phone.

You should say:
    when it was
    where it was
    why you could not use your mobile phone

and how you felt about it.

You will have to talk about the topic for one to two minutes. You have one minute to think about what you are going to say. You can make some notes to help you if you wish.

PART 3

Discussion topics:

The use of mobile phones

Example questions:
Do you think it's necessary to have laws on the use of mobile phones?
What do you think of children having mobile phones?
At what age should children have mobile phones?
Are people politer now than in the past?

Test 4

PART 1   *Questions 1–10*

Complete the notes below.

*Write **ONE WORD AND/OR A NUMBER** for each answer.*

Theatre Club

Postal address: 117 Green Street

The club house: for holding **1**............................

Roles available: actors and **2**............................ singers

Errands needed: taking care of props and **3**............................

Meetings

* Members get together: every **4**............................ at 7 pm
* Summer holiday: in **5**............................

Membership

* 60-pound fee includes a club **6**............................
* Concessions for jobless or retired people: **7**............................ pounds
* Minimum age: **8**............................

Plays

* Generally perform: **9**............................ plays
* Christmas charity performance: raise funds for a children's **10**............................

PART 2   *Questions 11–20*

Questions 11–15

*Choose the correct letter, **A**, **B** or **C**.*

11 What is the new activity in the zoo in November?

    A evening tours

    B bonfire nights for adults

    C various parties

12 What is the most popular species in the zoo?

    A kangaroo

    B koala

    C sheepdog

13 What is the key to feeding kangaroos?

    A feeding more than one at a time

    B gently touching the baby kangaroos

    C standing up straight when feeding

14 Why is the wild dog area closed?

    A The wild dogs are unwell.

    B The enclosure is under repair.

    C The dogs have not arrived.

15 Where can visitors get discount tickets this year?

    A at the café

    B on the official website

    C at the gift shop

Questions 16–20

Label the map below.

*Write the correct letter, **A–G**, next to Questions 16–20.*

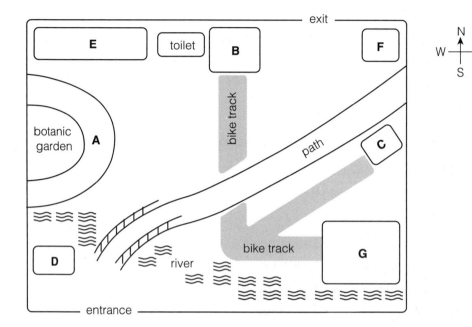

16 Arena ....

17 Educational hall ....

18 Picnic spot ....

19 Photo printing shop ....

20 Gift shop ....

PART 3   *Questions 21–30*

Questions 21–26

Choose the correct letter, **A**, **B** *or* **C**.

Field Trip Report

21 Why did Natasha decide to write the report?

    A to get extra credits

    B to help her decide on a course

    C to practice report-writing

22 How does Mr. White advise Natasha to improve her report?

    A She should include some more details.

    B She should take advantage of report templates.

    C She should revise the introduction.

23 How did Natasha choose the field trip site?

    A She chose a difficult place to get to.

    B She selected one that was recommended.

    C She chose one at random.

24 Natasha's main aim in going on the field trip was to

    A apply some of the techniques she learned in class.

    B measure the density of grasses in the area.

    C analyse the soil content of sand dunes.

25 Why did Natasha include data from other students?

    A to make her result more reliable

    B to compare her data with other data

    C to make her report more complete

26 How did Natasha produce such a detailed map?

    A She made careful observations.

    B She took some photographs first.

    C She copied relevant material.

Questions 27–30

What problem does each of the following part of data collecting have?

Choose **FOUR** answers from the box and write the correct letter, **A–E**, next to Questions 27–30.

Data collection issues

A   inadequately developed

B   time-consuming

C   redundant

D   poorly organised

E   too complicated

---

27 The test kit   ....

28 Data collecting sheet   ....

29 Literature Review   ....

30 Interviews   ....

PART 4 *Questions 31–40*

Complete the notes below.

*Write **ONE WORD ONLY** for each answer.*

Sense of Smell

Smell:

- Plays a key role in our enjoyment of life

- Common to all species

- Less developed in **31**........................... than people generally think, although some primates are able to distinguish **32**........................... odours from other types

Sense of smell in humans:

- Easy to recognise common aromas like that of **33** ....

- However, sense of smell is very subtle

- Scents trigger different emotions and can be used to influence behaviour
  e.g. in a club, the scent of **34**........................... promotes positive feelings

- Many scent reactions are subconscious
  e.g. being attracted to someone because of their scent
      or being aware of someone's **35**........................... because of their sweat

- We are gradually losing our sense of smell because we obscure odours
  It is potentially dangerous if we cannot detect the **36**........................... of a smell

Important because:

- Other senses may not be **37**........................... or available

- An important part of memory
  e.g. recalling experiences from **38**...........................

- Closely related to emotions
  e.g. may help treat patients who are **39** .... or depressed

- Can offer job opportunities
  e.g. coffee roasters or sellers of **40**...........................

READING PASSAGE 1

*You should spend about 20 minutes on **Questions 1–13**, which are based on Reading Passage 1 below.*

Stress of Workplace

A   Take some time to observe how busy is too busy. Some may consider it akin to missing one's long lunch; others may compare it with missing one's lunch altogether. For some, not being able to take a 'sickie' once a month is being too busy. However, there is another bunch of people for whom staying up on their toes, day and night, even on the weekends, is a norm. Notably, in the case of most senior executives, the pace of work can be awfully busy or even frantic. Neil Plumridge, the vice-president of AT Kearney (a management consultancy) and also its Asia-Pacific telecommunications head, states that his work time fluctuates between 45 hours to 80 hours every week.

B   Plumridge makes use of three scales to gauge his workload; they are scheduling, sleep, and family. He knows that he has a lot on his plate when he has to reschedule his appointments continually and when he can manage less than six hours of sleep for three nights, back-to-back. He is unable to spend time with his family, considering that he has a daughter of three and another one is on the way, hopefully in October. Whenever Plumridge misses an anniversary, it is a tip-off that things are out of order.

C   However subjective being too busy might be, any person can understand that being too engrossed in work can ultimately take a toll on one's health and it is the main reason behind their health problems. Visible symptoms include disrupted sleep, and a slump in physical and mental well-being. In fact, the maximum time lost in workplaces is attributed to stress rather than any other workplace injury, as per National Workers' Compensation figures. The effects are quite expensive, with workers taking off due to stress for an average of 16. 6 weeks. Another 2003–2004 report by the federal government insurer Comcare asserts that claims for psychological injury accounted for 7% of all claims but their costs took up approximately 27%, which was above the average.

D   According to experts, getting a break, be it through a game of golf, a massage therapy or a swimming session, is not adequate for dealing with stress; instead, there is a need to reassess one's workload. For instance, to deal with stress, Neil Plumridge identifies what needs to be changed and does something, like earmarking additional resources to a task or project, or extending the time limit or merely readjusting the final expectations, which may take him many days. His colleagues are of great help, as they coach each other with business dilemmas. A fresh pair of eyes over a subject is invariably beneficial.

E   But the issue of stress is not confined to large corporations. Vanessa Stoykov, who runs her own advertising and public relations venture and holds expertise in serving financial and professional firms, is also a victim of stress. Her brand, Evolution media, registered such a quick growth that it debuted on the BRW Fast 100 list for the fastest growing businesses last year, which was immediately after she delivered her first child. Running one's own business is, every now and then, replete with moments when one feels like the head will blow up in pieces juggling various activities. To unwind and unclutter her mind, she makes regular trips to the mountains whenever possible. These short doses of relief were helpful for her since her company was on a constant roll: hiring new workers, training them, guiding them about the work culture, clients, and a lot more.

F   Jan Elsner, a Melbourne-based psychologist that specialises in executive coaching, offers a reprieve from such stressful situations. She states that it is typical of senior executives and business people to flourish in demanding work engagements. She also suggests that there is no one-size-fits-all approach, as some may perform their best during the days of acute stress, while others may prefer a sustained pressure level for optimal performance. While a psychologist may consider hormonal standards to pass the verdict for a patient being stressed or not, it is hard to gauge if the same level of stress is having an equal (emotional or cognitive) impact on any two individuals, or their experiences.

G   Elsner's practice revolves around the school of thought called positive psychology, according to which, feeling positive, engaged, challenged or contributive towards a cause does not reduce one's stress but is effective in building one's resilience to deal with stress over time. Therefore, the good stress which brings about the feeling to face it all with courage and willingness is as cumulative as bad stress. She also reveals that most of her corporate clients rely on yoga and meditation to keep a check on their bad stress. Elsner also points to a study which concluded that meditation has the power to modify the brain's biochemistry, rewiring the brain and the body to respond to stress distinctively. Both meditation and yoga can help you reconfigure your mind and body's reaction, and if people master it, they are in full control.

H Coming back to Neil Plumridge, he affirms that our unrealistic goal setting precipitates stress. For instance, when someone promises a client that he will deliver task A tomorrow, then promises another client that he will deliver task B tomorrow, at a time when he is aware that he can deliver only one task in a day, he puts himself under extreme pressure to stay true to his words. The fact is that he could have easily told one of the clients to give him additional time. Over-commitments like these are stress incubators. He further explains it with reference to procrastination — that work expands to fill the available time. And some researches signify that many humans may be hard-wired to do this.

I Another study, published in the *Journal of Experimental Psychology*'s February edition, finds that most of us tend to believe that we will be less busy in the future than we are now. This is, though, a fallacy, according to Professor Gal Zauberman from the University of North Carolina and Professor John Lynch of Duke University, Who are authors of the report. They make it clear that, on average, a person will be simply as busy as he or she is right now in a couple of weeks or a month in the future. But in routine life, things are a tad different. Many people make commitments to tasks long in advance, which they will otherwise avoid or deny if they have to work on them immediately. In other words, it means that people view future time investments with relative clumsiness. It is fascinating that we generally perceive that there will be more 'surplus' time in the future than in the present. While it is a question to ponder over, researchers suggest that one major cause of stress is that we underestimate the time required to complete a prospective task, and fail to gauge competition of our own time in the future effectively.

Questions 1–5

Look at the following statements (Questions 1–5) and the list of people below.

*Match each statement with the correct person, **A–D**.*

*Write the correct letter, **A–D**, in boxes 1–5 on your answer sheet.*

NB   *You may use any letter more than once.*

1   Coping mechanisms can vary according to an individual's condition.

2   Spending time in nature is an excellent antidote to feeling overwhelmed.

3   People need to maintain a realistic expectation of their pace of life.

4   To cope with stress, it is sometimes necessary to amend the current arrangements.

5   Meditation is a common method for managing stress.

List of People
A   Neil Plumridge
B   Vanessa Stoykov
C   Jan Elsner
D   Gal Zauberman and John Lynch

Questions 6–8

Choose the correct letter, **A, B, C** *or* **D.**

Write your answers in boxes 6–8 on your answer sheet.

6 What is the primary cause of poor health for employees?

   A They could not sleep well at night.

   B They may commit excessively to their jobs.

   C They lack solutions to mental illnesses.

   D They constantly work under great pressure.

7 The writer refers to positive psychology in order to suggest that

   A we should keep pushing ourselves till our brain can respond to stress positively.

   B courage and willingness are the keys to controlling stress.

   C our ability to tackle stress can be strengthened by confronting it with the right mentality.

   D stress would never be reduced if we do not face it.

8 What point does the writer make in paragraph I?

   A People are not as busy as they think in the present.

   B People may lack objectivity when evaluating the amount of time available in the future.

   C People will have more available time in the future.

   D People will avoid tasks in the future to allow for more availability.

Questions 9–13

Complete the summary below.

*Choose **NO MORE THAN TWO WORDS** from the passage for each answer.*

Write your answers in boxes 9–13 on your answer sheet.

According to a report from early this century, **9** .... resulting from stress may account for over a quarter of all insurance claims' costs. While finding a good work-life balance is essential for reducing stress, it may not be enough. Although scientists can measure stress levels quantifiably with **10** .... , these measurements only help identify stress, and do not help us determine the **11** .... or intellectual effects of stress. Positive psychologists try to support people by strengthening their **12** .... to stress through practices such as meditation. In terms of over-commitments, the problem can be related to **13** .... After all, it is well known that when we put off working, stress increases. An article from the *Journal of Experimental Psychology* supports this commonly held belief and argues that time management is essential for reducing stress.

READING PASSAGE 2

You should spend about 20 minutes on **Questions 14–27**, *which are based on Reading Passage 2 below.*

Mammoth Kill

A Mammoths were characterised by long and curved tusks and the northern species were covered by long hair. These species belonged to the Elephantidae family which also included the two classes of the current elephant species and their antecedents. Similar to their close relatives, mammoths had a reputation for being huge. The largest of these species got to as high as four metres at the shoulder level and used to weigh up to eight tonnes. Male mammoths that were extraordinarily large would reach more than twelve tonnes. In most cases, however, mammoth species would only reach the size of current Asian elephants. At about six months of age, a small set of tusks first appeared and they were later replaced by a long-lasting set. The new set of tusks grew at approximately one to six inches per year. Studies conducted on the current elephant species indicated that mammoths most likely had twenty-two months of gestation before culminating in the birth of one calf. These mammoth species almost certainly had social structures resembling the current Asian and African elephants which are comprised of an all-female herd and a matriarch leader, while the males had solitary lives or formed lax groups after they reached maturity.

B It is hard to fathom in the current age of modernisation, urbanisation and automobiles, North America was once the home of mammoths, cow-size ground sloths, bear-size beavers, camels, and other strong beasts. About 11,000 years ago, these huge mammals, approximately 70 species in total, became extinct. The extinction of the species nearly corresponded with the arrival of the human species in the New World and dramatic climatic change factors that bore theories concerning perishing. Despite years of scientific research, the precise cause is still unknown. There are recent findings that support the contentious hypothesis that human beings were responsible for hunting that resulted in the extinction of the megafauna. The overkill model came about in the 1960s when Paul S. Martin brought the agenda at Arizona

University. From that point, critics of the model have proposed that there is no evidence to sustain the argument that early Americans hunted the animals to the level of extinction. However, John Alroy, a paleoecologist at the University of California, argued in an annual meeting of the vertebrate paleontology that extinction as a result of hunting was believable and inevitable. By using computer simulation, he demonstrated that even an ordinary volume of hunting was enough to wipe out the animals.

C   Assuming there were 100 human beings at the beginning with a population growth of 2% per year, Alroy found that a group of 50 human beings was able to kill 15 to 20 mammals each year, so human beings could wipe out the entire animal populations within 1,000 years. In particular, large mammals are susceptible to pressure because their gestation period is longer as compared to the smaller mammals and their offspring need protracted care.

D   The assessment by Alroy does not have universal consensus though. To start with, the outcome is subject, in part, to the estimated population size of extinct animals and the estimates are not reliable. Ross MacPhee, a mammologist from New York City's Natural History Museum, presents a deeply pointed criticism of Alroy's findings by calling attention to pertinent archaeological records that only contain a handful of stone tools embedded in the bones of mammoths and none of them are recognised as coming from other megafaunal corpses. This is contrary to the expectation that hunting drove these mammals to their extinction. Certain animal species had vast ranges and an example is the humongous ground sloth that lived in the far north region up to Yukon and far south down to Mexico. The range itself would make it improbable to slaughter the animals to the extent of causing extinction.

E   MacPhee agrees that human beings were most likely responsible for the extinction of the mammoths and other species that existed at the same time, but not in a direct way. His suggestion is that people likely initiated very lethal diseases, probably through parasites or the dogs, occasioning a widespread epidemic among species with poor immunity in the new biosphere. Similar to Paul Martin's overkill model, large mammal populations would find it hard to recover. The recurrent lethal disease outbreaks would quickly lead to extinction. MacPhee does not present any empirical evidence to support his hypothesis. Also, it can be difficult to find the evidence since lethal disease would have killed these animals far too quickly to leave signature on the bones. However, MacPhee is confident that DNA and tissue analyses from the last species of mammoths would reveal the deadly microbes.

F   Another proposition on what caused the extinction of North American mammoths has nothing to do with human beings. Supporters of the new proposition blame the weather for the loss. Pleistocene epoch era was characterised by significant climatic instability as Russell Graham, a paleontologist, explains. The harsh weather caused the disappearance of some habitats and some of the species that had formed communities were driven apart. Some animals seized the opportunities and flourished. However, the intensifying harsh environment may have been too much for megafauna and caused their geographic range to diminish. This spelled doom for the huge animals which needed larger spaces to survive. As Graham stated, although sizeable populations survived the Pleistocene, the Younger Dryas occurrence was too much for them. Alroy is certain that the demise of the titans can be traced to human hunters in the period of extreme cold, the Ice Age. However, Graham believes that changing climate scenarios could predict with accuracy that these species would still become extinct eventually.

Questions 14–20

Complete the summary below.

Choose **NO MORE THAN TWO WORDS** *from the passage for each answer.*

Write your answers in boxes 14–20 on your answer sheet.

Being a member of the family **14** ...., the mammoths were a group of animals that were closely related to modern elephants. They were large, highly social, and had long **15** .... periods for their young. Today, many scientists are trying to determine the cause of their extinction. A researcher from the University of California believes that human hunting was the cause. However, this argument does not have **16** .... According to MacPhee, the **17** .... do not provide evidence of humans killing the mammoths. Another argument is that disease may have killed the mammoths, but there is no **18** .... evidence to support this idea. A paleontologist points that the era — **19** .... is a possible cause by arguing that megafauna may not have been able to adapt to the changing environment which reduced their **20** ....

Questions 21–27

Look at the following statements (Questions 21–27) and the list of people below.

*Match each statement with the correct person, **A–C**.*

*Write the correct letter, **A–C**, in boxes 21–27 on your answer sheet.*

NB *You may use any letter more than once.*

21 We can calculate the rate of extinction by measuring the rate of hunting against the stable increase of population.

22 We should analyse the bodies of extinct mammals to look for signs of disease.

23 Some species can thrive in more challenging environments.

24 We would expect to see stone tools near mammoth remains if they were extensively hunted.

25 The mammoths were fated to become extinct, regardless of human activity.

26 Humans could have brought parasites that could kill mammoths.

27 Mammoths were vulnerable due to the way they raised their young.

List of People
A   John Alroy
B   Ross MacPhee
C   Russell Graham

READING PASSAGE 3

*You should spend about 20 minutes on **Questions 28–40**, which are based on Reading Passage 3 below.*

Facial Expressions

A A facial expression is best defined as one or more motions or positions of the muscles on the face. It can often be used to convey an emotional state of a person and is easy for anyone paying attention to understand. As notable author Charles Dickens once said, "The expression of a man's face is commonly a help to express his thoughts, or a glossary on his speech." Facial expressions are also classified as a form of non-verbal communication and a way of conveying information. This is not unique to humans, as many animals can exhibit facial expressions that are just as easy to understand.

B A major misconception when discussing facial expressions is to assume that they are voluntary. Facial expressions are very much tied to emotion and are more often than not involuntary. Someone who is sad could attempt to exert a lot of internal effort to convey the opposite and declare to the world they are in fact happy. But they are likely to show their true feelings involuntarily in the end, even though they attempt to show their feelings in quite opposite ways.

This nature of facial expressions is not unique to how someone feels about themselves. Sometimes it can lead to embarrassing social situations. For example, a person could involuntarily give the message that they find someone they just met unattractive by showing a brief expression of disgust. They may intend to show a less offensive expression yet they just cannot help but show how they truly feel.

C Not all emotions are easy to understand. Quite the opposite holds true, as the feelings of disgust and fear are difficult to tell apart. The reason for this is simple: the face has minimal ranges of movements and the difference between disgust and fear breaks down to very minuscule differences in the relative position of facial features.

Sometimes a person's face could express a neutral emotion — as is typically the case during a period when everything is normal and there is no stress. However, it is possible that the specific proportions of a neutral facial expression closely resemble a face associated with a specific emotion. A scenario where someone is looking at their new coworker or friend and assuming they are sad when they are not is a daily occurrence and happens quite often.

D   A person's eyes can also reveal how they are feeling at any given moment. William Shakespeare once said, "The eyes are the window to your soul." — And it is for a good reason. Boston College professor Joe Tecce found a correlation between blinking and stress. He explained that rapid blinking is related to unpleasant feelings, especially among liars.

However, the key to the theory is that the person needs to feel bad about lying. People who gain pleasure from lying, such as psychopaths, will not show a similar rapid blinking trait. As such, non-verbal traits and cues are multi-channeled and focusing on only one cue is reckless.

Poker players are best known for being experts in evaluating facial characteristics. A novice poker player who is bluffing will more likely than not blink when putting chips on the table. An expert facial expression reader will not hesitate to take advantage of his advantage to win a hand. Similarly, all it takes is a brief nanosecond for a novice poker player to visually tell the world he is holding excellent cards. The expert poker players will instantly fold their hand and avoid falling into a potential trap.

E   Charles Darwin stated in his book *The Expression of the Emotions in Man and Animals* that people of all ages, along with animals, show emotions through similar behaviours. He also thought at the time that a human face could show just a few emotions. This theory contradicted French physician Guillaume-Benjamin-Amand Duchenne who argued a human could express at least 60 different emotions.

F   In the 1960s, studies by scientist Paul Ekman supported Darwin's stance to a large degree. Ekman evaluated adults and children from a very isolated region in New Guinea to see if there are any differences in responses compared to people in less isolated societies. Participants listened to a story which describes one particular emotion and were then shown either two or three pictures of facial expressions.

They had to match the facial expression with the overall theme of the story.

Isolated people from the South Fore region of New Guinea were able to identify the accurate facial expression at the same rate as the non-isolated control group. The study also found that emotions for fear and surprise were consistently misidentified.

G The reason for selecting New Guinea was based on early feedback to similar tests among people in Argentina, Brazil, Chile, Japan, and the United States. Ekman had found that the participants across the five geographically dispersed locations had similar facial expressions for emotions.

He questioned his own study and asked, "What if these five cultures had all grown up watching the same movies and television shows? Could it be that the reason they all agree is they have learned these expressions from the same place? Could the reason for their agreement be their similar backgrounds and experiences? Learned from media or actors for example?"

Exploring the highlands of New Guinea where ancient traditions and ways of life are supreme should remove all doubts to his findings. The people in New Guinea most certainly did not grow up watching the same movies like those in the United States. His study has stood the test of time as more modern approaches have come to the same conclusion.

H Finally, certain expressions of emotions are also found to be universally accepted. Among those are anger, disgust, joy, sadness, and surprise. Of particular note, none of these emotions has a definitive social component, such as shame or pride.

Findings on contempt (which has a social component) are less clear. There is some preliminary evidence to suggest that the expressions of contempt and other social emotions vary across cultures.

Questions 28–32

Complete the summary below.

Choose **NO MORE THAN TWO WORDS** *from the passage for each answer.*

Write your answers in boxes 28–32 on your answer sheet.

It is not difficult to **28** .... the emotion another person is feeling if you watch their facial expressions carefully. This is because such expressions are a method of **29** .... our emotions to others. Even if you try to hide how you are feeling, your facial expressions may still show the truth as they are usually **30** .... However, some emotions are more difficult to distinguish than others. For example, people often have difficulty telling the difference between **31** .... and **32** ....

Questions 33–38

Reading Passage 3 has eight sections, **A–H**.

Which section contains the following information?

Write the correct letter, **A–H**, *in boxes 33–38 on your answer sheet.*

NB *You may use any letter more than once.*

33 a contradiction between two theories on the range of emotions humans can express on their faces

34 an explanation of how involuntary facial expressions can result in embarrassment

35 a reference to social factors causing cultural difference in conveying emotions

36 the reason why relying on a single physical cue to determine one's emotions can be wrong

37 a reference to an experiment of how geographical location does not affect people's understanding of facial expressions

38 a common mistaken assumption made about facial expressions

Questions 39 and 40

*Choose **TWO** letters, **A–E**.*

Write the correct letters in boxes 39 and 40 on your answer sheet.

Which **TWO** of the following ideas were shown by Ekman's studies in New Guinea?

    A People generally learn facial expressions from watching TV.

    B Darwin's belief was correct to a great extent.

    C Fear and surprise were the most commonly expressed emotions.

    D The expression of many emotions appears to be the same across cultures.

    E There were no similarities between the results of the study in New Guinea and those of similar tests in other countries.

WRITING

WRITING TASK 1

You should spend about 20 minutes on this task.

> **The map below shows the development of the village of Ryemouth between 1995 and present.**
>
> **Summarise the information by selecting and reporting the main features, and make comparisons where relevant.**

Write at least 150 words.

1995

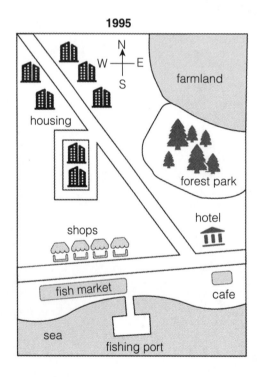

Present

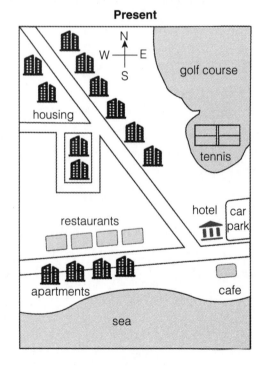

WRITING TASK 2

You should spend about 40 minutes on this task.

Write about the following topic:

> *Some people think that the best way to reduce the time spent in travelling to work is to replace parks and gardens close to the city centre with apartment buildings for commuters, but others disagree.*
>
> *Discuss both these views and give your own opinion.*

Give reasons for your answer and include any relevant examples from your own knowledge or experience.

Write at least 250 words.

SPEAKING

PART 1

The examiner asks the candidate about him/herself, his/her home, work or studies and other family topics.

EXAMPLE

Number

- What is your favourite number?
- Are you good at remembering phone numbers?
- Do you usually use numbers?
- Are you good at math?

PART 2

Describe a crowded place you went to.
You should say:
when you went there
who you went there with
why you went there
and how you felt about it.

You will have to talk about the topic for one to two minutes. You have one minute to think about what you are going to say. You can make some notes to help you if you wish.

PART 3

Discussion topics:

Congestion and public facilities

Example questions:

Do people like to go to crowded places? Why?

How can the problem of traffic congestion be solved?

Why do people like to live in big cities even though there are severe traffic jams?

What public facilities does your city have?

IELTS PREP
ORANGE
BOOK

第二部分
解　析

Test 1

Listening / 104

Reading / 116

Writing / 129

Speaking / 133

Listening

1	Pennington	6	flat
2	greenfield	7	forest
3	66 Lake	8	organic
4	radio	9	bike
5	UK765024EG	10	dance

Audioscripts

MARK: Good afternoon, Lakeside Eco Farm, Mark speaking.

HELEN: Oh, good afternoon, my name is Helen. I was listening to a programme the other day and it said that you are a member of the Northern Hotel Group.

MARK: Yes, that's correct. Are you a member of the Group?

HELEN: Yes, I am, and I would like to find out about staying with you for a week during the school holidays.

MARK: No problem, Helen. May I have your full name?

HELEN: Helen Pennington. That's P-E-double N-I-N-G-T-O-N. ❶

MARK: Thank you, Helen. And your email address?

HELEN: helen123@email.com. No dashes or underscores. Oh sorry, actually it's probably better if I give you my work email address, which is more convenient for me. That is helen123@greenfield.com, and greenfield is one word. ❷

MARK: Okay, and your home address?

1 此题考查单词拼写，需要注意 double N，因为题目中有 Name 这一定位词，所以在听到 full name 时需要准备好拼写出答案。

2 此题定位词为 E-mail address，需要注意在听到第一个地址后还不能确定答案，因为后面又说"Oh sorry, actually..."，可知又改变了想法，换了地址，所以后面说的地址才是答案，最后需要注意 greenfield 是一个词。

HELEN: It is 66 Lake Road, Sheffield. ❸

MARK: May I ask where you heard about us. You mentioned a program. Is it on TV or?

HELEN: Actually, I heard about you on the radio ❹ and I thought it might be a good place to take my children during the summer holidays. What kind of activities do you have?

MARK: Well, here we have lodges in the woods, a couple of lakes, lots of activities and great food so I'm sure your whole family will love it. I can give you prices for all these. But first could I have your membership number?

HELEN: Oh yes, I think it's UK765042GE, but I will just check. It has been a while since I used it... just a moment... ah, actually it is UK765024EG. ❺

MARK: That's fine, thank you.

HELEN: Can you see my information on your system?

MARK: Yes, I've found you. So, regarding accommodation here at Island Eco Farm, for families I recommend our family chalets, as they are large and suitable for both adults and children.

HELEN: Ah okay, that sounds nice. But a lodge is probably too big for us and I don't think we have much time and energy for cleaning, so we would like to stay in a flat, ❻ preferably near the farm.

MARK: I'm afraid there's no accommodation near the farm. Would you want to be located near the lake? It's got a great view.

HELEN: Actually, my daughter would prefer to stay in the

3 此题定位词为 Home address，填空处后为 Road，故只需要听 Road 前面的内容，为 66 Lake。

4 此题定位词为 Source of information，即信息来源，文中 where you heard about us 即问信息来源，需要注意听后面的内容，听到 on TV 时还不能确定答案，因为只是一个猜测，接着听到单词 actually，表事实，所以后面的内容才是真正的信息来源，故填 radio。

5 此题定位词为 Membership number，可预判填数字或字母，或数字和字母的组合，在听到 UK765042GE 后，因为说话者继续说 I will just check，即核对一下，故有可能更正信息，仍需要仔细听后面的内容，后面由 actually（事实上）可知正确答案为 UK765024EG。

6 此题定位词为 Accommodation type，因为填空处前面有已经给出的信息 lodges，故听到 lodge 后需要注意答案词将会出现，would like（想要）和题目中的 preferences（偏好）为同义替换，故填 flat。

7 此题定位词为 location，填空处前面有已经给出的信息 lakeside，原文中虽然没有出现 lakeside，但出现了 near the lake，两者都是湖边的意思，为同义替换，故注意听后面的内容，prefer 和 preferences 为同义替换，故填 forest。

8 此题定位词为 Food，由题目可知 seafood 和答案词为并列关系，故需要注意听与 seafood 相关的内容，文中 seafood 没有出现同义替换，听到 seafood 后可直接判断其后面的 organic 为答案。

9 此题定位词为 Transport，train 和答案词为并列关系，故需要注意听与 train 相关的内容，文中提到 train 后紧接着提到了 bike trail，因为问的是交通工具，故填 bike。

10 此题定位词为 Courses，题目中给出的信息为 flower planting course，原文中的 planting flowers 与之对应，需要注意听后面的内容，接着提到 a little more energetic，为 active 的替换词，根据其后的 a dance course 举例，可知填 dance。

forest if possible. ❼

MARK: That's fine, we have some lovely log cabins with room for four people which would suit your family.

HELEN: Yes, that's the kind of thing we want. I hope you have a wide range of food available. My husband is a meat-eater, I like seafood and my children like organic food, ❽ including plenty of vegetables.

MARK: Yes, we cater for all different types of diet so you can get all of those preferences here, don't worry.

HELEN: Great. So, what is the transport situation? Can we get there by ferry or van, for instance?

MARK: No, the best way is by train. There's a regular service from Sheffield, or there is a bike trail all the way here. ❾ It generally takes about six hours to ride here from Sheffield.

HELEN: That sounds good, but it might be difficult with our luggage. It's a pity you don't have vans or ferry boats, but I think we will take the train. So, what activities do you have there?

MARK: We have a gardening course on planting flowers. Would that be suitable?

HELEN: I was hoping for something a little more energetic, to give us more exercise, a dance course, ❿ for example.

MARK: Hmm, that is something guests requested in the past but it's not something we are doing at the moment. I will bear that in mind for the future, though.

HELEN: Okay that would be great. I need to get back to work, so can you email me through the prices and all the details?

MARK: Certainly, I'll send all the details through to your work email address right now.

HELEN: Great, thank you.

MARK: You're welcome and we hope to see you here at Lakeside Eco Farm soon.

HELEN: Thanks, goodbye.

Part 2

Listening Keys,
Questions 11 – 20

11	C		16	A
12	A		17	F
13	B		18	G
14	A		19	D
15	C		20	B

Hello, I'm Edward and I'm here to tell you about road conditions in various areas of the UK. I am also going to tell you about driver's licences in the UK.

Audioscripts

If you have never had a driver's licence, or you have one from another country and you want to get a UK licence, you must be a UK resident. You will need to show a medical report when

11 此题定位词为 basic requirement 和 UK driving licence，原文说想获得英国驾照，必须是英国居民，后期更新驾照才需要医疗报告，也就是说获得英国驾照的基本要求是英国居民，a UK resident 与 current residency in the UK 对应，must 和 requirement 对应，故选 C。

12 此题定位词为 translation of original licences，在听到 translate your original foreign driving licence 后可知道答案在其后面，原文接着说需要访问一个官方机构，visit an official agency 和 go to a recognised organisation 对应，故选 A。

13 此题定位词为 type of photos，需要注意题目中说的是 NOT be approved，原文说大多数被拒绝的照片是用奶油色背景拍摄的，rejected 对应 NOT be approved，故选 B。

14 此题定位词为 licence checking service，说话者认为理想情况下，他希望看到这个服务过程进展得更快，因为目前要花几小时才能完成，言外之意是说这个服务过程进展太慢，故选 A。

your UK licence needs to be renewed. ⓫

If you are trying to translate your original foreign driving licence to apply for a UK licence which is a must if you want to be able to drive here, you will need to visit an official agency. ⓬ These are scattered throughout the London area and are well-equipped to assist you with any questions you might have, and any services they offer are included in your licence fee. If you already have a translated licence, but need some personal information updating, you do not need to pay for the update — they'll do it for free. When you are getting a new driving licence, you may need to have a new photo taken, as some photos are rejected. It's actually okay if your photo is too small, since we can get it enlarged with our printer. The majority of rejected photos are the ones that were taken with a cream backdrop instead of a monotone grey background. ⓭ We've now found that photos with the latter allow us to identify the licence holder much more easily. If you were wearing glasses on the previous photo, you don't need to worry about it since it is still allowed.

If you are not sure whether your previous licence is still valid, then the licence checking service is for you. The procedures are quite clear and you just have to follow them. Ideally, I would like to see the process going faster since it can take hours to finish. ⓮ From my standpoint, it will help if all the applicants bring the necessary identification with them. Then all they have to do is just fill in the forms accordingly, step by step.

I'm often asked whether I have a personal recommendation about the fastest or cheapest place to get all this done, but I think it really depends on where you are. They can all get busy at some point and when it is quiet at one branch it may be busy in another, so take your pick. All I would say is that there is absolutely no difference in price — it's a standard fee. The only advice I would give is that the quickest way to complete an application is to fill out the form on the internet and then bring a print copy with you to the agency location of your choice. ⓯

Next, people frequently ask me what I think of the road conditions in some of our cities. London is obviously the biggest and busiest, and there are lots of parking restrictions, one way systems, and so on, but on the whole, I find the traffic signs are very clear. ⓰ In Edinburgh, most people use digital maps to get to know local traffic and road conditions, which can be estimated through different traffic flow lines. It is a city of lights — traffic lights — but they're extremely efficient as they're timed perfectly to get the traffic flowing smoothly. ⓱ That's important because pedestrian areas and crossings are always packed with people on foot, which needs strong regulation. The city of Cardiff has tackled traffic flow in a different way. It recently completed a road expansion scheme and the extra lanes of the dual-carriageway are easing congestion. ⓲ It's a similar story in Manchester, instead of going through the town centre, most vehicles choose ring-roads so as to avoid the downtown congestion. ⓳ It can still happen, though, so there's a possibility that the city will introduce check points where the police can intervene to direct traffic at peak periods. And finally, they say all roads lead to Rome, and you could say that about Oxford. I like the many options for getting in and out of the city because drivers can always find alternative routes. ⓴ The other cities in the UK are …

15　此题定位词为 recommend，需要注意推荐或者建议内容，在听到 The only advice 后可确定答案在其后面，说话者说他唯一的建议是，最快完成申请的方法是在网上填写表格，fill out the form on the internet 与 complete the forms online 对应，故选 C。

16　此题定位词为 London，地名一般不会同义替换，故听到 London 后可判断答案，原文说伦敦的交通标志很清楚，traffic signs are very clear 对应 good signage，故选 A。

17　此题定位词为 Edinburgh，原文说交通灯非常高效，traffic lights—but they're extremely efficient 对应 effective traffic lights，故选 F。

18　此题定位词为 Cardiff，原文说该地政府最近完成了一项道路扩展计划，并增加了双车道的行车线，extra lanes of the dual-carriageway 对应 additional lanes，故选 G。

19　此题定位词为 Manchester，原文说该地大多数车辆选择环城公路而不是穿过市中心，以避免市区的交通堵塞，故选 D。

20　此题定位词为 Oxford，原文说进出这个城市有很多选择，many options for getting in and out of the city 与 multiple access roads 对应，故选 B。

Part 3

Listening Keys,
Questions 21 – 30

21	C	26	G
22	B	27	B
23	A	28	D
24	B	29	E
25	A	30	F

Audioscripts

21 此题定位词为 Joy 和 finish this assignment，需要注意 Joy 说话的内容，implement the results of our research 即实施研究结果，与 put their findings into practice（将他们的研究结果付诸实践）相对应，且学期即将结束，对应题干 before the semester ends，故选 C。

22 此题定位词为 Tim 和 ignore，需要注意 Tim 说话的内容，由 doesn't have much bearing on the subject we're researching 可知理论章节和他们做的研究没有太大关系，后面接着说他们的项目是课堂管理，而不是公司结构，说明他们项目的重点和课本的重点不一样，故选 B。

JOY: Hi, Tim！I thought you'd never get here. We still have so much of our classroom management project to complete; I don't know how we'll get it done！

TIM: Take it easy, Joy. Our results for this course won't be high enough if we rush to finish. It's our final assignment for the semester. We don't have any other projects to do, so we can focus on this.

JOY: I'm not worried about my results. But we need to finish it, because part of the project is to implement the results of our research and make the classroom a better learning environment. If we don't start soon, we'll run out of time, you know the semester will finish next month. ㉑

TIM: That's true. What do you think of the theory chapter in our textbook? I don't think we should bother with it.

JOY: Are you saying that because you find the theory in that chapter too difficult to understand or is the chapter just too long？

TIM: Neither. My real issue is that it doesn't have much bearing on the subject we're researching. Our project is on classroom management, not on company structuring. ㉒

JOY: There are parallels though: we're learning about management and structure for careers in business management. This classroom-based project is just a training-ground.

TIM: Maybe. Anyway, last time we were considering the benefits of a discussion board in each home-group room. What have you come up with?

JOY: The role of the discussion board is for sharing ideas — each of us can learn from what others have done before us. I thought, instead of the students merely stating what textbooks they think will be beneficial, it would be more useful to document what they've already studied and the reactions they had to the material. ❷❸

TIM: In that way others can find books that will further their own research. That's great!

JOY: What about you? How have you been getting on with your analysis of classroom structure?

TIM: I've been thinking about what we should discuss in our essay on that topic. The teacher's role has been discussed in previous research papers, as has the important relationship between teachers and their students. But I haven't come across much research on the place an individual student holds in the classroom. So this is what I want to talk about. ❷❹

JOY: That could be a controversial topic. The roles have slowly evolved. Traditionally, the teacher dominated the classroom. Now the general idea is that the teacher is a mentor to guide students learning, rather than telling them what to do.

TIM: I agree. It places the students on a more equal footing with the teacher, so the students have more respect for their teachers. Should we conduct interviews with the teachers regarding this developing interaction? It's not required that we do it — we could interview the students instead.

JOY: I was considering it, but I think it may be difficult for many of the teachers to find the time. I tried to have a

23 此题定位词为 Joy 和 discussion board，需要注意 Joy 说话的内容，他认为学生记录下他们已经学过的东西和他们对材料的反应会更有用，reactions they had to the material 与选项 A 中的 responses to materials they have studied 对应，故选 A。

24 此题定位词为 Tim，需要注意 Tim 说话的内容，他说教师的角色在之前已经讨论过，教师和学生之间的重要关系也讨论过，但他还没讨论过学生在教室中扮演的角色，the place an individual student holds 即每个学生起的作用，和 the role of individual learner 对应，接着说这是他想要讨论的话题，故选 B。

discussion with some of the professors, but they were all tied up with marking the first-year students' exam papers and suggested I come back in a week or so.

TIM: Hmm ... If that's the case, we'd better not bother them. ㉕

TIM: What about this last research question about the factors that contribute to successful learning outcomes?

JOY: Well obviously, classroom management comes into it. I think for students, it's impossible to gain the full benefits of studying without it. In fact, I'd say it is the single most important factor of success in learning. ㉖

TIM: I agree, but I think feedback is pretty important, too. There has to be a real dialogue going on between teachers and students and constructive criticism is essential to students' progress and development. ㉗

JOY: True, and I've been thinking about the shift in roles in recent years, but the essentials are still the same. For instance, effective lesson planning is pretty fundamental. Teachers have the responsibility to do it properly. ㉘

TIM: I agree, that is a requirement for every teacher. I believe that each student learns at his or her own pace. Some students may need individual tutoring. I think it should be a matter of choice, though, as it doesn't work well for everyone. ㉙

JOY: You are right. I'd like to see more supervision in the lab, too. Some of the students need a lot more help than they're getting.

TIM: Yes, that's true. And it would also be beneficial if students had more access to technology. Nowadays,

25 此题定位词为 Joy and Tim，需要注意听他们不采访老师的原因，前面 Tim 说并不需要采访老师，可以采访学生，Joy 认为老师没有时间接受采访，接着 Tim 说如果是那样的话，就不要去打扰他们了，故选 A。

26 此题定位词为 classroom management，Joy 认为课程管理是学习成功的最重要的因素，后面 Tim 也同意这一观点，the single most important factor of success 与 the key to success 对应，故选 G。

27 此题定位词为 feedback，Joy 和 Tim 认为反馈对学生的进步和发展很重要，essential to students' progress and development 和 necessary for progress 对应，故选 B。

28 此题定位词为 lesson planning，Joy 和 Tim 都认为有效的上课计划是根本，fundamental 和 a basic requirement 对应，故选 D。

29 此题定位词为 individual tutoring，Joy 和 Tim 认为个人辅导并不是对每个人都有用，看个人选择，即可有可无，故选 E。

students and teachers can use few simple clicks with a computer to finish something that might take them hours or even days in the past . ㉚

JOY: I agree. Even though funding technology can be expensive, it pays in the long run.

TIM: I am not sure. We can record it in our research though, as a recommendation.

30 此题定位词为 access to technology, Tim 认为现在的学生和老师可以很快通过电脑完成一些事情, 相比以前节省了很多时间, Joy 同意这一观点, 虽然后面也提到了 funding, 但是根据 Tim 说的 I am not sure 可知不确定, 故选 F。

Part 4

Listening Keys,
Questions 31 – 40
🔑

31	rivers	36	storms
32	3/three	37	guard
33	estimate	38	fences
34	farming	39	locator
35	eggs	40	media

Thank you for attending this conference which is about the plight of our local terns. Firstly, I will provide you with some background information. Terns are sea birds that live all over the world. They are normally to be found near wetlands and other places where there is water. There is one species in particular that warrants our attention — our New Zealand fairy tern, which is often called the tara-iti.

Audioscripts

This small and dainty tern is New Zealand's most endangered bird. As you may know, it has grey plumage on its upper parts, and white underneath, along with a forked tail. Adults have a yellow beak and a black cap of feathers on their heads.

These lovely terns breed between Whangarei and Auckland on

31 此题定位词为 alongside coastlines，通过连接词 and 可判断答案词为与 coastlines 并列的名词，原文说燕鸥通常在海边或河边筑巢，seashores 对应 coastlines，along 对应 alongside，故填 rivers。

32 此题定位词为 1983 和 breeding pairs，虽然提到了数字 15，但并不是 breeding pairs，接着听到了 3 breeding pairs，故填 3。

33 此题定位词为 difficult，因为填空处前为动词不定式 to，可判断答案为动词，problematic 对应 difficult，numbers 对应 population，故填 estimate。

34 此题定位词为 Increased coastal 和 animals，原文说由于近年来海岸附近的农业增加，未受保护的巢穴可能被家畜践踏，coasts 对应 coastal，故填 farming。

35 此题定位词为 predators，原文说燕鸥的蛋很容易被捕食，predation 对应 predators，也就是捕食者会捕食燕鸥的蛋，故填 eggs。

New Zealand's North Island. Terns do not nest in trees like most birds, instead the nest is usually constructed along seashores or rivers. **㉛** They usually choose sites where a large number of shells have accumulated, as these provide a hiding place for the nest and the young chicks. The birds are so endangered that their nests are protected by the Department of Conservation to ensure that people — or other animals — do not disturb the nests.

It's currently estimated that there are around 40 individual birds in the wild, including about 10 breeding pairs. This may sound like a dire condition; however, their situation has improved dramatically since 1983 when only 15 birds were found, of which there were 3 breeding pairs. **㉜**

Research into populations is not always easy to carry out. There aren't many fairy terns, and because these birds move around quickly and rarely stay in one location for long, it is always problematic to estimate bird numbers. **㉝**

So why has the number of terns declined to such an extent? They were once thought to be widespread on both of New Zealand's islands. Well, firstly human activity is to blame. The construction of new homes in prime coastal locations means that there is much more human activity on the beaches formerly used as nesting sites by the birds. Also, unprotected nests can be trampled by domestic animals since farming has increased near coasts in recent years. **㉞**

Wildlife can also threaten the birds' survival and while adult birds are not normally caught and eaten, populations suffer because the terns' eggs are very vulnerable to predation. **㉟**

Those are reasons for their decline which has been caused by humans, but there are also environmental reasons. Their nests are basically a scrape in the sand, usually only just above the high tide mark. This means that the nests are vulnerable to bad weather; for instance, they are likely to be washed away by storms. ㊱

So what is being done to protect and grow the number of fairy terns? There are a variety of methods in use. Some conservation groups have a trained guard responsible for each nest 24 hours a day. ㊲This is actually a very practical method which has already brought good results. Another approach has received widespread support and it's already taking place in several locations. Fences are built around the nesting sites, which greatly reduces the risk of people undertaking recreational activities — such as driving on sand and kite surfing — accidentally disturbing nests. ㊳ Also, young chicks are often caught, and tagged with a locator band to help monitor their progress and track their movements. ㊴ In one case, conservationists even assisted feeding two wild chicks following the loss of one of their parents. There are also some programs where wild breeding pairs are caught and transferred to a suitable captive site where breeding security can be guaranteed, but some believe this may not be in the best interests of the birds, so more research in this area is needed.

This afternoon, we'll have a press conference as we believe that media can play an important role in assisting us to educate the public and publicise the importance of protecting these lovely birds. ㊵ Next, we are going to talk about...

36 此题定位词为 at risk of destruction，填空处前为介词 by，可判断答案为名词，题目要求只填一个单词，因此前面 bad weather 不适用。原文说它们很可能被风暴冲走，也就是有被风暴破坏的风险，故填 storms。

37 此题定位词为 securing，在听到 protect 后可知答案即将出现，因为填空处前面有 a，故答案很可能为名词，原文说一些保护组织有一个训练有素的警卫，负责每天 24 小时看护鸟巢，由于字数限制，故填 guard。

38 此题定位词为 humans，因为填空处前后为 introducing 和 to，故答案很可能为名词，原文说在筑巢地点周围筑篱笆，这大大降低了人们从事娱乐活动时对鸟巢造成的风险，故填 fences。

39 此题定位词为 chicks 和 monitor activity，原文说幼鸟经常被捕捉，并贴上定位带，以帮助监测它们的进展和跟踪它们的活动，monitor their progress and track their movements 和 monitor activity 对应，故填 locator。

40 此题定位词为 raising awareness，由 through the 可判断答案为名词，原文说相信媒体可以发挥重要作用，帮助教育公众，宣传保护这些鸟的重要性，educate the public and publicise the importance of 和 raising awareness 对应，故填 media。

Reading

Passage 1

Reading Keys,
Questions 1 – 13

1 E	6 G	10	environmental conservation
2 B	7 C	11	herbal healthcare
3 D	8 F	12	rejuvenate
4 A	9 B	13	fundamental concept
5 D			

■ 思路解析

Questions 1 – 4 ※题目类型：从属关系配对题

1 题干意思是"这是新婚夫妇最喜欢的目的地"，重点词为 newlyweds，原文只有 section F 第三句提到了与新婚夫妇相关的 honeymoon，即蜜月，section F 对应地区为 Belize，故选 E。

2 题干意思是"威胁旅行者的健康忧虑还没被解决"，重点词为 health concerns，原文 section C 第二句提到了 fungal infection 即真菌感染，已经可以基本定位，且往后读还有 epidemics（传染病）have become a common health occurrence for travellers，section C 对应地区为南美，故选 B。

3 题干意思是"它以吸引不同年龄阶段的人口为目的"，demographics 指特定年龄阶段的人口，原文 section E 列举了不同年龄阶段的旅客如 55 ~64 岁、35 ~54 岁、18 ~29 岁等，section E 对应的地区为 Indonesia，故选 D。

4 题干意思是"它提供宣传传统药物的课程"，重点词为 course 和 traditional medicine，section B 第三部分提到了 herbal medicine，可以基本定位，往后读还有 imparts herbal healthcare knowledge to the students，与题干的 course 对应，section B 对应的地区是 Cuba，故选 A。

Questions 5 – 9 ※题目类型：段落细节配对题

5 题干意思为"一项通过生态旅游减少野生物种消失的提议"，重点词为 suggestion、

loss、wild species。由 section D 第三句话 "Peter Lindsey... illegal wildlife hunting has robbed wildlife resources more so"，Lindsey 说到非法捕杀已经大量掠夺了野生动物资源，可知资源的减少对应 loss of wild species，"This value can be realised through alternatives like ecotourism" 即为通过生态旅游对野生动物的价值重新重视，减少更多的损失，故选 D。

6　题干意思为 "一个作为生态旅行者旅行过程中的亮点产品的例子"，重点词为 product、highlight、eco-tourists。由 section G 最后一句话 "The cheese is a delicacy for tourists and the distinct eating experience is a famous form of ecotourism." 可知，这种芝士对于旅行者来说是一种较为特殊的食物（a product），且品尝的过程使得整个经历很独特，也是生态旅游的一种很出名的形式，对应原文中 tour highlight，故选 G。

7　题干意思为 "提到一些特定活动需采取的安全措施"，重点词为 safety precautions，即安全措施，section C 提到了南美旅行者患上的传染病，第一部分的倒数第二句说到了 it is advisable to hose off boots... after wearing them，这些都是安全措施的内容，末句提到特定群体的旅客 travellers with cardiovascular diseases，即有心血管疾病的旅客，文章建议他们不去洞穴探险，故选 C。

8　题干意思为 "对于一个特定群体的游客的一系列体贴服务"，重点词为 a series of considerate services。section F 第一部分第三句至第一部分最后一句 "Tourists receive champagne after arriving... rainforest tours." 描述了这个地方为度假的 lovers（对应 typical guests）提供的一系列服务，从到达时的香槟到若干定制化的行程，这些都体现了 considerate services（贴心服务），故选 F。

9　题干意思为 "提到一个文化遗产的保护"，重点词为 cultural heritage 和 conservation。section B 第三部分首句提到了 introduced an initiative aimed at salvaging an important Cuban practice，其中 salvage（抢救）和 conservation 为同义替换，an important Cuban practice 对应 a cultural heritage，故选 B。

Questions 10 – 13　※题目类型：摘要填空题

10　题干第一句是对 ecotourism 的概括，空格问的是 "生态旅游可以让游客提升当地社区并支持什么"，是并列考点，可通过 "empower local communities" 对应 "enhances the livelihoods of the citizens" 定位 section A 中第一句对生态旅游的定义 "ecotourism can be defined as... that promotes environmental conservation and..."，promote 对应 support，因此填 environmental conservation。

11 题干主语 a Cuban institution，需要定位到提到古巴的相关段落，由 section B 第三部分 "An ecotourism community school in Las Terrazas imparts herbal healthcare knowledge to the students by teaching them the application and the cultivation of herbal medicine..." 可知，一所古巴的社区学校（对应 institution）教授学生（对应题干 learners）与草药保健相关的知识，包括应用和种植（即为不同角度 different angles），故填 herbal healthcare。

12 题干主语为 African nations，因此定位到 section D 谈论东非的内容，题干问 "非洲国家用生态旅游 XXX 动物数量"，因此答案填动词或动词词组，section D 第二句提到了 This will rejuvenate the wildlife population，其中 wildlife 与 animal 为同义替换，故填 rejuvenate。

13 题干的定位词为 development、governments、all segments of tourists、young、old。因此需定位到提到政府采取促进生态旅游措施的 section，同时该 section 还应提到不同年龄的游客。由 section E 第一、二句可知，在印尼，生态旅游已成为一个基本的理念，而政府必须针对不同游客群体做相应的优化措施（to enhance 对应题干 further development）。第一部分剩余的内容提到了不同年龄段，符合题干中的 young、old，故填 fundamental concept。

■ 译文 ｜ 发展中国家的生态旅游

A 根据生态旅游协会的定义，生态旅游可以被定义为在自然中旅行，从而促进环境保护和提高公民的生活水平。生态旅游被认为是提高和丰富旅游业水平的一种有利方式，因为这种旅游方式尊重当地人和他们的自然遗产。生态旅游也符合每个遗址和自然景点所能承受的人口阈值。

B 很明显，古巴是一个生态旅游目的地。它有令人惊叹的生态水体、保护区、海滩和乡村景观。此外，公路基础设施的改善和通信网络促进了生态旅游。在加勒比海地区，古巴是第二受欢迎的旅游目的地。

生态旅游提高了当地和外国游客学习环境意识的能力。更好的生态旅游激发了人们为环境保护采取行动的意愿。此外，生态旅游与促进和平密切相关，这是通过增加文化交流和教育机会来实现的。游客的健康和安全得到了保证。

古巴前总统、菲德尔·卡斯特罗的弟弟劳尔·卡斯特罗提出了一项倡议，该倡议旨在挽救古巴一项重要习俗。他重振了草药在医疗体系中的使用。Las Terrazas 的一所生态旅游社区学校向学生传授草药保健知识，教授他们如何应用和培育用于面霜、酊剂、茶和软膏的草药。

生态旅游已成为古巴消除贫困的有效工具。它为当地人带来了经济财富，创造了就业机会。劳尔·卡斯特罗的努力增加了生态旅游社区居民的就业机会，也增加了古巴整体生态旅游的就业机会。

C 南美洲很可能是展示生态旅游负面影响的地区。荚膜组织胞浆菌是一种双态真菌，也是美国最常见的真菌感染。这种双态真菌与接触鸟类或蝙蝠粪便有关。近年来，对于从南美洲和中美洲返回的旅行者来说，流行病已成为一种常见的健康事件。从事探险旅游、洞穴探险、生态旅游和其他娱乐活动的旅行者最容易受到伤害。他们在旅行中忽视适当的卫生措施是一个普遍的现象。参加完危险活动后，最好先用水管把靴子冲洗干净，然后把衣服放在密封的袋子里待洗。那些患有心血管疾病的旅行者应该远离危险的环境，避免诸如洞穴旅行这些行为。

尽管存在着生物多样性，但在拥有丰富野生动物资源的偏远地区探险，与自然探索相比，它提供了生态旅游的机会。可持续旅游促进了生态旅游，使社区和自然在一个优越的环境中同时发展。旅行者通常会在旅行的各个阶段中找到乐趣，从而提升他们的可持续发展之旅的体验。南美洲热带森林面临的一些最严重的威胁是：因想要扩大耕地而滥伐森林、非法古柯种植、采矿、石油泄漏和开采、伐木、殖民活动、牧牛等。由于森林砍伐，土著居民失去了他们的领土，人口大量减少。越来越多的人开始接受生态旅游，并试图持续有效地利用所有资源，促进旅游业的可持续发展。

D 为了促进生态旅游和提高经济效益，东非应更加注重减少非法狩猎。这将恢复野生动物的数量，因此有机会进行战利品狩猎。《新研究》的作者彼得·林赛（Peter Lindsey）说，非法猎杀野生动物更严重地掠夺了野生动物资源，因为这种行为降低了野生动物的价值。这种价值可以通过生态旅游和狩猎等方式来实现。许多东非居民认为生态旅游有潜力提供解决方案。他们支持社区赋权。彼得·林赛赞扬了当地正在进行的保护工作，他说这促进了生态旅游，培养了环境意识。

E 1995年，生态旅游开始成为印度尼西亚的一个基本理念。为了促进国内旅游，政府必须瞄准合适的市场，以促进生态旅游。印度尼西亚生态旅游的细分市场包括：a) 55~64岁年龄段或"沉默的一代"。这些人有足够的财富，受到良好的教育，没有孩子依赖他们。他们可以旅行一个月。b) 35~54岁年龄段或"婴儿潮一代"。这些人是富裕的初级经理，他们很可能会带着孩子和家人旅行两到三周。对他们来说，旅行有助于缓解压力。c) 18~29岁或"新一代"。这一代人喜欢背包环游世界。他们的旅行时间通常在三到十二个月之间，每个月的花费在300到500美元之间。在印度尼西亚，应该针对不同的人群设计不同的生态旅游套餐。这个国家吸引了各种各样的游客。

F 生态旅游提供的服务与传统旅游一样多。伯利兹位于加勒比海、墨西哥和危地马拉之间。人们都喜欢去伯利兹的哈玛纳斯度蜜月。游客到达后会得到香槟，第一天晚上的私人服务，一日三餐，以及一次由他们选择的冒险。哈玛纳斯也提供 6 到 7 晚的蜜月选择。情侣们将会有几次定制之旅，包括硫磺山要塞和邻近的岛屿之旅。有些由导游带领的旅行还包括种植园、火山和雨林之旅。

格雷戈里·佩雷拉（Gregory Pereira）是一位性格外向、知识渊博的导游和徒步旅行者。他说，生态旅游冒险包含特别设计的陆虎车作为交通工具、有益健康的热带果汁、岛屿糕点野餐、知识渊博的岛屿导游以及为参与者准备的综合保险。

G Kodai 对于那些喜欢亲近大自然的人来说是一个极好的去处。想要身心得到滋补的游客会发现 Kodai 十分壮美。据说那里的每只鸟都要唱歌。对于游客来说也是一样的，因为他们应该在陡峭的山峦和深谷中规划出自己的路线。坐落在森林里的 Kodai 芝士厂以出口大量芝士闻名于世。奶酪对游客来说是美味佳肴。独特的饮食体验是一种著名的生态旅游形式。

Passage 2

Reading Keys,
Questions 14 – 26

14	A	19	NO	24	E
15	D	20	NO	25	D
16	A	21	YES	26	B
17	B	22	YES		
18	NOT GIVEN	23	NO		

■ 思路解析

Questions 14 – 17 ※题目类型：单选题

14 题干问 A 段中作者如何看待 Musicophilia，A 段最后一句 "my reactions… are rather ambivalent"，其中 ambivalent（矛盾的）与 A 选项 mixed feelings 相对应，故选 A。若不认识 ambivalent，也可以从倒数第二句中 "had high hopes" 和最后一句 "But with a sense of guilt" 推导出作者对这本书有复杂感情。

15 题干问 Sacks 的书除了探索音乐和神经科学之间的联系，还是怎么样的？B 段第二句提到了 "He… chronicled his life in the book and unveiled… personal events."，即他在书中

记录他的生活和私事，与 D 选项 autobiographical（自传的）相对应，故选 D。

16 题干问当治疗病人的时候，Sacks 更喜欢做什么，原文 C 段第二句提到了 "He also accentuates the value of... observation as well as the human context and looks to blend the two with the latest diagnostic method in the tech world... in order to penetrate into the experiences of his patients and subjects"，Sacks 想利用科技手段来促进 observation 和 human context 的融合，帮助他洞察病人的经历，对应题干中的 improve the effectiveness of observation，故选 A。

17 题干问作者对书的第二部分有什么评价，重点词为 second part，据此定位 F 段首句 "In part two of the book, ... most of the chapters have little to nothing remarkable, or nothing we do not already know"，即第二部分几乎没有什么非同寻常的或者我们不知道的内容，与 B 选项相对应（没有提供新颖独特的见解）。

Questions 18 - 23 ※题目类型：正误判断题

18 题干是 Sacks 需要多花时间讨论他的家庭生活，重点词为 home life，B 段讲了 Sacks 在这本书中描写了自己的个人生活，并没有提到 home life 的信息，故填 NOT GIVEN。

19 题干是封面不足以比喻这本书的内容，重点词为 cover、inadequate。根据 cover 定位到 B 段倒数第二句 This cover aptly summarises the contents of the book，即封面适当地总结了书的内容，其中 aptly（适当地）与题干的 inadequate 相反，故填 NO。

20 题干是这本书需要对 Sacks 的病人进行更完整的描述，重点词为 needs、complete、descriptions，根据 descriptions 定位 D 段第一句 The book has comprehensive accounts of cases concerning the patients，其中 comprehensive 为题干中 complete 的同义替换，因为书已经有关于病人案例的完整描述，不需要更完整的描述，故填 NO。

21 题干是造成 Cicoria 情况的确切原因还未知，重点词为 Cicoria、unknown，E 段开头提到 what could be the reason behind this sudden interest，即探讨 Cicoria 情况的原因，故定位 E 段，该段最后提到了 Cicoria refused to undergo them（指代 more sensitive tests），因 Cicoria 拒绝接受测试，故他的情况原因未知，答案为 YES。

22 题干说 Sacks 应对音乐方面的紊乱症治疗有效的方法进行拓展说明，重点词为 effective remedies、music、disorders。根据 remedies 定位 I 段第一句 "While the reasons behind music brain oddities...Sacks could have done a little more to outline... successful treatments

…" 及第二句 "Sack could have divulged…in the case of losing the ability to comprehend harmony", successful treatments 对应题干 effective remedies, music brain oddities、losing the ability to comprehend harmony 与 music-specific disorders 对应, 故填 YES。

23 题干是 Sacks 的治疗神经问题的方法可以呈现出一致且可预测的成果, 重点词为 consistent、results, J 段倒数第一句提到了 "Most treatments mentioned by Sacks are… though their efficacy varies extensively", 其中 efficacy（功效）对应题干 results, 即 Sacks 治疗方法的疗效相差很大, 与题干的一致且可预测相反, 故填 NO。

Questions 24 – 26 ※题目类型：完成句子配对题

24 题干内容是人们口头清晰表述观点的能力会下降, 重点词为 orally state opinions、deteriorate, 据此定位到 G 段… those suffering from Expressive Aphasia（a condition that inhibits a person from expressing their thoughts verbally generally as an aftermath of a stroke or other cerebral incident）, 即表达性失语症的病人会有因为中风等大脑损伤造成的表达障碍, 故选 E。

25 题干内容是人们灵活地移动会有困难, 重点词为 difficulty、move around、flexibly, 据此定位到 G 段 Sacks illustrates how music can bring life and movement into patients with severe Parkinson's disease or other body movement disorders that confine them to specific postures, 即音乐可以给患有严重帕金森症的病人带来移动的便利, 而帕金森症和其他运动障碍都会造成患者局限于特定动作, 即无法灵活移动, 故选 D。

26 题干内容是人们即使听懂旋律, 也可能听不懂和声, 重点词为 melody、harmony, 据此定位到 I 段 "Sacks could have divulged on the many specific dissociations among components of music perception, as in the case of losing the ability to comprehend harmony but not melody, signifying that the music centre in the brain is missing.", 即大脑中负责音乐知觉的部分无法建立联会导致理解和声的能力丧失, 尽管能理解旋律, 故选 B。

■ **译文** | 《音乐迷恋》书评
对奥利弗·萨克斯最新音乐作品的评论

A 作为一个在听觉学习和记忆方面有专长的神经学家, 我认为大脑和音乐都是迷人的主题, 而且这两者似乎特别令人着迷。因此, 我对奥利弗的最新作品《音乐迷恋》寄予厚望。但带着一种内疚感, 我承认我对这本书的反应相当矛盾。

B   萨克斯本人是一位神经学家，也是一位多产的作家。他在书中充分地记录了自己的生活，并公开了一些隐私。在这本书的封面上，他戴着耳机，闭着眼睛，沉浸在音乐中，与此同时，艾尔弗雷德·布伦德尔正在演奏贝多芬的《悲怆奏鸣曲》。这本书的封面很好地概括了这本书的内容，或者说，封面就是从书的内容里诞生的。在整本书中，萨克斯的语言清晰而博学，但他一点都没有显得自大、自我推销或偏执。

C   萨克斯完美地解释了他从广泛而快速发展的音乐感知和意象方面的神经系统经典作品中收集到的深刻见解，并解释了这些作品中表现得复杂而奇怪的地方。他还强调了观察艺术以及人类环境的价值，并试图将两者与科技界最新的诊断方法结合起来，以便深入了解他的病人和研究对象的体验。此外，如果你读过他的《音乐迷恋》，你就会发现，尽管他从事神经病学已经有30多年了，但他还是在古老的观察方法和现代的高科技方法之间左右为难，他知道现代的方法更合适，但是，他内心更倾向于选择传统的方法。

D   这本书对萨克斯在行医期间所见过的病人的情况作了全面的叙述。许多当代神经科学报告都以简短讨论的形式在书中大量出现。在第一部分，即"被音乐萦绕"部分，托尼·西科瑞亚的一个特殊案例尤其引人入胜，因为他是一位完全没有音乐细胞的中年外科医生，但一次被闪电击中的经历让他内心产生了对音乐的强烈热爱。他开始有一种听钢琴音乐的突发冲动，这是他以前从来没有想过的。他对音乐的热爱逐渐发展到弹钢琴和作曲，他自然而然地就能将大量的音符编到曲子中。

E   但这种突如其来对音乐的兴趣或音乐技能背后的原因是什么呢？这可能是心理上的，因为当闪电击中他时，他曾有过一次濒死的遭遇。或许，这一事件对他大脑皮层的听觉区域有直接的影响。最早的脑电图（EEG）检查是在该闪电击中事件发生后立即进行的，那时他对音乐的热爱也变得很明显，脑电图显示他的脑电波完全正常。虽然更敏感的测试可以更深入地探究这个谜团，但西科瑞亚拒绝接受测试。

F   在这本书的第二部分，萨克斯涵盖了一系列的主题，但遗憾的是，大多数章节没有什么特别的，或者是我们不知道的内容。例如，第十三章只是反映了一个知识点，即盲人比其他人对音乐更敏感。当然，最奇怪的案例最能引起人们的注意。第八章的内容与"失乐感"有关，失乐感指无法听到一些声音，比如音乐，这一章也提到了另外一种障碍，观察对象无法听到和声，但他们仍然能理解旋律，萨克斯将其称为"失和声感"。你会从他的经历中发现更多的案例，这些案例贯穿他的书《音乐迷恋》中。

G   第三部分为"记忆、运动和音乐"，与音乐治疗相关，但这一领域还没有研究成果。他明确提到了"旋律语调疗法"是如何帮助那些患有表达性失语症（一种通常在中风或其他脑损伤后人们无法口头表达自己想法的状态）的人重新获得流畅表达的能力。在另一章中，萨克斯举例说明了音乐如何能给患有严重帕金森症或其他身体运动障碍（这些运动障碍会使患者局限于特定的身体姿势）的患者带来生命力和运动能力。迄今为止，音乐的这种非凡力量还没有被任何科学现象合理化。

H 然而，对于那些不熟悉神经科学和音乐行为概念的人来说，《音乐迷恋》充满了迷人的信息。但正如萨克斯所提到的，它并不能满足那些渴望了解这种现象的原因和含义的人。与讨论实验相比，萨克斯似乎更乐于讨论病人，此外，他较为轻率地相信科学发现和理论。

I 虽然大脑对音乐的奇怪反应背后的原因还没有得到准确的理解，但萨克斯其实应该进一步概述他和其他神经学家所做的成功治疗以及通过仔细观察发现的影响。例如，萨克斯本应透露音乐感知各个组成部分之间的许多特殊的分离关系，比如失去了理解和声而不是理解旋律的能力，这意味着大脑中的音乐中枢缺失了。由于许多读者会认为所有的心智功能都与大脑的特定部位有关，即大脑定位，所以他可能错过了教育大众的好机会。

J 人们可能还会得出结论，认为音乐是无法治愈神经系统疾病的。一种药对不同的病人可能有不同的效果；它可能减轻一个人的疼痛，或者使另一个人的疼痛加剧，或者也可能让同一个病人受到积极和消极的影响。萨克斯提到的大多数治疗方法都是使用专门用于抗癫痫的药物，这些药物通常会略微降低大脑的兴奋性；尽管它们的功效差别很大。

K 最后，在《音乐迷恋》这本书中，不考虑患者的大脑对音乐产生的症状的变化，大多数病例中患者的脑电图都是正常的。虽然萨克斯深知许多新技术能比神经脑电图测试更加细致地研究病人的脑电波，但他并没有要求使用这些技术。事实上，尽管他对患者的研究充满热情，但他并没有表现出在音乐脑障碍的诊断和治疗方面寻求创新途径的紧迫性，也没有呼吁大家去寻找新的途径。在这本书的开头，也就是前言中，有一点是显而易见的，即他表达了他的担忧——如果我们过于依赖现代科技，"简单的观察艺术可能会丢失"。然而，他对这两种方法都持肯定态度，我们也可以相信神经学界会做出回应。

Passage 3

Reading Keys,
Questions 27–40
🔑

27	A	32	FALSE	37	theory
28	C	33	NOT GIVEN	38	climate change
29	B	34	FALSE	39	complex
30	A	35	TRUE	40	the public
31	D	36	esoteric		

思路解析

Questions 27 – 31　※题目类型：单选题

27　题干问作者在 section A 中指出科学会怎么样，原文提到 it is the essence of better understanding what we think we know and developing new knowledge，即科学是更好地理解我们认为我们知道的以及形成新知识的关键（扩展我们的视野），与 A 选项相符，选项中 further discoveries 和原文 new knowledge 对应，故选 A。

28　题干问 section C 中作者提到了什么观点，首句提到了 Ambiguous language... can have more than one interpretation which leads to misunderstanding... among the scientific community，即含糊语言导致科学界有误解，其中原文 ambiguous（含糊的）对应 C 选项的 imprecise，原文 misunderstanding 对应 C 选项的 confusion，故选 C。

29　题干问当提到气候变化术语改变时，作者强调的是什么，section F 第三部分提到了科学家正在讨论是否改名，但 such change will not generate any benefit to the research itself，即改名对研究没有任何好处，与 B 选项 "对科学家没有任何意义的帮助" 一致，故选 B。

30　题干问作者在 section H 暗示什么，文章主题是科学研究的沟通问题，第二部分第一句提到在科学家表示得不出结论的情况下，下 "研究完全是一个失败" 的论断是错误的，后面接着说研究可能具有数学意义，也就是说尽管一个研究没有结果，它仍然可能是有价值的，故 A 为正确选项。

31　题干问 section I 中作者强调了什么观点，第三部分第一句 "avoiding every conflict, misunderstanding... is simply impossible"，即完全避免冲突和误解是不可能的，和 D 选项 "在科学领域，我们总是会遇到理解错误" 一致，conflict 和 misunderstanding 和 D 选项 miscommunication 相对应，故选 D（误解总会发生）。

Questions 32 – 35　※题目类型：正误判断题

32　题干是科学家总是认为使用非正式用语是合理的，重点词是 informal terms，section C 第一部分第二句 Scientists sometimes feel guilty of using colloquial language，其中 colloquial 是题干 informal 的同义替换，guilty 与 reasonable 矛盾，故 FALSE。

33　题干是不确定原则意味着我们不能对测量有绝对信心，重点词是 uncertainty principle，根据重点词定位 section D，首句提到不确定原则经常被误用，第二句提到 Some people take a look at the term and conclude it refers to a limitation on… the ability to make measurements，即描述了有些人对不确定原则的错误的理解版本，没有正面描述这个原则的准确含义，故 NOT GIVEN。

34 题干是当有实验基础时理论就是正确的，重点词是 theories、scientific experiments，由重点词定位到 section E 第二部分 Theories… are never completely correct，即理论从来不是完全正确的，与题干 Theories are true 表述相反，故 FALSE。

35 题干是科学家性别不影响研究结果，重点词是 gender，根据重点词定位 section G，第一句提到了 the ability of a scientist to generate results，结尾说 "there is no correlation between gender and scientific ability"，scientific ability 指代开头的 generate results 的能力，故这句话意思是性别和产生研究结果的能力没有联系，故 TRUE。

Questions 36 – 40 ※题目类型：摘要填空题

36 题干空格问有人认为现代科学什么样的性质是一个相关的原因，重点词为 confusion、nature、current，要填的是形容词。section A 内容都是 confusion，因此原因要在后面的 section B 找，通过 nature 找到 section B 第二部分第一句 many people wrongfully assume the esoteric nature of new scientific research，其中形容词 esoteric（深奥的）为答案。

37 题干是作者举几个迷惑性术语的例子，其中一个例子为一个什么词被用来提及一个没被证明的想法，重点词为 not proven，原文 section C、D、E 都是例子，只有 section E 提到 "the word 'theory' is problematic. Many people define 'theory' as a yet to be proven idea"，其中 yet to be proven 对应题干 not proven，many people 对应 commonly，define as 对应题干 referred to，故 theory 为答案。

38 题干是一些科学家质疑使用什么术语来重新定义他们研究领域的必要性。重点词为 scientific communities、term、redefine、research。section F 第三部分 "there is a controversy within the scientific community of this field about whether it is necessary to have a name change from global warming to climate change, though such change will not generate any benefit to the research itself." 提到这个领域的是否需要从 global warming 更名为 climate change，controversy…whether it is necessary（争论……必要性）对应题干 question the necessity of。题干 redefine 为重新定义，根据原文，更名后的名称 climate change 将起到重新定义的作用，故填 climate change。

39 题干是我们要意识到科学是 XXX，重点词是 realise，section I 开始讲到需要我们意识到的事情，第一部分开头 one of the biggest takeaways is to recognise that science is complex，其中 recognise 是 realise 的同义替换，故填 complex。

40 题干是谁应该多花些时间理解科学进程，重点词为 take more time、scientific process，空格应填入有关的词汇或短语，section I 第二部分第三句提到了 The public should…be more patient to comprehend how scientists process their studies，patient 对应 take more time，process their studies 对应 scientific process，故填 the public（公众）。

译文 | 科学中的沟通

A 科学是生命的基石——它是了解已知事物并开发新知识的关键。尽管科学在人类的进步中扮演着重要的角色，传播科学发现比以往任何时候都更加困难。错误传达和曲解会导致不必要的混淆和误解。

B 也许推进科学知识的最大挑战始于科学家他们自己。科学家们倾向于使用复杂的语言，而这语言有时使目标受众难以理解。

此外，许多人错误地认为，新科学研究的深奥本质意味着研究结果是错误的。相反，它应该被视为人类的聪明才智在解决一些更紧迫的问题上取得成功的体现。

一些很值得注意的例子包括当前占据媒体头条的紧迫的全球问题。人们会考虑解决全球变暖的危机，就像会考虑改善癌症患者的生活那样。当然，科学可以扩展到其他话题，不一定要生死攸关，比如了解饮食如何影响减肥。

C 根据定义，含糊的语言可以有多种解释，从而导致误解，并造成科学界中进一步的辩论。科学家们有时会使用口语，包括俚语和行话，这让他们有时感到内疚，因为这些语言对某些人来说可能是容易理解的，但对另一些人来说则是难以理解的概念。

"相对论"就是这样一个例子，它的定义本身就具有误导性。有人会说，这意味着一切都是相对的，没有绝对。以爱因斯坦的"相对论"为例，它侧重于发现物理现象的内部变量描述。

D "不确定性原理"是科学界中经常误用的另一个术语。有些人看到这个术语后认为它指的是一种对观察者和测量能力的限制。

E 人们也可以认为"理论"这个词是有问题的。许多人将"理论"定义为有待验证的、需要进一步评估的想法。这一过程在科学界中有所差异，例如，物理学家看待一个确定的物理框架时，会利用一套对于这个世界的基本假设，而这些假设可以产生一系列的预测。

从定义上来说，理论永远不能代表真理，它们也永远不可能完全正确，尤其是在科学发展的早期阶段。其中一个比较著名的例子是爱因斯坦近十年的探索以完善相对论的研究。即使在今天，它仍然是一种理论，因为它不能被证明是正确的。

F　全球变暖继续占据着媒体头条，但这个名字本身就有问题。气候科学家的任务是模拟温度的潜在波动，而不应被认为可以预测未来几个月的天气趋势。

然而，许多人不了解气候研究背后的科学。相反，如果即将到来的冬季比往常更冷，许多人很快就会对科学界不屑一顾，并质疑他们的可信度。

因此，在这一领域的科学界存在着争议，即是否有必要把名字从全球变暖改为气候改变，尽管这种改变不会对研究本身产生任何好处。

G　哈佛大学是探讨性别是否决定了科学家产出能力的辩论的起点，虽然这一辩论毫无意义。数据显示很清楚：一些社会因素可能导致男女之间的细微差异，但总体而言，性别和科学能力之间没有相关性。

一个完美的类比是，从无人操控的航天任务中收集的信息，其合理性等同于由宇航员收集同样的数据的合理性。

H　如果认为质疑科学家收集的数据就是对科学家本人的直接攻击，那就错了。对于那些在重要领域工作的科学家来说，这可能是一个更重要的话题。

此外，如果一位科学家承认得出结论几乎是不可能或完全不可能的，那么认为这个项目完全失败是不对的。更具体地说，这项研究可能具有一定的数学意义，尽管公众往往对数学持怀疑态度。

I　归根结底，我们最大的收获之一就是认识到科学是复杂的。只接受简单易懂的科学发现可能会让我们感觉良好，但是世界不会进步。

科学家也可以在帮助世界理解重要话题方面发挥作用。他们可能会考虑从繁忙的日程中抽出时间，为自己所做的工作提供一个简单易懂的解释。公众应该支持那些付出更多努力的科学家，并更耐心地去理解科学家们是如何进行他们的研究的。

不过，避免每一次冲突、误解或困难都是不可能的。科学是一项永无止境的实验，没有期限，没有人知道全局——至少现在还没有。

Writing

Task 1

审　题

这个表格显示了 2003 年和 2013 年在美国的留学生学业的主要资金来源。

图表类型

表格动态图

分析思路

一般对于表格图，我们需要注意两点，一是对比数量，二是看懂趋势变化。在概述里，我们主要描述趋势变化。我们能发现一个明显的趋势是从现在的雇主以及外国政府或大学获得资助的学生的百分比增幅较大。

接着，我们具体分析数据信息。一般先看总数，只涉及到两个数字，该表格中为 572,509 和 886,052，那么我们可知这十年来，总数是增长趋势。

然后我们纵向对数字进行比较，如在 2003 年里，67%、23%（或其对应的两个数字 383,600 和 132,015）这两个数字与其他数字有较大差距，需要在作文中提到。

参考写作结构

首　　段：概述表格信息/改述题目
综 述 段：对总数、趋势或者对比数据进行描述（可与首段合并）
主 体 段：对表格中信息明显的数据（最大或最小）进行分析

参考范文[⊖]

The table shows how international students studying in the U.S. in 2003 and 2013 met their financial commitments.

Overall, in 2003, the vast majority of overseas students either paid for themselves or received financial support from their families. This percentage virtually remained at the

---

⊖ 范文中加色字为高分表达，后同。

same level in 2013, although the total number of international students attending colleges and universities in the U.S. increased dramatically.

Between 2003 and 2013, the number of foreign students in the U.S. nearly doubled, rising from around 570,000 in 2003 to about 886,000 a decade later. In 2003, 67% of international students were self-funded and this figure had changed very little by 2013, just falling marginally by 2%. In both 2003 and 2013, the second most common source of funding was scholarships from educational institutions in the U.S. In 2003, just under a quarter of international students (23%) received scholarships from American colleges and universities whereas this percentage was noticeably lower, at 19%, in 2013.

In 2003, just 2% of overseas students were financially supported by governments or universities in their own countries. Although this figure was relatively insignificant, it skyrocketed over the next ten years, reaching 7% by 2013. Only 3% of students were sponsored by their employers in 2003, but this percentage had doubled by 2013.

Overall: 7.5

Task 2

审　题
如今在很多国家，城市人更喜欢独居或与小家庭住在一起，而不是和一个大家族一起生活。这一趋势是好是坏？

讨论对象
城市中独居（家庭人数变少）的现象，写作文章为议论文（讨论是好是坏）

写作观点选择
有所侧重（趋势是好/坏）vs 无侧重（有好有坏）

写作论据准备

positive：
◇ 个人有更多的自由和私人空间 more freedom and personal space
◇ 减少日常生活中的矛盾和摩擦 reduce conflicts in daily life
◇ 让个人变得独立 become more independent and self-reliant
◇ 增加住房需求，促进经济发展 increase demands for housing and promote economic development

negative：

◇ 育儿压力大 great pressure from childcare

◇ 租房/买房带来经济压力 renting or buying a house brings financial pressure

◇ 与人的互动减少，感到孤独或患精神疾病 reduced human interaction leads to feeling of isolation or mental illness

参考写作结构

1 首   段：引出讨论对象＋表明观点 positive

   主体段1：positive 论据1

                论据2

   主体段2：negative 论据（可省略）

   末   段：重申观点 positive

2 首   段：引出讨论对象＋表明观点 negative

   主体段1：negative 论据1

                论据2

   主体段2：positive 论据（可省略）

   末   段：重申观点 negative

3 首   段：引出讨论对象＋表明观点 positive & negative

   主体段1：positive 论据

   主体段2：negative 论据

   末   段：重申观点 positive & negative

参考范文[⊖]

These days many people, especially those in metropolitan areas, choose to live on their own or in a small family rather than an extended one. Considering the potential pressure brought about by this lifestyle, I contend that this trend has more negative consequences than positive ones.

Admittedly, living alone can benefit both individuals and the development of the society. For one thing, it offers opportunities for young people to develop basic life skills, such as cooking, cleaning, paying utility bills, and managing personal finance. This makes those who live by themselves become more self-dependent. Another benefit is that family

---

⊖ 范文中加色字为高分表达。

members, by living separately, will have more living space and privacy which are essential for avoiding quarrels and conflicts. As for the society, this lifestyle can increase demands for housing and thus boost the construction industry.

However, living independently or in a nuclear family has its downsides. One problem is that people may have to carry enormous financial burden considering the soaring housing prices and other living expenses. For example, single occupants who cannot rely on others to share the rent or other expenditures will have to work hard to make their ends meet. Without the support from senior family members, working parents in nuclear families may have to turn to babysitters or nurseries, an extremely pricey option, to look after their children.

Apart from the financial pressure, those living alone are more likely to experience mental problems. Since there is no one available to talk with in their daily life, they may tend to immerse themselves in electronic devices to kill time. Such lifestyle, if lasting for a long time, might lead to the feeling of loneliness, isolation or even depression, which will eventually damage their mental health.

In conclusion, although it seems beneficial for people to gain independence by living alone, I believe the financial support as well as spiritual connection offered by larger families are more advantageous for the well-being of individuals; therefore I would consider living by oneself or in a smaller family unit as a negative trend.

Overall: 7

Speaking

Part 1 | Cake & Dessert

Do you like dessert?

Desserts are my absolute favourite part of a meal and they are my guilty pleasure. It goes without saying that I have a sweet tooth and the pleasure of indulging in a creamy chocolate mousse makes my day. In my opinion, the right indulgences can fuel our body and mind. Therefore, I am powerless to resist my fondness for sweet cravings.

高分表达

- ◇ guilty pleasure 有罪恶感的享受
- ◇ it goes without saying 不用说
- ◇ have a sweet tooth 爱吃甜食
- ◇ indulge in 沉溺于
- ◇ make my day 令我开心

- ◇ indulgence /ɪn'dʌldʒəns/ n. 沉溺
- ◇ fuel /'fjuːəl/ v. 给……提供燃料/能量
- ◇ powerless to resist 无法抵抗
- ◇ fondness /'fɒndnəs/ n. 喜爱
- ◇ craving /'kreɪvɪŋ/ n. 渴望

Do you like eating cakes?

I absolutely love eating cakes and I often submit to the irresistible temptation to enjoy a rich, moist home-made cake. There is nothing that tastes better than a fresh-out-of-the-oven cake and the delightful moment of delving into it is priceless. Of course, cakes should be eaten moderately, but rewarding myself once in a while with a delicious cake can have a highly positive effect on my mental health.

高分表达

- ◇ submit to 屈服于
- ◇ irresistible temptation 无法抗拒的诱惑
- ◇ fresh-out-of-the-oven 新鲜出炉的
- ◇ delightful /dɪ'laɪtfl/ a. 令人愉快的

- ◇ delve into 探索
- ◇ reward /rɪ'wɔːd/ v. 奖励
- ◇ once in a while 偶尔
- ◇ mental health 心理健康

What desserts do Chinese people like?

One of the most popular desserts in China is moon cake. It represents a profound cultural tradition with a spiritual feeling of the Mid-Autumn Festival or the Moon Festival. Moon cakes have a remarkably long history in China and their flavor varies according to different regional styles and local traditions. There is a great variety of moon cakes, but my absolute favourite would be the chocolate moon cake because of its thick and irresistible chocolate scent.

高分表达

◇ a profound cultural tradition 深厚的文化传统

◇ spiritual /'spɪrɪtʃuəl/ *a.* 精神的

◇ remarkably /rɪ'mɑːkəbli/ *ad.* 非常地

◇ vary /'veəri/ *v.* 变化

◇ a great variety of 各种各样的

◇ irresistible /ɪrɪ'zɪstəbl/ *a.* 无法抗拒的

Have you ever made cakes?

I often make them, and I consider it a truly relaxing activity. Even though some people claim that making cakes is a matter of talent, I truly believe that it's a practical skill that can be easily honed. Since I have a sweet tooth, I often reward myself with a delicious, home-made cake.

高分表达

◇ truly /'truːli/ *ad.* 非常

◇ a matter of talent 天赋问题

◇ a practical skill 实用技能

◇ hone /həʊn/ *v.* 训练

◇ have a sweet tooth 爱吃甜食

◇ reward /rɪ'wɔː(r)d/ *v.* 奖励

Part 2

Describe a person who taught you something.
You should say:
   who this person is
   what he/she was like
   what he/she taught you
and how you felt about him/her.

You will have to talk about the topic for one to two minutes. You have one minute to think about what you are going to say. You can make some notes to help you if you wish.

A person who had a profound influence on me and taught me knowledge is my English teacher in high school.

She was a dedicated professional, an extremely knowledgeable person who would apply various teaching styles to generate student motivation and instill a love of learning in her students. She could always recognise individuality and would go out of her way to actively encourage all her students to achieve their learning goals.

Since the process of learning a foreign language is often time-consuming with numerous obstacles to overcome, her remarkable personality had a far-reaching effect on me because she believed in my talents. She provided me with wholehearted support and demonstrated kindness and patience when I needed them most. She imparted invaluable knowledge of English and helped me improve my speaking skills. My teacher also taught me the importance of trust, patience and hard work, which helped me become a better person. Furthermore, she was the one who made me realise that I can be the best at anything I set out to be.

I have always admired my English teacher because of her incredible talent to teach, her genuine willingness to treat her students as individuals and help them embrace their mistakes.

高分表达

◇ a profound influence 深远的影响

◇ dedicated /'dedɪkeɪtɪd/ a. 有奉献精神的

◇ professional /prə'feʃənl/ n. 专业人士

◇ knowledgeable /'nɒlɪdʒəbl/ a. 知识渊博的

◇ apply... to... 把……应用于……

◇ instill /ɪn'stɪl/ v. 逐渐灌输

◇ individuality /ˌɪndɪˌvɪdʒu'æləti/ n. 个性

◇ go out of one's way 努力做

◇ time-consuming a. 费时间的

◇ numerous obstacles 很多困难

◇ remarkable /rɪ'mɑːkəbl/ a. 非凡的

◇ a far-reaching effect 深远的影响

◇ wholehearted support 全心全意的支持

◇ demonstrate /'demənstreɪt/ v. 展示

◇ impart /ɪm'pɑːt/ v. 传授

◇ invaluable /ɪn'væljuəbl/ a. 极宝贵的

◇ set out (怀着目标) 开始努力

◇ embrace /ɪm'breɪs/ v. 欣然接受

Part 3

What qualities do you think a good teacher should have?

In my opinion, a good teacher should possess comprehensive knowledge of their subject matter and high expectations for all students. He or she should use different teaching methods to challenge students to think outside the box. Another important quality is to offer invaluable classroom experience, the opportunity for students to explore, understand and apply new ideas and information. A good teacher will always share best practices, demonstrate their thirst for knowledge, engage students with creative lessons and provide students with timely and constructive feedback.

高分表达

- ◇ comprehensive /ˌkɒmprɪˈhensɪv/ *a.* 全面的
- ◇ high expectations 高期望
- ◇ think outside the box 跳出固有思维模式
- ◇ invaluable /ɪnˈvæljuəbl/ *a.* 极宝贵的
- ◇ apply /əˈplaɪ/ *v.* 应用
- ◇ demonstrate /ˈdemənstreɪt/ *v.* 展示
- ◇ thirst for knowledge 求知欲
- ◇ engage with 引起（某人的兴趣或注意力）
- ◇ timely /ˈtaɪmli/ *a.* 及时的
- ◇ constructive /kənˈstrʌktɪv/ 建设性的

Who do you think can learn better, old people or youngsters?

I genuinely believe that youngsters learn better than old people. Unfortunately, learning becomes more complicated and challenging as we grow older and old people no longer possess the ability to absorb new information quickly. Even though old people are usually self-directed in learning and have great control over motivation and results, young people are more efficient in gaining practical knowledge. Furthermore, youngsters have a strong motivation and a personal sense of achievement. Nowadays, younger learners highly value real-world learning so they actively put their knowledge into practice, which enables them to learn from their mistakes and improve more.

高分表达

- ◇ genuinely /'dʒenjuɪnli/ *ad.* 真诚地
- ◇ possess /pə'zes/ *v.* 拥有
- ◇ absorb /əb'sɔːb/ *v.* 吸收
- ◇ self-directed /selfdɪ'rektɪd/ *a.* 自主的
- ◇ efficient /ɪ'fɪʃ(ə)nt/ *a.* 高效的
- ◇ a strong motivation 强烈的动机

- ◇ sense of achievement 成就感
- ◇ value /'væljuː/ *v.* 重视
- ◇ put knowledge into practice 将知识应用于实践中
- ◇ enable /ɪn'eɪb(ə)l/ *v.* 给……能力/机会

What do you think is the best age for children to go to school?

Although there is variation in the ideal age when children should start formal schooling, I truly believe that the best age would be when children are 5 years old. By the time they turn 5, children will have learned how to be fairly independent and how to keep to a regular schedule while broadening social horizons through interaction with other children. Furthermore, they will possess certain basic skills to adjust themselves to a new environment as well as become emotionally, physically and cognitively ready to participate in various school activities.

高分表达

- ◇ variation /veərɪ'eɪʃn/ *n.* 差别
- ◇ ideal /aɪ'diːəl/ *a.* 理想的
- ◇ formal schooling 正规学校教育
- ◇ keep to a regular schedule 保持规律的作息时间
- ◇ broaden social horizons 拓展社会视野

- ◇ adjust... to... 使……适应……
- ◇ emotionally /ɪ'məʊʃənəli/ *ad.* 情感上地
- ◇ physically /'fɪzɪkli/ *ad.* 身体上地
- ◇ cognitively /'kɒɡnətɪvli/ *ad.* 认知上地
- ◇ participate in 参加
- ◇ various /'veərɪəs/ *a.* 各种各样的

Do you prefer to study by yourself or with your friends?

I am a night owl and I usually study at night, so I definitely prefer to study by myself. I find it really difficult to maintain focus if there are distractions. However, when I learn on my own, I devote my full attention to the learning material and I have absolute control over my study environment. The freedom to choose when I want to study is a must for me. For example, if I feel mentally exhausted, I can take a break. The absence of peer pressure is truly liberating because I can study at my own pace.

高分表达

◇ a night owl 夜猫子

◇ maintain focus 保持注意力

◇ distraction /dɪ'strækʃ(ə)n/ *n.* 干扰

◇ devote one's full attention to 全神贯注于

◇ have absolute control over 对……有绝对控制

◇ a must for 对……是必需的

◇ mentally exhausted 心力憔悴

◇ absence of peer pressure 没有同辈压力

◇ liberating /'lɪbəreɪtɪŋ/ *a.* 解脱的

◇ at one's own pace 按自己的节奏

Test 2

Listening / 140

Reading / 152

Writing / 164

Speaking / 168

Listening

Part 1

Listening Keys,
Questions 1 – 10

1	Atkinson	6	flashing
2	EL14 2BF	7	bright
3	Queens	8	Central
4	1986	9	screen
5	5	10	strain

Audioscripts

JACKSON: Good afternoon, take a seat.

ANU: Oh, thank you, Doctor Jackson.

JACKSON: How can I help you?

ANU: I'm feeling a bit unwell these days. I hope you can give me some advice.

JACKSON: OK. Could we start off with some basic details so that I can fill in the Patient Form?

ANU: Sure.

JACKSON: First of all, what's your full name, please?

1 此题定位词为 Name，考查单词拼写，需要在听和拼写的时候注意力集中。

ANU: It's Anu Atkinson.

JACKSON: Could you spell your family name?

2 此题定位词为 Post code，可预判答案为数字或字母，或数字和字母的组合，这里出现了信息更正，由 oh sorry 可知，前面说的邮编不正确，故填 EL14 2BF。

ANU: A-T-K-I-N-S-O-N, Atkinson. ❶

JACKSON: Do you know your postcode?

ANU: Yes, I think it's E-L-2-14-F-B, hmm, let me check, oh sorry, it's actually E-L-14-2-B-F. ❷

140

JACKSON: Thanks. And where are you living now?

ANU: At the moment, I'm living with my parents on Queens Avenue. ❸

JACKSON: OK, got that. And your date of birth?

ANU: October 1st, 1986. ❹

JACKSON: Oh, what a coincidence, it's my birthday too, but I was born in 1984. Do you have a telephone number that I can contact you with?

ANU: Yes, it's 875934, but I'm out and about a lot in the afternoon and evening.

JACKSON: So, would the best time to ring you be in the morning?

ANU: Yes.

JACKSON: Fine. Got that.

JACKSON: Now, what exactly brings you here?

ANU: Well. My eyes seem to have some problems whenever I spend more than half an hour reading books or working on the computer.

JACKSON: Hmm. I see. Is this a new problem or an old one? I mean, has it been happening for a long time?

ANU: No, it started just 3 days ago. Oh, no. I think it was 5 days ago in the gym after I played badminton. ❺

JACKSON: So, it was after you played badminton. What is the symptom exactly?

ANU: I see these flashing lights . ❻ I can't figure out what happened. Do you know what it is?

3 此题定位词为 Current address, 即现在的住址, 听力中的 I'm living...为我现在住在……, 注意听 Avenue 前面的内容, 故填 Queens。

4 此题定位词为 Birthday, 题目中已给出月份和具体某一天的日期, 故注意听年份, 一般不会记错自己的生日信息, 故听到 1986 后可确定为答案。

5 此题定位词为 lasted for, 即问持续了几天, 听到 it started just 3 days ago 还不能确定为答案, 因为后面接着说 "Oh, no", 说明前面的信息不正确, 后面是更正后的信息, it was 5 days ago, 即 5 天前就开始了, 故持续时间为 5 天, 故填 5。

6 此题定位词为 Symptom, 听力中直接问 "What is the symptom exactly?", 即可判断其后面的内容为答案, 故填 flashing。

7 此题定位词为 the room，根据填空处前面的 too 可知，答案为形容词，原文首先提到了"Was it very dark?"，此时不要急着确定答案，接着根据回答 it was very bright 可确定答案为 bright。

8 此题定位词为 Previous hospital，即之前去过的医院，题目中已给出 Hospital，故只需要注意听 Hospital 前面的内容，可预判答案为名词，根据回答可知填 Central。

9 此题定位词为 Suggestions，文中没有出现同义替换，即根据 Suggestions 后面的内容来判断答案，looking at a screen 与 staring at a screen 表达的意思相同，故填 screen。

10 此题定位词仍是 Suggestions，由题目可知共有两个建议，所以在听到"what about the second one?"时可确定后面的内容中会出现答案，听到 eye drops 时可知对应题目中的 medicine，继续往后听，reduce 对应 ease，故填 strain。

JACKSON: Em, I didn't know that either at the moment. What was the condition of the room where you played badminton? Was it very dark?

ANU: Oh, it was very bright. **❼**Sometimes I couldn't even open my eyes. Since then I haven't been able to see things clearly.

JACKSON: Oh, that might be the reason. And have you ever been treated before for anything like dizziness?

ANU: Well, I went into Central Hospital last month because of severe headache. **❽** And they kept me in for observation for a couple of days, but they couldn't find anything wrong.

JACKSON: OK, I'll make a note of that, too.

ANU: Thank you.

JACKSON: I think I've got all the information I need right now. And there are two suggestions for you. One is that you should take a good rest. If you find yourself looking at a screen for too long, **❾** you should look away, focus on a point in the distance for approximately 10-20 seconds, and then focus on something closer to you. Repeating this a few times should keep your eyes from getting tired.

ANU: Thanks. And what about the second one?

JACKSON: I'll give you some eye drops. You can use it before bed. That should reduce levels of eye strain. **❿** Here's the prescription. If the situation doesn't improve in a week, come back and see me again.

ANU: I see. Thank you for your advice, I will give it a try. Goodbye.

JACKSON: Bye.

Part 2

Listening Keys,
Questions 11 –20

🔑

11 submission	15&16&17 *IN EITHER ORDER*
12 election	A D F
13 library	18 B
14 Over 100	19 D
	20 A

Hello, all. My name is Samantha. I am a senior at the university and I am here this afternoon to introduce you to the student union on our campus.

As a student of this university, you are registered in our student union automatically and can enjoy all the benefits. No submission fees are required; ⓫ those are included in your tuition. With this in mind, we encourage you to take advantage of all of the different services our student union offers.

The student union is governed by students who are chosen by their fellow students in an annual election. ⓬ Nobody else is allowed to vote in these elections — not even university faculty or staff.

The student union is housed at the aptly-named Union House on the southeast corner of the campus where you will also see the library beside it. ⓭

A complete list of all clubs governed by the student union is available if you are interested. Compared to the number last year, we have 50 more non-sports clubs available, so that the union now governs 30 sports clubs and over 100 non-sports clubs on campus. ⓮ These include clubs for each of the majors offered by the university: political clubs, language clubs, international student clubs, sororities and fraternities, etc. We encourage you, as newly enrolled students of this university, to join any of the clubs available. It's a great way to meet fellow

Audioscripts

11 此题定位词为 no requirement 和 fees，当听到否定词 no 时则可判断后面紧跟着的 submission fees 为答案信息，故填 submission。

12 此题定位词为 yearly 和 selecting candidates，原文说学生会由学生管理，这些学生是由他们的同学在每年的选举中选出，annual 对应 yearly，故填 election。

13 此题定位词为 location，并根据题干关键词 next to 可判断原文可能出现方位的参照物。题干 location 与原文中 is housed at 对应，当听到 library 的时候注意听完整句描述，beside 为 next to 的同义替换，故填 library。

14 此题定位词为 30 和 non-athletic activities，原文说学生会现在管理 30 个体育俱乐部和 100 多个非体育俱乐部，non-sports 和 non-athletic activities 对应，故填 Over 100。

students, and to have some fun. This university prides itself in developing its students completely, not just academically!

But the student union does more than that. It is also available to help you with various problems you might encounter in your time here. If you feel that your civil rights have been seriously violated, for example, the student union can arrange a legal consultation for you. **⑮** Unlike most consultations offered outside the university, we will do this for you for free since most of the staff are working as volunteers. If you struggle with paying tuition, the student union has a placement agency for part-time jobs which are available exclusively to students of this university. **⑯** For health-related problems, we can direct you to the doctors at the campus clinic or to the local hospital, although we're not qualified to give medical advice ourselves, obviously. And if you're feeling a bit overwhelmed or a bit down, then you shouldn't hesitate to call the mental health line in our local area, which is 555 632 1987. They are very professional in this respect. If you have problems with your courses or exams, on the other hand, the student union will organise regular sessions to help you improve. **⑰** I'm afraid it can't solve communication problems with a roommate, a girlfriend, or a boyfriend at the moment, but you should certainly make use of most of the services that are available.

Before I go, I would like to highlight three of my personal favourites from the many clubs or teams which are part of the student union. The first is The Movie Makers, which travels to different locations during semester breaks and produces films and documentaries. They have achieved great success and are recognised among the film community for their work. **⑱** They have won numerous international awards as well as some national awards at the prestigious Sundance Film Festival.

15 此题定位词为 offer help，即在哪些方面提供帮助，原文说如果觉得自己的公民权利受到了严重侵犯，学生会可以安排法律咨询，civil rights 为公民权利，与法律问题相关，后面的 legal consultation 也为一个辅助定位点，因此可确定选 F。

16 原文说如果学生为交学费发愁，学生会有一个专门为这所大学的学生提供兼职工作的介绍机构。也就是解决学生在经济方面的问题，paying tuition 对应 finance，故选 D。

17 原文说如果在课程或考试中遇到问题，学生会将会定期组织课程来帮助你提高，即解决学生学业上的问题，problems with your courses or exams 与 academics 对应，故选 A。

18 此题定位词为 The Movie Makers，原文说他们取得了巨大的成功，工作得到了电影界的认可，are recognised among the film community for their work 对应 good reputation，故选 B。

The Team Travel club is an organisation that arranges discounted trips for many of our students and staff. It negotiates discounts with airlines, hotels and hostels, car rental companies, and long distance transport companies, so if you are planning a trip at mid-semester or semester break, consult Team Travel and you'll definitely get a better deal for your dollar⑲— and they don't charge a cent for planning!

And finally, Campus Radio, 94.7 FM. is manned mostly by students who are communications majors, marketing, or business majors. The schedule features a campus news show, live sporting events, and lots of great music. No other university campus radio station is bigger than ours,⑳ so if you want to stay informed about what's happening on campus, turn your dial to the Campus Radio.

Okay, thanks for your time and attention today. I hope you enjoy your time here at the university and that you utilise the many resources offered by our student union.

19 此题定位词为 Team Travel，原文说咨询团队旅游能省钱，而且不收取规划费，a better deal for your dollar 对应 low price，故选 D。

20 此题定位词为 "Campus Radio, 94.7 FM"，原文说其他大学校园的广播台都没有我们的大，也就是我们的广播台是最大的，对应 large size，故选 A。

Part 3

Listening Keys,
Questions 21-30
🔑

21	A	26	C
22	C	27	A
23	B	28	D
24	C	29	E
25	B	30	B

AMY: Hi Mike! Aren't these New Zealand carvings we've been studying in class fascinating?

MIKE: Oh hi, Amy. Oh, the Maori greenstone tikis? They're all a bit organic for my taste; you know, all curves and twisting shapes. I like modern stuff, geometric shapes, but I can see

Audioscripts

the skill involved in making them.

AMY: But the stories behind the tikis are what make them interesting. Besides, I imagine it would be difficult to create geometric patterns. The shape of each tiki seems to follow the natural contours of the stone. It's extremely hard, and it requires expertise and time to shape. ㉑

MIKE: That's true. I suppose that's why modern greenstone carvings are so expensive, but there aren't that many genuine old ones around. Archaeologists rarely discover such treasures, which is odd, given they are such a huge part of Maori culture. I wonder if archaeological dig sites were raided, and the tikis were taken to sell.

AMY: I believe it's because the owners valued them, and so preserved them. Many of them would have been passed down through the generations, and remain in the possession of the families today, like heirlooms. ㉒ Do you know what they were used for?

MIKE: I thought they were just an art form or a means of decoration, but Professor Matiu says that the Maori believed tikis were sacred and could be used as a pathway to their ancestors. They believed the dead could speak to them through these talismans. ㉓

AMY: So they don't represent tribes or anything? Interesting. How many different kinds are there? There must be hundreds of variations.

MIKE: There are other greenstone carvings beside tikis, although I can't remember all their names. Traditional tikis themselves can be divided into two distinct groups though.

AMY: Can they? By the materials? I've seen some with metal

21 此题定位词为 Amy and Mike agree，即两人都认可的内容，Amy 说 tiki 的形状很难塑造，需要专业知识和时间来完成，接着 Mike 表示同意（That's true），requires expertise 对应 take great skill，故选 A。

22 此题定位词为 Amy 和 archaeological dig sites，即只需要抓住 Amy 提出的观点即可。此处 Amy 表示相信许多人把 tikis 像传家宝一样代代相传，直到今天还保留在家族的手中，也就是说 tikis 作为继承物品，故选 C。

23 此题定位词为 Maori people，由 I thought 可知 Mike 只是猜测，接着说教授指出毛利人相信 tikis 是神圣的，可作为与先人建立联系的一个途径。他们相信死者可以通过这些护身符和他们说话，选项 B 中的 religious 和此处语境高度相关，故选 B。

features. Or is it to do with size or where they were made?

MIKE: Actually, it is the ways that their feet, heads and hands are placed that make the major difference. ㉔

AMY: Is it easy to discern the difference between the ancient stones and more modern reproductions? Are the styles very different?

MIKE: Modern reproductions usually use a different type of stone, although they may be of the same design. They may also be of a smaller size. But it's actually quite easy to tell if you are buying a genuine carving or a mass-produced souvenir.

AMY: How?

MIKE: Nowadays, they are produced by machine — using lasers, even — so they have no blemishes. In genuine carvings, they aren't always perfect, because the Maori used simple hand tools. For example, the hole that the cord is fed through isn't perfectly round. ㉕

AMY: That makes sense.

AMY: Actually it's amazing that they produced such detailed tikis with such simple tools and materials. Talk me through the process. I know the basic shape is carved from New Zealand greenstone.

MIKE: Yes, but first they had to get a blank of the right size.

AMY: You mean a piece of stone of the right size and basic shape?

24　此题定位词为 classified，即 tikis 是通过什么来被分类的，Amy 说的内容都是猜测性的，故还不能确定为答案，接着 Mike 说实际上……由 actually 可知后面的内容才是答案，"their feet, heads and hands" 摆放方法对应身体姿势，故选 C。

25　此题定位词为 distinguished，即问两者的区别，Mike 说真正的雕刻品并不总是完美的，因为毛利人使用简单的手工工具，比如，绳索穿过的孔并不是完全圆的，也就是说现代复制品的形状过于完美和规整，故选 B。

26 此题定位词为 blank，Mike 说他们使用一种坚硬的石制工具在一块绿石头上刻上一个凹槽，然后刻痕，stone tool 和 scored 对应 Stone scoring tool，故选 C。

MIKE: That's right. They used a hard stone tool — something rough — to wear a groove into a piece of greenstone. After they'd scored it with that, they could just snap it in two. **❷❻** I guess they could have used some kind of hammer though. They repeated the process until they had a piece of stone suitable for what they wanted to carve — usually flat pieces for tikis.

AMY: Right, because they're fairly small and quite thin. Then they started carving?

MIKE: Not right away. Before they could start carving they needed an absolutely smooth, flat surface. Nowadays when we want to do something like that we'd clamp the stone in a vice and use a sander, but they used a heavy block of sandstone and rubbed the piece of greenstone on it — over and over — to prepare it for carving. **❷❼**

27 此题定位词为 smoothing the surface，Mike 说他们用一块很厚的砂岩来使表面光滑，故选 A。

AMY: It must have been very time-consuming. So how did they cut out little details like hands and feet?

MIKE: They had carving tools. They used small chips of stone glued and tied onto a wooden handle, then they also used a piece of sharpened bone, made into a point. **❷❽**

28 此题定位词为 carving details，Mike 说他们还用一块削尖的骨头，并做成一个尖，故选 D。

AMY: Is that what they used to make the holes?

MIKE: Actually, they had a special tool to make holes. It was a stick tied between two heavy pebbles with a point at the end. They would wrap string around it, pull it back and forth to wear a hole into the tiki. **❷❾** They used the same technique to make round shapes, too, but didn't make the hole go all the way through.

29 此题定位词为 making holes，Mike 说他们把一根一头尖的棍子绑在两块重的卵石中间，然后会用绳子缠绕它，来回拉动，在 tiki 上钻一个洞，wear a hole 对应 drill，故选 E。

AMY: And I've seen some tikis with coloured eyes or decorations, are they painted?

MIKE: Mostly they are inlaid with different coloured stone, or mother of pearl from shells, or sometimes dyed pieces of bone. They were fixed in place using tarata gum, a sticky plant resin. ㉚ They used plants to make the natural strings, too.

AMY: That's right. The Maori were very resourceful, weren't they?

MIKE: They certainly were.

30　此题定位词为 fixing coloured decorations，Mike 说它们是用一种叫 tarata 的黏性植物树脂来固定的，也就是植物胶，故选 B。

Part 4

Listening Keys,
Questions 31- 40

🔑

31	preserved	36	affordable
32	trace	37	dimensions
33	buried	38	rocks
34	minerals	39	images
35	exhibitions	40	sediments

Welcome, students, to the daily talk on the fossils found here at Green Mountain Fossil Park. First, I will tell you a little about the history of our park. The park is designed to educate you on what the environment was like in this area around 5 million years ago, when most of the area was at sea level and near water bodies such as lakes and seas. These bodies of water provided moisture and significant plant and animal variety, which has resulted in the fantastic collection of fossils which you will see today. The fossils here were discovered by mine workers during the 1960s, and the park itself was opened to tourists and students back in 1985.

We have three types of fossils here in the park — the first are transitional fossils. These are rare fossils that appear to exhibit

Audioscripts

31 此题定位词为 common，这里需要注意很明显的顺序词 Next，即第二种化石，对应填空处答案，在说了 preserved fossils 后接着说了 common，和题干给出的信息一致，故填 preserved。

32 此题定位词为 animals，这里需要注意顺序词 Thirdly，即第三种化石，对应填空处答案，原文没有直接说出化石名称，先提到了 animals 对应题干信息，最后才说这种化石称为（we refer to as）痕迹化石，故填 trace。

33 此题定位词为 Petrifaction，根据填空处前后内容可推测答案很可能为动词被动语态或者形容词，原文说动物死后被埋在泥土或淤泥下面，is 对应 becomes，故填 buried。

34 此题定位词为 replace the bones，即什么代替了骨头，推测填空处为名词，原文说骨头腐烂，被矿物质取而代之，故填 minerals。

35 此题定位词为 Shop，问购物的地点，原文说公园外面可以买东西，也可以从展览中购买，make purchases 和题干 Shop（动词）为同义替换，故填 exhibitions。

36 此题定位词为 Prices，根据题干中 generally 可推测答案为形容词，原文说不要认为所有的化石都是昂贵的，大多数都是负担得起的，即大部分化石的价格都是可负担的，故填 affordable。

traits of the animal's evolutionary ancestors and its descendants, such as an animal showing both dinosaur and bird-like features. Next, we have preserved fossils, which are more common fossilised remains. **31** These are fossils in which the structure of an animal or plant remains intact and you can clearly see something like a plant or a fish. Thirdly, we have fossils which indirectly show the activities of animals, such as their tracks and burrows, and we refer to these as trace fossils. **32**

You may wonder how fossils are formed. Well, many people think it happens when organisms are caught in a volcanic eruption and are trapped in ash, but in reality, these formations are rare. The most common way a fossil is formed is through petrifaction. An animal dies and becomes buried under mud or silt. **33** Over time the mud hardens around the bones of the animal. Eventually the bones also decay and are replaced by minerals which form the shape of the fossil in stone. **34** You will see many of this kind of fossil today.

After you finish today's tour, you may wish to take home a souvenir. We encourage you to do so. There is a shop outside the park, but you can also make purchases from our exhibitions. **35** The money raised helps to fund our work of preserving this wonderful site. Of course you can also buy fossils and take them home. Please don't think that all fossils are expensive to buy — the majority are small and affordable samples that are as wonderful as the larger ones. **36** — Don't forget to check them out.

As you can see, you all have some worksheets to go through here today. These will help you to learn as much as you can from your visit. There are also some tools you will find as you go around the site. For example, there are tape measures available beside each fossil so that you can note the dimensions of each fossil. 37 This can help us to identify different species. We also encourage you to use your specially-designed notebook to record as many different types of rocks as you can. 38 Geology forms an important part of the study of fossils, and so we want you to focus on the types. If you brought a camera along with you today, don't hesitate to use it as the images of the fossils will be worth reviewing later. 39 You may wish to experiment with the settings to see what they are like. Here in the information centre, you can pick up an information sheet which contains some useful tips on how to do that.

Last of all, you can practice using a compass. Even though you cannot locate the fossils themselves using the compass, it will help you find the sediments which are the key to the location of the fossils. 40 These are very soft, so to protect the delicate fossils, trowels and plastic covers are needed. You will find these throughout the site, please use them.

Please feel free to ask any of our staff as you tour around, and enjoy your day! We hope you leave us today with a greater passion to study fossils further.

37 此题定位词为 A tape measure，根据填空处前面内容可推测答案为名词，原文说化石旁边都有卷尺，这样就可以记录每块化石的尺寸，故填 dimensions。

38 此题定位词为 A notebook，根据填空处前面内容可推测答案为名词，原文说使用特别设计的笔记本来记录尽可能多的不同类型的岩石，故填 rocks。

39 此题定位词为 A camera，根据填空处内容可推测答案为名词，原文说不要犹豫使用相机，因为化石的图像很值得回看，也就是用相机获得图像，故填 images。

40 此题定位词为 A compass，根据填空处前面的内容可推测答案为名词，原文说用指南针可以帮助找到沉积物，find 与 detect 为同义替换，故填 sediments。

Reading

<table>
<tr><td rowspan="7">

Passage 1

Reading Keys,
Questions 1 – 13

🔑

</td><td>

1   F

2   C

3   G

4   D

5   limited time

6   continuous
product growth

</td><td>

7   surplus

8   icons of culture

9&10 *IN EITHER ORDER*
     A   E

11&12&13 *IN EITHER ORDER*
     C   E   F

</td></tr>
</table>

■ 思路解析

Questions 1 – 4   ※题目类型：段落细节配对题

1   题干是运营一个重磅展览需要的费用，重点词为 outlays（开支，费用）、required，根据重点词定位 F 段开头 Huge capital expense is required for blockbuster，其中 expense 是题干 outlays 的同义替换，即运营一个重磅展览需要的费用，故选 F 段。

2   题干是如今运营一个画廊需要的资格，重点词是 qualifications、today，C 段首句 New museology（新博物馆学）对应题干 today，初步定位 C 段，该段最后两句 "To become an art gallery director today a degree in art is not necessary…stating that skills in public relations and business intellect…were fundamental requirements for the director…"，其中 To become an art gallery director，即为题干中 to run a gallery，skills in public relations and business intellect 对应题干 qualifications，故选 C。

3   题干是重磅展览好处与坏处的对比，重点词是 benefits、drawbacks，G 段第一句 The unfortunate thing 对应 drawbacks，第三句 the hiring or creation of blockbusters can have many positives，其中 positives 对应题干 benefits，故选 G 段。

4   题干说提到艺术和文化场所对重磅展览的展示并非必要，重点词是 artistic and cultural venues，D 段最后一句说不需要通过艺术画廊、科学中心或者博物馆来展示重磅展览，an gallery 对应 artistic venues，museum 对应 cultural venues，do not require 对应

unnecessary，故选 D。

Questions 5 – 8 ※题目类型：摘要填空题

5　填空处前面有 lasts for，主语为 A blockbuster，推测问的是重磅展览开放多长时间，A 段第六句提到了 A blockbuster can be understood as... that is only displayed for limited time，即只有有限时间内展出，故填 limited time。

6　空格问的是重磅展览采用了什么关键方法来增加访客，推测空格处是一个名词或名词性短语，重点词为 a key、increase visitors，据此定位 C 段第一、二句 "New museology is a means implemented to... grow the number of visitors. This can only be achieved through continuous product growth."，即增加访客的核心方法为 continuous product growth，grow the number 对应题干 increase，this can only be achieved 对应题干 a key，故填 continuous product growth。

7　空格问的是重磅展览这些活动为画廊其他较少盈利的项目提供了经济上的什么，重点词为 financial，据此定位 E 段第一句 The question is whether blockbusters... can generate the surplus needed to finance other initiatives，即重磅展览产生的盈余能否为（画廊的）其他项目提供资金，故填 surplus（盈余）。

8　空格问展示重磅展览以及推广新的博物馆学将特定的场所从什么变为娱乐场所，重点词为 entertainment venues，据此定位 G 段最后一句 "the trend in favor of blockbusters... make art galleries... the entertainment industry instead of as icons of culture..."，即这种趋势将画廊等文艺场所从文化标志变成娱乐产业，philanthropic and government support 对应 support from charity organisations and the government，故填 icons of culture。

Questions 9 – 10 ※题目类型：多选题

9-10　题干问澳大利亚的博物馆和机构展示重磅展览的原因是什么，重点词是 museums and institutions in Australia，根据重点词定位 E 段第四句 "Some Australian museums... demonstrate their attempt to recover some of the costs of operation..."，即澳大利亚的博物馆试图通过展示重磅展览回收运营成本，其中 costs of operation 指这些机构每天投入在维护和管理方面的开支，对应 A 选项，故选 A（它们可以抵消运营成本）。

根据重点词定位 F 段倒数第二句 "As Australian institutions seek to grow their visitors... for better revenue through blockbuster..."，即澳大利亚的机构通过重磅展览增加参观者数量，以带来收入的提升，for better revenue 对应 achieving further profit targets（达到更远的收益目标），故选 E。

Questions 11 – 13　※题目类型：多选题

11-13　题干问针对重磅展览，哪些是批评言论，重点词是 criticisms，应在文中寻找负面的评价和此类展览的缺点。

根据重点词定位 B 段第三、四句 " Literature items from the USA and UK apply the word blockbuster for non-elitist, less scholarly... aims to attract the public. "，即批评家认为重磅展览是不太具有学术性的，且目标在于吸引大众，scholarly 和 academic 为同义替换，the public 和 the majority 为同义替换，故选 C。

G 段倒数第三句 although they subject staff to stress and the unpredictability of the market，前文介绍的是好处 positives，从 although 转折词看出，此处为展览的缺点，即重磅展览让员工有压力，其中 staff 对应 E 选项 employees，stress 对应 pressure，故选 E（重磅展览给员工很大的压力）。

F 段首句 Huge capital expense is required for blockbusters 与 G 段第二句 the actual costs in the entire institution are hard to calculate 均强调了运营重磅展览的高费用，故选 F。

■ 译文 ｜ 博物馆重磅展览

A　重磅展览（Blockbuster）是一个从 1980 年就开始使用的时髦术语。这个词代表艺术画廊展览、科学展览或令人惊叹的博物馆展览。埃尔森在 1984 年说，重磅展览是一个大规模的展览，吸引了一般不会去参观博物馆的人群。这些人要等很长时间才能看到这些展览。詹姆斯·罗森菲尔德在 1993 年的《直接营销》一书中写道，重磅展览的成功是营销和策展能力的成功。一个重磅展览可以理解为一个著名且突出的展览，只在有限的时间内进行展示。罗森菲尔德和埃尔森对重磅展览的定义忽略了这样一个事实：人们愿意花钱来观看重磅展览。他们的定义还忽略了一个事实，即重磅展览适用于电影展览。

B　给一部电影或一个展览取名为重磅展览并不意味着它们确实是重磅展览。"重磅展览"这个术语只有在产品获得巨大反响和成功的情况下才算被有效使用。美国和英国的文学作品将重磅展览一词用于非精英主义、非学术性和大众化目的的情况下。批评者认为，重磅展览的设计目的是吸引公众。一些重磅展览试图激发学者的项目合作，并提供覆盖广泛的社会领域的展览，而不是局限于特权阶层。

C　新博物馆学旨在研究如何维持和提高访客数量。这只能通过产品的持续增长来实现。这种增长不应局限于组织或引进重磅展览，而应着眼于创新和展览的定期变化。重磅展览的访客正在成为顾客，而不是普通的访客。博物馆、画廊和科学中心用来吸引更多顾客的技能正在改变。企业家素质、市场营销和商业技能是最重要的。策展人变成了管理者。如今，要成为一名美术馆馆长，不一定要有艺术学位。1994 年的《经济学人》对其进行了最好的总结，它指出公关技能、商业智慧和提供吸引大众的旅游展览与对手竞争的能力是做馆长的基本要求。

D   随着新博物馆学的兴起，博物馆旅游、文化产业、游乐、盈利等方面受到了广泛的关注。这引发了一场激烈的争论，争论的焦点是让机构活动适应市场的需要是否合适，以及是否应该将博物馆视为主要的旅游景点。尽管评论家们认为科学中心、艺术画廊和博物馆的管理者们在全球范围内寻找融合商业和文化的好办法，重磅展览仍处于领跑地位。虽然重磅展览是新博物馆学的组成部分，但你不需要艺术画廊、科学中心或博物馆来获得轰动效应或展示重磅展览。

E   问题在于，在一家机构上演的重磅展览能否产生盈余为其他项目提供资金。如果目标是盈利，那么许多主要的画廊和博物馆已经证明了这种能力。一些博物馆可能需要钱来修复它们的藏品或维修建筑物。一些澳大利亚的博物馆和画廊希望有机会能够收回部分运营成本，或者用未列入预算的收入资助其他项目。这将使经济理性主义者欢欣鼓舞。有些被誉为"重磅"的展览，其实并不是重磅展览。有些不能产生收入。机构中的大多数会计系统很可能不会承认引进或创作一个重磅展览的实际成本。

F   重磅展览需要巨额的资金投入，因为需要所有组织部门的资源。这涉及到更多的成本。除了巨额的资本投入外，人力资源管理成本也增加了实际成本。巡展要花很多钱。重磅展览还需要项目管理中来自各种管理结构的资源。每一个人，包括服务单位、普通劳动者、培训、技术、行政和前厅人员都被期望做更多的事。澳大利亚的机构试图通过大型展览来增加他们的访客和会员，以获得更好的收入，但由于市场竞争激烈，能将盈余继续用于资助其他项目的机会更少了。来自客户的资源是有限的，并且重磅展览的参观者将不得不从各种各样的重磅展览中选择产品。

G   不幸的是，当净利润成为重磅展览的基本目标时，就很难维持这种结果了。机构人员在引进和创作重磅展览的过程中筋疲力尽，整个机构的实际成本难以计算。另一方面，引进或创作重磅展览也有很多积极的方面。例如，一个著名的重磅展览可以提高一个机构的形象，使得博物馆更受欢迎。重磅展览通过增加餐馆、酒店、零售商、运输行业和商店的就业机会来促进经济，尽管它让员工承受压力和市场的不可预测性。重磅展览的成功或失败可能预示着决策者和管理者需要重新考虑他们的方法。然而，有利于重磅展览和新博物馆学的趋势可能会使美术馆、博物馆，尤其是科学中心一同被视为旅游业和娱乐业的组成部分，而它们不会被视为是值得慈善机构和政府支持的文化标志。

H 也许最好的办法是中和一下定期展览和重磅展览。只有在有足够的空间和其他资金来源来进一步支持那些不那么激动人心的展览时，中间立场才有可能发挥作用。要想让展览和定期的项目更吸引人，有必要探索当地人还希望从展览中得到什么。大多数人都希望参观经济实惠的海外场馆（如科学中心和博物馆）。

Passage 2

Reading Keys,
Questions 14 – 26

14　C	19　A	24　B
15　E	20　C	25　A
16　F	21　C	26　E
17　D	22　B	
18　H	23　C	

■ 思路解析

Questions 14 – 18　※题目类型：段落细节配对题

14　题干意思是书写系统对一个文明来说很重要的例子，重点词为 importance、a civilisation。由 C 段第三、四句 "For instance... the epics tales of the... were so captivating that there was a need to preserve them... the Greeks... borrowed the alphabet system..." 可知，为了记录两个史诗级的故事，古希腊人专门借用了一套书写系统，即以事例证明了书写系统的重要性。故选 C。

15　题干意思是提到一个现代的故事讲述形式的受欢迎程度，重点词为 popularity、modern form。由 E 段第一、二句 "Each year, over seven billion people head towards the silver screens... the chief storyteller of the day is none other than the Cinema！" 可知，当今故事讲述之王——影院在全球拥有超过 70 亿的观影人群，对应题干受欢迎度以及现代形式，故选 E。

16　题干意思是提及一个让观众惊叹的概念，重点词为 concept、take audience's breath away。由 F 段最后两句话 "He states that when a story fascinates us... which he calls—

'the suspension of disbelief'" 可知，由于"暂停怀疑"这一概念可以使得观众忘却时空、恐惧，进而接受虚构的故事，fascinates us 对应题干的 take audience's breath away，故选 F。

17 题干意思是"口头叙事由于其他叙事形式出现而失宠"，重点词为 oral、losing popularity、other forms，D 段倒数第二句"oral storytelling is … taken over by journals, novels…"，taken over 为 losing popularity 的同义替换，journals 等属于 other forms，故选 D。

18 题干意思是"提到两种不同的故事类型"，重点词为 two、types，H 段第三句提到了 "Two theatrical storytelling types, tragedy and comedy"，可以确定答案为 H，往后的内容是两种故事的解释。

Questions 19 – 22 ※题目类型：单选题

19 题干意思是"作者用召集猫的比喻是为了说明……"，通过 B 段第一句的"Finding the initial stories … as these were preserved in the minds of the storytellers"和最后一句 "However, while such memorisation seems like art or sorcery, the essential idea… helps one recall specific information in one's mind"可知因为原始版本的故事存在于讲述者的大脑里，且没有一个记号系统，所以研究原始的故事难度很大，故选 A。

20 题干问的是希腊人创造书写系统是为了什么，从题干的 Greeks 可以定位到 C 段第三句的 the onset of literacy in ancient Greece is… the epic tales of… were so captivating that there was a need to preserve them，其中 tales（传说）对应 C 选项的 stories，captivating（迷人的）对应 C 选项的 like，故选 C（记录他们喜欢的故事）。

21 题干问作者提到现代电影院的目的，原文 E 段谈到电影院，大部分选项有关 storytelling，E 段关于 storytelling 的是倒数第一、二句"visual storytelling must … the conventional patterns… are indispensable for a good story"，其中 visual storytelling 与电影院相对应，conventional patterns are indispensable（传统模式不可或缺）与 C 选项"叙事原则怎样保留"相对应，故选 C。

22 题干问鼓励编剧读亚里士多德的原因，根据 screenwriters 和 Aristotle 可以定位 F 段开头 an aspiring screenwriter needs to… Aristotle，但原因要继续往后读，F 段倒数第四句是 he had ample perception of how to gather and retain large crowds，如何聚集并留住观众对应 B 选项的保持观众兴趣，故选 B。

Questions 23–26　※题目类型：完成句子配对题

23 题干问过去故事讲述者创造了什么，重点词是 storytellers in the past，原文 B 段第一句提到了早期的故事讲述者记忆方法，可先定位答案在 B 段，倒数第二句中 recite thousands of verses and proses 对应 C 选项中 large pieces of information，倒数第一句中 have a system of reminders or mnemonics that helps one recall…提示或者助记系统即为记忆储存的工具，故选 C。

24 题干问好故事会激发什么，G 段第二句 "They might have… astonishment or ecstasy … or even days after the show" 中 days after the show 对应 B 选项中 long-lasting 的效果，astonishment 等皆为强烈的情绪，故选 B。

25 题干问的是雅典人对什么特别感兴趣，根据 Athenians 定位 H 段，第三句 "Two theatrical storytelling types, tragedy and comedy, made Athenians immerse themselves in gloom and glee"，即悲剧和喜剧让雅典人沉浸在悲喜之中，对应 A 选项的 sorrowful events or stories with cheerful ending，故选 A。

26 题干问荷马通过什么使得故事吸引人，根据 Homer 定位 I 段，开头提到了荷马创造的角色 "credible heroes that were powerful and majestic but did not turn into fantasy figures… He made them sulk, quarrel, cheat, and whine"，powerful and majestic 对应题干 E 选项中的 admirable qualities，而 "quarrel, cheat" 对应 controversial behaviour，故选 E。

■ 译文 ｜ 古代的故事讲述

A 最初的故事可能是讲给蜷缩在篝火旁的人们听的。这些包括伟大的冒险故事，如濒死遭遇、狩猎远足、或一次从致命危险中的逃脱，或者也许是一个谜或神的轶事。然而，抛开这个话题，所有这些故事背后都有一个主要的目的：让听众好奇和投入，让他们忘却担忧或疲劳，只让一个问题占据他们的头脑——接下来会发生什么？

B 发现人类历史上最初的故事就像把猫聚在一起那样难，因为这些故事被保留在讲故事的人的脑海里。然而，这种储存或记忆，不应被视为无效。澳大利亚、巴尔干半岛和世界其他地区的口述传统记录告诉我们，当时讲故事的大师和诗人可以背诵成千上万的诗句和散文，一字不漏！然而，尽管这种记忆似乎是艺术或巫术，但它创造符号的基本理念是要有一个提醒系统或助记符，以帮助人们回忆脑中特定的信息。

C 在一些波利尼西亚社会里，讲故事的人用一根锯齿状的记忆棒来辅助连续的背诵。然而，在许多其他全球社群中讲故事的艺术导致了书写系统的发明或发展。例如，古希腊人识字的开始是由于特洛伊战争和奥德修斯航行的史诗故事是如此引人入胜，以至于有必要将它们保存下来。因此，在公元前 750 年至公元前 700 年，希腊人从他们的地中海东部的邻居——腓尼基人那里借用了字母系统。

D 在羊皮纸和其他材料上记录故事的原始做法或许可以追溯到许多古代文明。古埃及的祭司纸莎草档案，北美欧及布威族印第安人使用的桦树皮卷轴就是很好的例子。它已经成为一种久经考验的实践，多亏了这些实践，故事才成了纸上文字。甚至连口头讲故事的做法也认为是被期刊、小说、连环画等取代的。然而，书面文本不是人类获得故事的主要来源。那么，主要来源是什么呢？

E 每年，超过 70 亿人涌向电影院观看国内和国际电影院提供的最新电影。是的，如今主要的故事讲述者就是电影院！电影以动态画面的形式讲述故事，与阅读纸质信息或者静态摄影相比，电影是当代的奇迹。更确切地说，这是一种最初为人们所接受的按特定顺序排列图像而形成的错觉。即便如此，我们也必须承认视觉叙事艺术一定带有一种深刻的返祖氛围。尽管有上述的优点，传统的故事情节和人物塑造在很久以前就融入到了故事叙述中，这些模式对于一个好故事来说是必不可少的。

F 大电影公司的桌子上成千上万个剧本落满了灰尘，而一个有抱负的编剧需要仰视的是四世纪的希腊哲学家亚里士多德。在他未完成的作品《诗学》中，他留下了几篇讲稿，描述了在多种文学和戏剧媒介中讲故事的艺术。尽管他不太可能设想出当今多厅影院那种爆米花助燃的氛围，但他对如何聚集和留住大批观众到这样的创意中心有着丰富的经验。亚里士多德以令人印象深刻的理性主义来审视这一过程。他说，当一个故事让我们着迷时，我们不知道自己身处何地，无法感受到恐惧，只能接受虚构。这是亚里士多德的戏剧原理之一，他称之为"暂停怀疑"。

G 观众知道这种感觉！他们坐在剧院的座位上，经历恐惧、悲伤、惊讶或狂喜，甚至在演出结束几天后还会经历这些，他们知道这一切都是虚构的，却让它影响他们的精神状态。他们很少想清楚为什么他们会陷入讲故事的人的圈套中。

H 亚里士多德曾在雅典教书，在这座城市里，戏剧成为大众休闲娱乐的主要方式。所以很明显，他可能观察到的是"暂停怀疑"在起作用。悲剧和喜剧这两种戏剧叙事方式让雅典人沉浸在忧愁和欢乐之中。其中，亚里士多德明确地承认悲剧是激发观众最真挚情感的有力武器，因此他探寻叙述者的艺术中有哪些因素能引起这样潜意识的骚动。为此，他研究了欧里庇德斯、埃斯库罗斯、索福克勒斯，甚至荷马的古希腊悲剧杰作。即使在那个时候，荷马的故事也和今天一样令人敬畏。他的《伊利亚特》和《奥德赛》被认为是文学里程碑，并被用作衡量所有其他故事的标尺。

| 那么，荷马史诗背后的神秘之处是什么呢？荷马构想了可信的英雄，他们强大威严，但最终没有变成幻想中的人物。他们会生气、争吵、欺骗和发牢骚。他们有观众能够感同身受或愿意追随的特征。这自然激起了观众的好奇心，想知道接下来会发生什么。正如亚里士多德所观察到的那样，这些英雄有人性，有人类容易体现的缺点和弱点，恰好充满戏剧性。

Passage 3
Reading Keys,
Questions 27–40

27	v	32	ix	37	FALSE
28	x	33	iii	38	unfinished
29	vii	34	xi	39	volcanic stone
30	iv	35	TRUE	40	political and religious
31	ii	36	NOT GIVEN		

思路解析

Questions 27–34 ※题目类型：段落标题配对题

27　A 段提到这个岛鲜有人类居住，岛上居民的神秘吸引了 Heyerdahl 这样的早期探险者登岛勘察，故选 v。

28　B 段提到了岛上原住民（original inhabitants）在公元 318 年到达该岛，当时岛上还有很多树、海鸟及食物资源等，即描述了岛上早期的状况，故选 x（早期的小岛的环境）。

29　C 段提到了岛上的巨石像（gigantic stone statues），前面强调巨石像之多，后面强调巨石像之大，突出了古人所留巨石像的稀有性和其价值，故选 vii（岛民的遗产：雕像）。

30　D 段第五、六句提到了 the statues were symbols of both political and religious authority and power... they were sources of sacred spirits，即这些头像是政治和宗教的象征，是当时人们神圣精神的来源，对应 iv 选项（石像的文化方面的重要性）。

31　E 段主要讲这个岛还有其他的名字，并且表明这个岛有可能被用作天文台地点和测地标志，即这个岛可能用于古代做研究的地点，对应选项 ii。

32　F 段前半部分提到 20 世纪末和 21 世纪初，科学家和作家提出了许多理论，解释为什么复活节岛的文明在第一批欧洲人到该岛时就衰落了，暗示了两者的发生有某种巧合，对应 ix 选项。

33　G 段主要讲由于岛上没有充足的食物来养活居民，因此居民数量减少，对应 iii。

34　H 段主要讲关于复活节岛消失的理论和假设，其中最令人信服的假设是复活节岛的毁灭与欧洲人的到来有关，convincing 和 persuasive 为同义替换，对应 xi 选项。

Questions 35-37　※题目类型：正误判断题

35　题干是复活节岛上没有永久居民，重点词是 residents，据此定位 A 段第四句 it is also not inhabited，其中 inhabit 与题干的 residents 为同义替换，即这个岛屿没有人居住，故 TRUE。

36　题干是波利尼西亚人来到小岛后种了很多树，重点词是 Polynesians 和 trees，文中 B 段提到了波利尼西亚人来到小岛时，岛上有很多树木和丰富的食物来源，但没有提及波利尼西亚人是否在岛上种了很多树，故 NOT GIVEN。

37　题干是作者认同 Jared Diamond 的结论，重点词是 Jared Diamond、agrees，H 段提到了 These theories presented defective ideas starting with the racialist assumptions ... propagated by writers like Jared Diamond who had no historical archaeological knowledge ...，即一些有问题的和带有种族歧视的理论被 Jared Diamond 所鼓吹，并且此人没有历史考古知识，由此看出作者对他结论的负面态度，故 FALSE。

Questions 38 –40　※题目类型：摘要填空题

38　空格问的是岛上其他地方的一些雕像是怎么样的，C 段提到了巨石像的位置，该段中间部分提到除了这些坐落在 ahu plateaus 的巨石像，还有少数未完成的巨石像遍布岛的其他地方，故填 unfinished。

39　空格问的是巨石像是用什么做的，推测填的是名词或名词性词组，重点词为 formed out of，C 段后半部分提到了巨石像的外形特征，倒数第三句提到了 "they are mostly carved from Rono Raraku，a type of volcanic stone"，carved from 对应 formed out of，a type of 对应 a kind of，故填 volcanic stone。

40   空格问目前的理论认为巨石像有什么样的作用，推测空格填的是形容词，重点词为 function，D 段首句提到了 the purpose of the moai statues，对应题干 function，故定位 D 段，第五句提到了 the statues were symbols of both political and religious authority and power，其中形容词为答案，故填 political and religious。

■ 译文 ┃ 复活节岛的谜团

A   复活节岛是一座多丘陵、没有树木的小火山，是世界上最著名的考古遗址之一。然而，它罕有人迹，也无人居住。它被一位名叫雅各布·罗格文的荷兰船长命名为复活节岛。雅各布于 1722 年 4 月 5 日访问了该岛，他是第一个踏上该岛的欧洲人。为了揭开岛上居民的神秘面纱，挪威探险家托尔·海尔达尔（Thor Heyerdahl）在 20 世纪 50 年代初探访了该岛。海尔达尔认为岛上的原始居民是来自于美国南部海岸的印第安社会。然而，经过广泛的对民族志、语言学和考古学的研究，人们发现这一理论是不准确的。

B   根据研究以及从岛上挖掘出的骨骼中所提取的 DNA 显示，岛上的原始居民来自波利尼西亚的马克萨斯群岛。根据从坟墓中收集的芦苇的碳年代测定，这些人在公元 318 年来到岛上。人们相信，在那个时候，岛上有大量的树木和成群的陆鸟和海鸟，有丰富的食物来源——鱼、植物和鸟，这使得人口迅速增长，产生了丰富的艺术和宗教文化。

C   摩埃石像是当地居民最著名的文化特征之一，它们是巨大的石像。据说，至少有 288 座这样的摩埃石像竖立在 250 个被称为"阿胡"的石坪上，每个"阿胡"距另一个"阿胡"约 1.5 英里，围绕着这个岛形成了一条连续的线。除了坐落在阿胡高原上的摩埃石像，岛上还有其他未完成的摩埃石像。有的在采石场，有的在古道上和沿海地区。摩埃石像平均高 14.5 英尺，重 14 吨，大多由拉诺·拉腊库火山岩雕刻而成，质地坚硬。还有其他更大的摩埃石像，重达 80 吨，高约 33 英尺。考虑到这些石像的巨大尺寸，预计大约需要 50 到 150 人用树木制成的滚轴和雪橇在岛上搬运这些石像。

D   一直以来，人们很难对摩埃石像的用途做出明确的解释。然而，人们相信摩埃石像的产生起源于波利尼西亚的一个类似的做法，尽管波利尼西亚的石像与复活节岛的不同。这些石像有一些人类的特征。根据肖像学和考古学的分析，对雕刻神像的崇拜是建立在男性哲学的基础上，也建立在某一家族的权威之上。因此，这些雕像是政治和宗教的权威以及权力的象征。对使用它们的人来说，它们是神圣灵魂的来源。在波利尼西亚的宗教中，当木制品和雕刻的石头被仪式化地准备好时，人们相信某种具有神奇的被称为莫纳的精神力量会改变他们。因此，复活节岛的阿胡平原是庇护所，而摩埃石像是神圣的东西。

E 这个岛还有其他名字，比如 Mata-Ki-Te-Rani，意思是 "望着天堂的眼睛"，它还可以被叫做 Te-Pito-O-Te-Henua，意思是 "世界的中心"。这两个名字虽然被大多数考古学家忽略，但却表明这个岛有可能分别被用作天文台和大地测量标志。格雷厄姆·汉考克（Graham Hancock）在他的书《天堂的镜子》中指出，该岛可能是上古文明的一个重要的科学前哨。罗伯特·洛马斯（Robert Lomas）和克里斯托弗·奈特（Christopher Knight）等学者研究了古代的大地测量符号，并在《乌列尔的机器》一书中提出，这些符号被用于预测和应对未来的灾难。

F 在20世纪末和21世纪初，科学家和作家提出了许多理论，解释为什么复活节岛的文明恰好在第一批欧洲人与该岛接触的时候衰落了。贾里德·戴蒙德（Jared Diamond）在其著作《崩溃：社会如何选择失败或生存》中阐述了其中一个已被证明不准确的理论。

G 基本上，大多数理论都认为，随着殖民后人口的增长，对大量资源的需求增加，岛屿无法在生态上自我补充。结果，岛上的森林在15世纪就被砍伐殆尽，地面植被被移除，泉水干涸，成群的鸟也消失了。由于没有树木来建造独木舟用于近海捕鱼，而且鸟类和野生动物也消失殆尽，人们缺乏足够的食物。农作物产量也下降了，随之而来的饥荒导致同类相食。由于岛上没有食物来养活岛上的居民（包括牧师和管理人员），因此出现了社会和文化的崩溃。根据这些理论，人口数量下降到原来的十分之一，而且在17世纪和18世纪的部落战争中，大多数摩埃石像都被毁了。

H 这些理论从托尔·海尔达尔（Thor Heyerdahl）的种族主义假设出发，提出了一些有问题的观点。这些观点后来被像贾里德·戴蒙德这样的作家传播，而他们对复活节岛上发生的真实事件没有任何历史考古学知识。最令人信服的假说便是，复活节岛的毁灭是因为无情的欧洲到访者，尤其是奴隶贩子。他们把天花等疾病带到岛上，杀害了复活节岛上的土著人，并把他们作为奴隶运到南美洲。

Writing

Task 1

审　　题

这两幅图说明了瓢虫的生命周期和成虫的结构。

图表类型

流程图

分析思路

对于流程图，我们通常只需按图表提示来描述图中信息即可。在描述时需要注意两点：一是阶段数量，二是各个阶段的特点。在概述里，我们主要描述阶段数量，很明显有四个阶段。接着，我们具体分析流程图的各个阶段，每个阶段是什么，有什么特点（图中需要体现时间信息）。对于成虫结构，我们在概述里只需要说明主要的身体部位即可。接着，我们具体分析结构图，需要提到主要的身体部位，身体部位名称，有什么特点。

最后可进行总结，内容与概述内容相同。

参考写作结构

首　　　段：概述流程图和成虫结构信息
主体段1：流程图各个阶段的名称及特点
主体段2：成虫各部位的名称及特点
末　　　段：总结主要特点

参考范文[⊖]

The flow chart shows that there are four main stages from birth to maturity in the life of a ladybird and the other diagram provides the information of the structure of an adult ladybird.

To begin with, eggs are produced on leaves by mature ladybirds and it generally takes 2 to 5 days for each egg to become a larva. The larval stage then lasts for three weeks until

---

⊖ 范文中加色字为高分表达。

these young insects turn to pupae. After one week, the adult ladybird emerges from the pupa and the life cycle begins anew.

Looking closely at the anatomical picture of a ladybird, one would find that this insect has a dome-shaped body with six short legs and an oval black head with two antennae on the front. Its two small eyes are near the pronotum which is connected to two light coloured elytra which are evenly spotted. Under the hemispherical elytra are two transparent wings and a dark abdomen.

Overall, it takes about five weeks for a ladybird egg to become a mature bug; meanwhile the adult of this species possesses an over-proportionally large body compared to its other parts.

Overall：7

Task 2

审　题
当孩子开始上学，老师对他们的智力和社会性发展方面的影响比父母对他们的影响更大。你在多大程度上同意或不同意？

讨论对象
老师和父母对孩子在智力和社会性发展方面的影响，写作文章为议论文（讨论谁的影响更大）

写作观点选择
有所侧重（老师/父母的影响更大）vs 无侧重（两者对孩子的影响相当，没有较大差异）

写作论据准备
老师对孩子智力和社会性发展方面的影响
◇ 将学术知识传授给学生 impart academic knowledge
◇ 指导和帮助孩子们高效地学习 help children to learn more efficiently
◇ 发展孩子的社会技能 help children to develop social skills
◇ 帮助学习如何与别人相处 help to learn how to get along with others

父母对孩子智力和社会性发展方面的影响
◇ 通过自己的行为影响孩子 influence children through their own behaviour
◇ 教孩子良好的行为习惯 teach children good manners

◇ 教孩子他们在社会中扮演什么角色 teach children what role they play in society

参考写作结构

1 首　　段：引出讨论对象 + 表明观点
　主体段1：老师对孩子的智力和社会性发展方面有很大影响
　主体段2：家长对孩子的智力和社会性发展有很大影响
　末　　段：重申观点

2 首　　段：引出讨论对象 + 表明观点
　主体段1：老师对孩子的智力和社会性发展方面有很大影响
　让步段2：虽然家长也有影响，但是老师的影响更大
　末　　段：重申观点

3 首　　段：引出讨论对象 + 表明观点
　主体段1：家长对孩子的智力和社会性发展方面有很大影响
　主体段2：虽然老师也有影响，但家长的影响更大
　末　　段：重申观点

参考范文⊖

Some people argue that after children go to schools, teachers would exert a stronger influence on children's academic and social development than parents. I certainly disagree as educators only have a deeper impact on children's intellectual development rather than how they behave socially.

Admittedly, teachers can have a profound impact on children's intellectual development and social skills, which is why children are sent to school when they reach a certain age. Being trained professionally to impart academic knowledge to the students, teachers are experienced in guiding the young to explore their interests and learn efficiently. To some extent, children's social skills would be improved at school since they would need to learn how to communicate and cooperate with their classmates in group tasks.

Parents, on the other hand, can influence their children's social development even more deeply than teachers. As youngsters spend most of their free time with their parents, they are more likely to follow in their parents' footsteps when it comes to how they are expected to behave. To be more specific, children are inclined to observe and imitate their parents' words and deeds whether good or bad. Even if they are taught to express themselves in a particular way at school, they may subconsciously change the way they speak simply

---

⊖ 范文中加色字为高分表达。

because their parents prefer a different manner of speaking at home.

To sum up, teachers do extend certain influence on children's intellectual development as well as social skills; however, in terms of behavioural education, teachers can never replace the role parents play in their daily interaction with their children at home. It is therefore safe to say that parents wield more power in affecting their children's social development than teachers.

Overall: 7

Speaking

Part 1 | Pen & Pencil

Do you usually use a pen or pencil?

I usually use a pen instead of a pencil. I have been practising calligraphy with pens since I was young, so I feel more comfortable writing with a pen. I only use my pencils when I occasionally need to draw something.

高分表达

◇ calligraphy /kəˈlɪgrəfi/ *n.* 书法

◇ occasionally /əˈkeɪʒ(ə)nəli/ *ad.* 偶尔

◇ comfortable /ˈkʌmftəb(ə)l/ *a.* 舒适的

Which do you use more often? Pen or pencil?

I use pencils more often. I can hang loose without worrying about making mistakes. I'm able to erase what I have written or drawn at the drop of the hat. Furthermore, a pencil is eco-friendly and it is made of wood, meaning that it's biodegradable, unlike a plastic pen.

高分表达

◇ hang loose 放松

◇ at the drop of the hat 随时

◇ eco-friendly /iːkəʊ ˈfrendli/ *a.* 生态友好的

◇ biodegradable /ˌbaɪəʊdɪˈgreɪdəb(ə)l/ *a.* 可生物降解的

When was the last time you bought a pen or pencil?

Off the top of my head, I can hardly remember the last time I bought a pen or a pencil. It's not because I don't write or draw often, but because my schools often gave away pens and pencils with their logo, together with other promotional items. Last month, I just received a set of new pens for free, and I guess my school really expected students to hit the books in the upcoming academic year.

高分表达

- ◇ off the top of my head 不假思索
- ◇ give away 赠送
- ◇ promotional items 附送赠品
- ◇ expect /ɪkˈspekt/ *v.* 期望
- ◇ hit the books 用功学习

What do you think of giving a pen or pencil as a present?

Well, they are a practical and useful present that stands for intellect. It would be creative to personalise a pen when it is engraved with a powerful quote which can make someone jump for joy, as the pen becomes more than just a pen — it becomes a memory.

高分表达

- ◇ stand for 代表
- ◇ personalise /ˈpɜːsənəlaɪzd/ *v.* 个性化
- ◇ engrave with 在……上雕刻
- ◇ make someone jump for joy 让某人高兴得跳起来

Part 2

> **Describe an ideal house or apartment where you want to live.**
>
> **You should say**:
>   where it is
>   what it is like
>   who you would like to live with
>
> **and explain why you think it is ideal.**

You will have to talk about the topic for one to two minutes. You have one minute to think about what you are going to say. You can make some notes to help you if you wish.

I have always dreamed of living in a very big house. The perfect location would be somewhere between the city centre and the countryside. It is important not to be located in the middle of nowhere, but at the same time, I need to feel the sunshine every morning, without having a building that blocks my view.

The style of the interior space should be mixed between modern and contemporary design, and it should reflect simplicity. It would be perfect to have a backyard garden where I can do many interesting things, such as playing outdoor games, having a picnic, growing vegetables and so on.

But a beautiful big house makes no sense if I live on my own, so I would like to live in this house with my parents who will make my time in the house more enjoyable. They love to cook at home and often invite friends to dinner on weekends, and I guess the house will be a great place for doing what they love.

This house is ideal since it reflects the feeling of comfort and serenity because of who lives inside rather than how it looks from the outside. Somehow I think it is a sweet dream that can come true and an attainable goal too.

高分表达

- ◇ in the middle of nowhere 在偏僻的地方
- ◇ block /blɒk/ *v.* 阻挡
- ◇ interior space 室内空间
- ◇ contemporary /kən'temp(ə)r(ə)ri/ *a.* 当代的
- ◇ simplicity /sɪm'plɪsəti/ *n.* 简单
- ◇ make no sense 毫无意义
- ◇ on one's own 独自
- ◇ comfort and serenity 舒适和宁静
- ◇ attainable /ə'teɪnəbl/ *a.* 可达到的

Part 3

Where do people in China like to live, in a house or an apartment?

Most people in China prefer to live in houses if they can afford one. To start with, it feels good to have less noise from neighbours, more privacy and definitely more space. Houses are usually situated far away from cities' hustle and bustle, which imparts people the feeling of tranquility. They also allow people to make use of their creativity when designing and decorating the rooms.

高分表达

◇ to start with 首先

◇ privacy /ˈpraɪvəsi/ *n.* 隐私

◇ be situated 坐落于

◇ hustle and bustle 喧嚣

◇ impart /ɪmˈpɑː(r)t/ 赋予……

◇ feeling of tranquility 平静的感觉

◇ make use of 利用

◇ creativity /ˌkriːeɪˈtɪvəti/ *n.* 创造力

What are the benefits of living in a house?

Living in a house is the greatest thing since sliced bread. To begin with, at the time of purchase, you will have the choice between an existing construction or a project of your own, in which you can personalise each room according to your taste and needs. Second, a house is more than a building, it is a permanent address. It offers more facilities than an apartment does, not to mention large rooms, a space for gardening if you have green fingers and so on. Additionally, you have more privacy and freedom.

高分表达

◇ since sliced bread 有史以来

◇ personalise /ˈpɜːsənəlaɪz/ *v.* 使个性化

◇ facility /fəˈsɪləti/ *n.* 设施

◇ not to mention 更不用说

◇ gardening /ˈgɑː(r)d(ə)nɪŋ/ *n.* 园艺

◇ have green fingers 擅长园艺

Why do many people like to live in the city?

Life in the city directly exposes people to more job opportunities and the chances to move up in the world are higher. More educational opportunities like universities, colleges and academic institutions are available. There is for sure a lot of competition, but consequently, city dwellers have more chances to meet new people and easily build bridges. The city life offers people many varieties and choices because of the abundance and the mix of people and culture. After all, variety is the spice of life.

高分表达

◇ expose to 使……暴露于，使……获得

◇ move up in the world 获得成功，得到晋升

◇ competition /ˌkɒmpəˈtɪʃn/ *n.* 竞争

◇ city dweller 城市居民

◇ build bridges 连接不同的人或群体

◇ abundance /əˈbʌndəns/ *n.* 丰富性   ◇ spice of life 生活的调味品

◇ variety /vəˈraɪəti/ *n.* 多样化

Where do people like to live，in the city centre or the suburbs?

Like every decision people make in life，deciding where to live is a challenge too. Most people determine to choose by practical reasons，while some others by preferences. Because of work proximity or easy accessibility to services，people tend to choose locations in city centres. Despite that，there is a greater appreciation of suburbs as they help to blow off steam. This is not only because there is a possibility of finding cheaper options，but also because people find it as an escape from the hectic noisy city life in which they work during the day.

高分表达

◇ determine /dɪˈtɜː(r)mɪn/ *v.* 决定   ◇ a greater appreciation of 更看好……

◇ practical reasons 实际原因   ◇ blow off steam 释放压力

◇ preference /ˈpref(ə)rəns/ *n.* 偏好   ◇ an escape from 逃离

◇ proximity /prɒkˈsɪməti/ *n.* 临近   ◇ hectic /ˈhektɪk/ *a.* 忙碌的

◇ accessibility / əkˌsesəˈbɪləti/ *n.* 获取
……的便利

Test 3

Listening / 174

Reading / 187

Writing / 199

Speaking / 203

Listening

Part 1

Listening Keys,
Questions 1 – 10

1 Jamieson	6 licence
2 11(th) July/ July 11(th)	7 transport
	8 Thursday
3 waiter	9 resume
4 children	10 color/colour
5 sing	

Audioscripts

SAM: Hello?

AMY: Hello, is that Sam Walker?

SAM: Yes, it is. How can I help you?

AMY: This is Amy calling from the Harvey Entertainment Agency. How are you?

SAM: Oh, I'm well, thank you.

AMY: That's good to hear. I'm calling as you are registered with our job agency last year and we have had a job come up that you might be interested in.

SAM: Great! Can you tell me about it?

AMY: Yes, of course. The job is with a very popular family resort located on Jamieson Island. It's a temporary job until the beginning of September.

SAM: Sounds interesting. Let me just get a pen and paper to write that down. How do you spell Jamieson please?

AMY: It's J-A-M-I-E-S-O-N. ❶

1 此题定位词为 location, 需要注意听 Island 前面的内容, 由 located on Jamieson Island 可知答案为 Jamieson, location 与 located 对应, 后面接着给出了拼写, 即可根据拼写得出答案。

174

SAM: OK. When does the job start?

AMY: The resort opens on the 10th next month. So, you will start on the next day, 11th July. ❷

SAM: What will I do exactly?

AMY: Let me see. There is a vacancy for a tour guide. Oh, sorry, it looks like this position was filled yesterday. So, the other position here is for a waiter. ❸

SAM: Okay, that sounds interesting. What experience is required for the job?

AMY: They want someone with at least two years' experience on the same position, and also someone who knows how to communicate with children. ❹

SAM: No problem. I have over five years' experience related to this type of work, and I have also worked in a kindergarten before, so I'm sure I'm a good fit for the job.

AMY: Fantastic! There is another requirement which is a little more unusual — they would like someone who has musical talent!

SAM: Oh! Well, I can play the guitar pretty well.

AMY: It's not that exactly — they already have a resident band — they really want someone who can sing well. ❺ The activities at the club involve a lot of music to entertain the guests. Would you be able to do that?

SAM: Hmm… Maybe… can I think about it? What else do I need to know about the job?

AMY: They also want their employees to be able to drive.

2 此题定位词为 Start date，即填一个具体日期，虽然前面提到 The resort opens on 10th next month，但并不是开始工作的日期，根据 So 可知后面提到的信息才为答案，故填 11 July，或 11th July，或 July 11，或 July 11th。

3 此题定位词为 Job position，即工作岗位，前面提到 a vacancy for a tour guide，即缺导游，但后面又接着说 "Oh, sorry…"，可知会更正信息，So 后面的信息才为答案，故填 waiter。

4 此题定位词为 get along with，可预判答案为名词，题目中有已知信息 2 years' experience，其后面会出现答案，knows how to communicate with 与 get along with 同义替换，知道如何与小孩沟通则相处起来没问题，故填 children。

5 此题定位词为 can，可判断答案为动词，虽然有提到 can play the guitar pretty well 但不符合字数要求，且根据后面的 It's not that exactly 可知答案在其后面，故填 sing。

SAM: Yeah, I can do that, but I don't have my own car at the moment. Is that a problem?

AMY: I don't think so. They need a person with a licence so that they can travel around various parts of the resort by car, as it's very large. ❻But there are resort vehicles provided for that purpose.

SAM: Okay.

SAM: Are there any special benefits for employees with this job?

AMY: Yes, there are. Of course you get free accommodation. The resort also provides transport for employees, which is free of charge. ❼

SAM: That's good. What about meals? Since I will be staying on the island, I guess there won't be much choice regarding the food.

AMY: That is true, and so the resort provides lunch at a very low price. I think that's a pretty good perk.

SAM: Sure, that sounds great.

AMY: So, do you think you would be interested in attending an interview for this job?

SAM: Yes, I think it sounds interesting. And you said it finishes in September?

AMY: That's right. The 3rd September. Okay, I will book you in for an interview on Wednesday.

SAM: Oh dear, I'm sorry but I have an appointment at the hospital on Wednesday. Is there any chance for an interview

6 此题定位词为 can drive，且可通过空格前的冠词 a 预判出答案为名词，be able to drive 对应 can drive，Sam 说自己没有车，Amy 表示没有车没关系，有驾照就行，故填 licence。

7 此题定位词为 free accommodation，由题目可知 accommodation 和答案为并列关系，注意听与 accommodation 相关的内容，文中提到 accommodation 后接着提到了 transport 和 free of charge，即提供免费的交通，free of charge 和 free 为同义替换，故填 transport。

on another day?

AMY: Yes. No problem. We can do it on Thursday. ❽ How does 10 am suit you?

SAM: That sounds perfect. Thanks a lot. What do I need to bring?

AMY: A resume is a must — just to let you know that the one I have on file is from last year, so perhaps something has changed since then?

SAM: Yes, that's true, I do need to update it. I'll bring that with me. ❾

AMY: And also we need a colour photo of you taken within the past 2 months. ❿We will provide it to the resort for your ID card, so we don't accept black and white photos.

SAM: Okay, got it. Thanks, and I appreciate your call. Look forward to seeing you soon.

AMY: See you then. I'll send you an email confirmation.

8 此题定位词为 Appointment，即约定时间，前面提到了 on Wednesday，但由于后面说"Oh dear, I'm sorry"，可知 Wednesday 不是答案，需要接着往后面听，后面提到了 Thursday 和 10am 两个与时间有关的信息，由题目中的介词 on 可知与 Thursday 搭配合适，故填 Thursday。

9 此题定位词为 Bring、updated。根据 Amy 对于 Sam 的简历的疑问，可知已有的简历并非最新，且 Sam 后面提到会更新，两个定位词之间出现的 resume 为答案词，故填 resume。

10 此处定位词为 photo，根据原文语序，可先判断答案，后面的 black and white photos 为不符合要求的照片（该信息为干扰项），故填 colour。

Part 2

Listening Keys,
Questions 11 – 20

11	F	16	shower
12	B	17	basement
13	E	18	food containers
14	A	19	access code
15	C	20	11. 30 pm

As you will have noticed upon entering the main campus, the area is quite vast. I'd like to show you around today and get you familiar with the area. Right now, we are standing in the

Audioscripts

campus garden, which is the most conspicuous area in the whole campus. It is roughly in the centre of the campus and makes for a good reference point.

To the north-west of the garden, we have what we refer to as the Student service unit. ⓫This is where you can find course information, lodge complaints about registration, receive grades, and conduct other administrational tasks. You should become familiar with this place as you will likely be visiting it a lot in the near future, by which I mean, from tomorrow!

To the south-east of the garden near the south gate, we have quite a vibrant venue for both sports and concerts, ⓬ and it provides over 5000 seats. You can find a lot of posters on the billboard nearby advertising upcoming activities. We usually organise at least one big event each month and have a few regularly scheduled activities that are open to all students on weekends.

Take the lane leading to the northeastern corner of the campus, and you will find a new building at the end. It's where trained staff are ready to cater to your health needs and give advice for any health related problems that you might have. ⓭ Just to let you know, the first floor is for physical checkups while the second floor is for consultations.

If you're from abroad and need help, you'll need to go to the building directly adjacent to the campus garden. ⓮Go straight to the second floor, where we have staff there to assist you. By the way, that building is also where we hold most of our international conferences and seminars. It's a great place to listen to experts share their experience. I highly recommend it!

For those who need to find a place to live on campus, you can go to the accommodation office. Please note that we have closed the old office which is directly to the west of the campus

11 此题定位词为 Student service office，由原文可知在花园的西北方，以花园为中心，其西北方为 F。

12 此题定位词为 Stadium，原文中提到的 venue for both sports and concerts 即为 Stadium 体育馆的同义表达，位于花园的东南方，靠近南门，故选 B。

13 此题定位词为 Health centre，原文中提到的 cater to your health needs and give advice for any health related problems 与之对应，沿着通向校园东北角的小路走，在尽头的新建筑即为健康中心，故选 E。

14 此题定位词为 International student office，原文中提到的 from abroad 与之对应，原文中提到 the building directly adjacent to the campus garden 表示紧邻校园花园的建筑，故选 A。

garden, as it is too small. The larger building right next to the café is where the new one is located. **⑮** I am aware that some students have yet to receive their room keys. This is probably because you have not provided us with your proof of payment and identity card yet. Please don't worry though; I can assure you that there are enough rooms for everybody.

The students' dormitory is on the south side of the campus, and it is, of course, where you would be residing throughout your stay. Each room is equipped to accommodate two students. The kitchen space is shared, but you do have a shower for yourselves. **⑯**

After you move in, you will have to talk to the designated manager of your dormitory building before using any of the facilities in the basement, including washing machines and dryers. **⑰**

If you have signed up for our school meal program, please listen up. In order to prevent any mix-ups when distributing meals, most of our food containers will be marked with each student's name. **⑱** If the labeling isn't done correctly on yours, please let us know in time.

You should be aware that last semester we had some incidents involving theft in the dorms. As such, we've implemented some new policies this year to upgrade our security services. Every student will be provided with an access code, without which they cannot enter their rooms. **⑲** Please don't share it with anyone. If you want to renew its validity, you'll need to check your portal page and find the button under the tab 'on-campus dormitory'. We hope that this new system should limit the number of thefts this year.

15 此题定位词为 Accommodation office，原文中有直接提到，注意听其后面的内容，原文说已经关闭了原来的办公室（H），因为它太小了，咖啡馆旁边的那栋大一点的大楼是新办公室的所在地，故选 C。

16 此题定位词为 Each student 和 own，原文说每个房间都配备了两名学生可使用的设备，kitchen 是 shared（共用的），所以不是答案，由 but 转折，可知答案在后面，由 shower for yourselves 可知答案为 shower，for yourselves 和 his or her own 对应，故填 shower。

17 此题定位词为 Laundry facilities，原文中提到的 washing machines 与之对应，这些设备在宿舍楼地下室，故填 basement。

18 此题定位词为 Most 和 are named，即被写上名字的，可推测答案为名词，原文中 Most 后即为答案出处，大部分食品容器将标上每个学生的名字，be marked with each student's name 与 are named 对应，故填 food containers。

19 此题定位词为 An 和 go into the dormitory，可判断填空处为名词或名词词组，且发音开头为元音，原文说每个学生都将有一个访问码来进入他们的房间，故填 access code。

20 此题定位词为 Electric appliances，原文中的 all gadgets and appliances 与之对应，原文说晚上 11 点 30 分熄灯后，所有电子产品和电器都要关掉，后面虽然提到了 11 pm，但是与电子产品无关，故填 11. 30 pm。

Finally, I'd like to talk briefly about campus rules. It is expected that all gadgets and appliances are switched off after the lights are out, which happens at 11. 30 pm. ❷⓿ Most students' bedtime is around 11 pm, so please keep to this time and respect others' need for quiet. We take this quite seriously and are quite strict. Any gadgets that are seized for breaking this rule won't be returned until the end of the semester.

Part 3

Listening Keys,
Question 21 – 30

21	C	26	two/2
22	B	27	11(th) May/
23	A		May 11(th)
24	interview	28	layout
25	font	29	online
		30	procedure

Audioscripts

LINDA: Hi Mr Brown, you asked me to stay after class?

MR BROWN: Ah yes Linda, as you missed class yesterday I wanted to talk to you about the project proposal that was assigned.

LINDA: Oh thank you very much, I appreciate that. My friend Rebecca told me that it's an essay to propose a project on the topic of women as business leaders.

MR BROWN: That's right, Linda. As you are a passionate advocate of women in business, I am sure you will enjoy this topic!

LINDA: Yes, I'm excited to do some research in this area. Can I ask whether this proposal will be examined and marked?

MR BROWN: No, and its result won't be added to your grades either. The proposal will just be reviewed by your professors and then given back with comments which will be helpful when it comes to undertaking the project itself. ㉑

LINDA: That will be very helpful. So I need to come up with an idea on women as business leaders… I suppose that the main aim of the proposal is to talk about the topic, but the expected result of the research is also of great importance, so shall we place equal emphasis on these two aspects?

MR BROWN: You can mention both of those things, but I would say that the major purpose of the proposal is to talk about the method you will use to research the topic. ㉒

LINDA: Alright, that's good to know. And Rebecca mentioned the 6000-word limit…

MR BROWN: Yes, do not exceed it.

LINDA: Ok. Are there any other restrictions or limitations?

MR BROWN: Yes, there are. Some are mandatory and some are optional, but this sheet has guidelines for both the proposal and the eventual project. It's really important that you stick to the rules, ㉓because the marks for the final project itself, which you will undertake later in the year, will be an important component of your grades.

LINDA: So I'm wondering how much work to put into the proposal as opposed to the project itself. For example, should I talk to some women in business to get their thoughts?

MR BROWN: I think it would be beneficial if you did a preliminary interview with one woman, ㉔ and just take a look at what's happening in the workplace. That will give weight to

21 此题关键词为 project proposal，原文说提案将由教授们审核，然后给出反馈意见，given back with comments 和 be returned with feedback 对应，故选 C。

22 此题关键词为 focus on，原文说提案的主要目的是讨论用于研究这个主题的方法，the major purpose 和 focus on 对应，method 和 approach 对应，故选 B。

23 此题关键词为 Mr. Brown suggests，需要注意听 Mr. Brown 的建议，他说 proposal 和最终的项目都有指导说明（guidelines），对应 instruction，后面强调 stick to the rules，the rules 这里指代上面才提到的 guidelines，即为 follow the instruction，故选 A。

24 此题关键词为 Conduct，注意到填空处前面有 an，可判断答案为名词，且发音以元音开头，原文说先需要对一个女性进行采访，然后再看看工作场所发生了什么，take a look at what's happening in the workplace 和题目中的 Make a few workplace observations 对应，do an interview 和 conduct an interview 对应，因为有字数限制，故填 interview。

your proposal without costing you a lot of time.

LINDA: That's a great suggestion, thank you.

LINDA: I'm wondering about the presentation of the proposal itself. Can I format it in any way I like?

25 此题关键词为 in the correct, 可判断填空处为名词, 原文说需要使用正确的字体, right 和 correct 为同义替换, 故填 font。

MR BROWN: Ah, there are some rules around that. You can check the guidelines you have as to the formatting required, and we need you to use the right font, which is size 12 Arial. **㉕**

LINDA: Alright. And how many copies of the proposal do I need to present? I think only one printed copy was required last time, and one electronic copy. Is that correct?

26 此题定位词为 hard copies, 学生问是不是只需要一份打印件, 一份电子版就可以了, 但回答并未认可, 而是说两位教授各需要一份打印件, 所以是两份, 由 so 也可判断填 two。

MR BROWN: This time, apart from a soft copy, please give us one paper copy each for Professor Jones and Professor Smith who will be reviewing them, so that's two. **㉖**

LINDA: Sure, I have noted that. And what is the deadline for the proposal?

MR BROWN: It is 11th April.

LINDA: Wow, that is a really short timeframe — that's only a week away!

27 此题定位词为 Due date, 可知填一个日期, 先提到了一个日期 11th April, 但后面根据 " Oh, I'm sorry" 可知会更正信息, 所以这个日期不是答案, 接着听到 the due date, 可确定答案为 11 May, 或 11th May, 或 May 11, 或 May 11th。

MR BROWN: Oh I'm sorry — I forgot we're already in April, the year is going so fast. The due date is in May of course, the 11th. **㉗**

LINDA: Great, that sounds much better. So we are going to make some changes until the final version is settled — does that mean that we can change the proposed project if there is any problem?

MR BROWN: We may give you permission to change the

layout of the proposal, ❷❽ but not the topic, and only so long as there is enough time before commencing the actual project. The date for that hasn't been set yet.

LINDA: And how do I get permission if I need it? Do I need to send a letter or mail?

MR BROWN: The request should be submitted online, ❷❾ and it's best to follow up with a phone call or in person, to make sure I received it.

LINDA: Alright. So just to get it clear, my proposal needs to deal mainly with…?

MR BROWN: Begin with a short theory or hypothesis as to the results of the proposed project. After that, I would say that the procedure you are thinking of using is the aspect to concentrate on. ❸⓿

LINDA: Alright Mr Brown, thank you very much for your time. I have a few ideas, so I better get started.

MR BROWN: Okay Linda, see you next week.

28 此题定位词为 make changes，对什么进行更改，可判断填空处为名词，可能会允许改变提案的布局，change 和 make changes 对应，故填 layout。

29 此题定位词为 requests、applications，需要通过什么申请方式提出修改请求，虽然原文中前面提到了 a letter or mail，但后文没有给出肯定回答，故不是答案，回答说此类请求应该在线提交，即需要在线申请，故填 on-line。

30 此题定位词为 After 和 focus on，原文说 After that，也就是在提出假设后，听到这里可以确定答案会马上出现，原文接着说正在考虑使用的程序是要集中精力的方面，concentrate on 和 focus on 为同义替换，故填 procedure。

Part 4

Listening Keys,
Questions 31–40

🔑

31 population
32 fashion
33 material
34 participation
35 cinemas

36 mental
37 uncommon
38 angles
39 limited
40 privacy

As we know, sports have become increasingly popular in recent decades. Historically, many sports were only for the wealthy and privileged, but now certain games, such as

Audioscripts

31 此题定位词为 a large proportion，根据填空处前面内容可推测答案为名词，原文说运动让来自全国各地的很大比例的人口都参与进来，engage 和 involve 为同义替换，a large proportion 与 a large percentage 为同义替换，故填 population。

32 此题定位词为 such as，可推测答案为名词，在原文中着重听举例内容，原文说体育在许多经济行业中发挥了巨大的作用，如时尚，故填 fashion。

33 此题定位词为 invention 和 new，可推测答案为名词，原文说运动服装的新材料正在被创造，created 对应 invention，根据 new 也可确定答案为 material。

34 此题定位词为 Governments，原文说许多国家的政府都致力于提高国民对体育的参与度，故填 participation。

35 此题定位词为 such as 和 free，重点留意举例内容，听到 for example 后可确定答案在其后面，原文说电影院会发放免费电影票，即可以免费进入电影院，故填 cinemas。

football and basketball, have become available to ordinary people. They are now being taught in schools and at local clubs.

One reason that sport has become so widely popular is that they involve a large percentage of the population, drawn from all around the country, creating excitement and anticipation for the event. ❸❶

Also, in recent times, sport has played a huge role in many large sectors of the economy, such as fashion. ❸❷They often go hand in hand. Certain brand-names of sports clothing have become increasingly popular, creating a multi-million-dollar industry. Everywhere you go, people proudly wear such brand names. From being merely clothing for sports-players, these brands have now become must-haves for this season's wardrobe.

Since sport is becoming ever more competitive, with international events, such as the Olympics, being held regularly, there is a drive to create better products used in sports. For instance, new material is being created for sports clothing and other equipment to reduce drag and improve the efficiency of the players. ❸❸The technology incorporated in these is of a high standard.

Playing sports is a healthy activity, with different sports suitable for all ages from the very young to those getting on in years. To improve the overall health of the nation, and to create a greater sense of community involvement, governments in many countries aim to increase their citizens' participation in sports. ❸❹ In some areas, there are even incentives for taking part in sporting activities; for example, with cinemas handing out free tickets to those involved. ❸❺

Sports can be very competitive, and although some experts

warn that a spirit of competition isn't healthy, many agree that this competitive spirit can actually contribute to a greater feeling of achievement. With such a positive effect, many therapists recommend sport as a way to improve mental health, and many participate with this focus in mind. **36**

Of course, the media has had an enormous impact on sports. The rise in popularity of uncommon sports like underwater hockey and parkour is fuelled by the increasing availability of satellite television. **37** However, this can unfortunately lead to personal injury and sometimes even loss of life, as more people attempt to copy these sports players without the appropriate safety precautions.

Digital television has also played a great part in promoting sports. Every part of a sport event can be replayed and analysed. For example, controversial or exciting moments in each game can be filmed from different angles. Certain feats can also be presented in a more impressive way than they really are. **38** Partly because of this, games are becoming more and more prestigious, with players trying different tricks and techniques to make themselves appear more skilled than their opponents, and to draw attention from the crowd.

People often learn about sports through television and the internet. Many feel it is easier to remember certain elements they have learned from a visual source, rather than learning from a book, the traditional way of studying. Knowledge about sports in books is limited, as some sports manoeuvres cannot be accurately depicted in a picture or in writing. **39**

Newspapers, however, remain a popular means to gain information about the results of sports events, and many people still check the cricket scores in their local newspapers each week. Unfortunately, as sports stars are becoming ever

36 此题定位词为 a sense of achievement 以及 health，原文说成就感带来积极效应（positive effect 对应 positively contributes to）使得许多治疗师建议将体育运动作为改善心理健康的一种方式，故填 mental。

37 此题定位词为 Satellite TV，原文说卫星电视的普及推动了水下曲棍球和跑酷等不常见运动的流行，故填 uncommon。

38 此题定位词为 details 和 different，原文说运动游戏中有争议的或激动人心的时刻都可以从不同的角度拍摄，由 different 可确定填 angles。

39 此题定位词为 books 和 knowledge，原文说书本上关于运动的知识是有限的，故填 limited。

more famous, people are becoming increasingly interested in their everyday lives. The newspapers often publish articles about them, including personal details that the players may not want shared with the public. There needs to be a greater respect for the privacy of these individuals. ❹

With sports becoming more available to all, now is a good time to join a local team, or just spend some time playing a cricket match or a game of football with friends. This can improve your own fitness and lead to greater quality of life for you and your whole family.

40 此题定位词为 sporting celebrities，对应文中提到的 sports stars，需要注意听与 sports stars 相关的内容，原文说需要对他们的隐私给予更多的尊重，即有时候没有尊重他们的隐私，故填 privacy。

Reading

Passage 1 Reading Keys, Questions 1 –13	1	FALSE	6	NOT GIVEN	11	temples and residences
	2	FALSE	7	TRUE	12	absolute power
	3	TRUE	8	marriage or descent		
	4	TRUE	9	bows and arrows	13	class war
	5	FALSE	10	Danube valley		

思路解析

Questions 1 –7 ※题目类型：正误判断题

1　题干说宗族里存在经济权力的等级制度，重点词是 hierarchy of economic power 和 clans，section B 与 clans 相关，第一部分最后一句 the economic disparity is non-existent，其中 economic disparity 即经济差异，是题干 hierarchy of economic power 的同义替换，文中说经济差异在宗族里不存在，题干意思与之相反，故 FALSE。

2　题干说只有宗族被认为是游牧民族，重点词是 clans 和 nomadic，section C 第一部分提到 "People belonging to the tribe societal group are mostly farmers, but could also be nomadic with a mobile…"，可知部落也有游牧的特点，题干意思与原文矛盾，故 FALSE。

3　题干说部落由社区做支持，这些社区里的人基本通过家族关系而关联，重点词 connect、family relationships。section C 第一部分最后一句 "Tribes are generally multi-community societies, with the individual communities integrated into the large society through kinship ties."，其中 through kinship ties 对应题干 through family relationships；generally、integrated 对应题干 are mostly connected，故 TRUE。

4　题干说在酋邦，居民会向酋长提供物品和食物，重点词是 chiefdoms 和 items and foodstuffs，section D 第二部分第二句 Chiefs obviously benefit… local craft products and food which are paid as a tribute，即酋长能收到居民送的特产和食物，题干中 items and foodstuffs 和原文中 local craft products and food 对应，故 TRUE。

5 题干说在国家，公民被认为是土地的所有者，重点词是 state 和 owners of the land，section E 第一部分倒数第二句 "The ruling lineage is viewed as the ultimate owner of the land..." 说统治家族是土地的最终所有者，题干意思与原文不符，故 FALSE。

6 题干说公民从他们的首领那里得到好处前必须向他们的首领纳税，重点词是 taxes、benefits 和 before，section E 第一部分最后一句说低级公民有义务向他们的首领纳税，section F 第一部分最后一句说首领也会给他们的跟随者提供好处，但没有提到公民先纳税后得到好处这一点，故 NOT GIVEN。

7 题干说早期的国家受益于他们重新分配资本的能力，重点词是 Early states 和 redistribute capital，section E 第二部分最后一句 "Early states tend to have developed redistribution systems..." 说早期的国家倾向于发展再分配制度，redistribute 和 redistribution 对应，best support 和 benefit 对应，故 TRUE。

Questions 8 – 13　※题目类型：简答题

8 题目问在宗族里，什么让一群人互相联系在一起，重点词为 clans 和 connected，section B 第一部分提到 Members of the clans are typically related to each other through marriage or descent and the group...，即宗族成员通过婚姻或血统相互联系，connected with 和 related to 为同义替换，故填 marriage or descent。

9 题目问哈扎人用什么来抓猎物，重点词是 Hadza，section B 第二部分提到了与 Hadza 相关的内容，倒数第二句 They hunt animals with bows and arrows... 中 hunt animals 与题目中 catch their prey 对应，故填 bows and arrows。

10 题目问考古学家在欧洲哪个地方发现了早期农场的例子，重点词是 Europe 和 early farms，在文中迅速定位 Europe，section C 第二部分第一句 "Some of... the first farms of the Danube valley in Europe." 中 the first farms 与题目中 early farms 对应，且 Danube valley 位于欧洲，故填 Danube valley。

11 题目问哪两样东西是酋长有而社会上其他成员所没有的，重点词是 chiefs、two items 和 available，根据 chiefs 定位到 section D，第二部分第一句 "Chiefs also benefit... in particular temples and residences." 说酋长们拥有其他人没有的东西，尤其是寺庙和住宅，故填 temples and residences。

12 题目问政治家拥有的什么使他们与酋长区分开来，重点词为 statesmen 和 chiefs，section E 同时提到了 statesmen 和 chiefs，定位到第一部分第一、二句 "Statesmen share many of the characteristics of a chief... Statesmen tend to have absolute power...", 根据第二句可知政治家拥有绝对的权利，而酋长没有，故填 absolute power。

13 题目问 Service 在古代文明中发现什么是缺失的，重点词是 Service 和 ancient civilisations，section F 第二部分第一句 "Service's...class war was not present in ancient civilisation." 中，not present 对应题干中的 missing，阶级战争在古代文明中不存在，故填 class war。

译文 | 古代社会分类

A 社会学家和人类学家根据社会群体对资源、威望或权力的获取程度对其进行分类。社会通常分为四类，历史上一直如此。在社会等级的最底端是氏族，其次是部落和酋长国，而在社会等级的最顶端是国家。

B 氏族由一小部分人组成，通常是猎人或收集者。一个群体往往少于100人，并且没有特定的居所，这样可以灵活地探索野外环境和收集粮食资源。氏族成员通常通过婚姻或血统来联系彼此，整个氏族没有正式的领导级别。这样，由于巨大的相似性，不同成员之间就不存在经济差异。

如今，符合这一特征的社会团体已经寥寥无几，而且大多数都被归入像坦桑尼亚的哈扎（Hadza）这样的地区。他们被认为是非洲地区最后的狩猎采集者部落之一，共有1300人。专家认为这一小群人非常重要，因为他们最能代表人类在过去是如何存在并生存下来的。事实上，哈扎的猎人使用的许多方法与数千年前相同。他们用手工制作的弓和箭捕猎动物，并用干草和树枝搭建自己的庇护所。正如几个世纪前的情况一样，这个群体拥有的财产非常少，尤其是与现代西方社会的人相比。

氏族的流动性也很强，他们的短期住所往往由季节性居住的营地和其他更小或更具专门用途的土地组成。始终不变的一点是：氏族寻找大型哺乳动物可以被捕杀和屠宰的地方。对于他们来说，同样重要的是能够制作工具或执行其他敏感活动。

C 部落大多比流动的狩猎采集氏族大，部落的人口超过几千人是很寻常的。部落群体主要以栽培植物和驯养动物获取食物来源。属于部落社会群体的人大多是农民，但在以饲养牲畜为基础的流动经济中，他们也可能是游牧民族。部落通常为多社区组成的社会，由单个小社区通过家族联系融合到部落的大社会中。

在世界各地发现的一些部落证据包括欧洲多瑙河谷地的第一批农场。其他还包括美国西南部的普韦布洛人，或组成现代土耳其一部分的早期农业村庄卡塔霍裕克。虽然有些部落有官员，甚至有"首都"或政府所在地，但这些官员缺乏有效使用权力所必需的经济基础。

D 酋长按照声望等级进行分级，高级成员拥有更多权力。更高级别的酋长还负责管理社会。一个人的声望和等级是由他与一位高级酋长的亲密程度决定的，但是没有真正的阶层划分。

酋长们还可以从权力中受益，坐享其他人几乎无法获得的奢华，特别是寺庙和住宅。酋长显然能以他们的权力和声望获得最大利益，即得到用不完的地方工艺品和食物，这些都是贡品。酋长保留贡品并用它们去满足工人，或将它们（贡品）重新分配给他的臣民。不同社会之间的首都规模通常差异很大，但典型的范围是5,000至20,000人。

E 政治家具有酋长的许多特征，但有一个关键的区别。政治家往往像国王或王后那样拥有绝对权力，这种权力明确赋予他们制定法律，并通过武装部队执行法律的权威。统治家族被视为土地的最终所有者，他们的奢侈品超越了酋长们所享有的寺庙。这是由于地位较低的人民有义务向政治家纳税才得以实现的。

政治家通常离首府不远，在那里，官僚机构强制征收税收并强化他们的关键职责。集中的地点能更容易地将收入分配给其他政府成员、武装部队和工艺专家。早期的国家倾向于发展再分配制度，以最好地支持基本服务和政府的正常运作。

F 埃尔曼·瑟维斯、威廉·桑德斯和约瑟夫·马里诺是社会等级领域的专家，这个知识的发现都有他们的部分功劳。通过各种论文和书籍，瑟维斯提供了一个良好的框架，帮助组织我们的思想。他尤其被认为发展了一种社会的"管理利益"理论，该理论假设包含一个中央集权领导的并有四个层级的社会，对所有人都是有益的。在最高级别的领导中，政治家或领导人为追随者提供利益，随着时间的推移，这些利益的复杂性越来越高，并改善了整个社会。

瑟维斯的研究也使他得出阶级战争在古代文明中并不存在的结论。事实上，那些处于社会底层的人渴望自愿地完成任务，而不是被领导者强迫去完成。他还发现，争论或斗争发生在政治精英之间。

Passage 2

Reading Keys,
Questions 14 – 27

🔑

14	C	19	I	24	conditioners
15	B	20	wastewater	25	Algaculture
16	H	21	indigenous	26	patent
17	A	22	bioremediation	27	Photosynthesis
18	F	23	mineral		

■ 思路解析

Questions 14 – 19 ※题目类型：段落细节配对题

14 题干意思为 "提及生物柴油的不同使用方法"，重点词为 different ways，快速浏览全文，C 段第二句 "However, apart from cars, boats, and buses, it can also be used for heating and power generation." 提到了该产品除了可在不同的交通工具上使用，还可以用于发热和发电，与题干意思相符，故选 C。

15 题干意思为 "一个宣布某公司领先地位的声明"，重点词为 an announcement 和 firm，重点在文中找声明和公司，B 段中 Barrie Leay 说道 "...we are the first-ever company in the world..."，表明了该公司在这个领域的领先地位，pioneering role 与 first-ever 为同义替换，firm 与 company 为同义替换，故选 B。

16 题干意思为 "提到藻类是如何作为食物被食用的"，重点词为 consumed as food，需要在文中寻找与 food 相关的词，详细提到藻类食品的只有 H 段，该段提到藻类富含维生素，可作为保健品，且在多个国家中作为食品，符合题干意思，故选 H。

17 题干意思为 "对现实中的一个试验的描述"，重点词为 real-life experiment，A 段主要写了 David Parker 在惠灵顿进行了成功试验且受到广泛关注这一事件，故选 A。

18 题干意思为 "使用藻类作为家畜的食物"，重点词为 food for domestic animals，可在文中找和家畜相关的内容，F 段中第一句提到除了生物燃料，藻类已经被用作肥料、牲畜饲料和土壤改良剂，livestock feed 和 food for domestic animals 相对应，故选 F。

19 题干意思为 "种植藻类并不需要很多资源这一事实"，重点词为 growing algae，I 段主要说培育藻类不需要特别的照顾，藻类不需要与粮食作物争夺土地、化学品和肥料等资源，种植藻类所需要的资源大量存在于自然中，cultivating algae 和 growing algae 为同义替换，故选 I。

Questions 20 –27　※题目类型：完成句子填空题

20　根据填空处前面重点词 be found in、nutrient-rich 可知，需要定位到讲述 algae 发源地的段落，C 段倒数第二句 "...as they are naturally produced in nutrient-rich wastewater"，其中 naturally produced in 和题干中的 found in 意思相近，且文中和题干都有 nutrient-rich，故填 wastewater。

21　题干问 "藻类除了可持续利用，在很多地方还是什么样的"，填空处内容应与 sustainable 形成并列关系，且为形容词，C 段最后一句 "They are both indigenous and renewable..."，renewable 对应 sustainable，可知填 indigenous。

22　题干问 "在从特定的 EMS 池提取藻类的同时，Aquaflow 对某种清除污水中有害成分的过程做出的贡献"。重点词为 extract、EMS ponds，快速浏览原文发现在 C、D 两个段落中提到了 EMS，由 D 段第一句话可知 Aquaflow 是在 Marlborough District Council 的 EMS ponds 中对藻类进行提取，符合题干意思，再由 D 段第二句 "Aquaflow is also aiding the Council's bioremediation process of cleaning up water discharge"，cleaning up water discharge 即净化排放的污水，与题干意思相符，故填 bioremediation。

23　题干问 "通过结合生物柴油和什么来生产这种燃料"，重点词为动词词组 combine with，E 段第一、二句 "The biofuels are blended with mineral diesel..." 说明该燃料里混合了 mineral diesel，其中 are blended with 和 combine with 对应，meet the target 和 comply with the requirement 对应，故填 mineral。

24　题干问 "藻类在农业中广泛应用，诸如什么样的方式用于土壤"。关键词为 agriculture、for soil。根据 F 段第一句话 "...algae are already used as fertiliser, livestock feed, and soil conditioners" 可判断被用于化肥、牲畜食物皆为应用在农业中的方式，soil conditioners 与题干对应，故填 conditioners。

25　题干问 "在池塘这样的地方种植藻类来处理水中污染物的方法称为什么"，填空处应为名词，根据 F 段第二、三句 "Both aquatic and microscopic species can be cultivated in ponds and clear tanks to treat effluents in ponds. This process is known as Algaculture"， treat effluents 为处理污水的意思, 对应题干中 addressing water contaminants, 可知填 Algaculture。

26 题干问 "Aquaflow 通过什么必要措施来保护他们对于 algae 生物柴油的知识产权", 由 G 段第一句 "the production of Aquaflow is subject to a provisional patent which prevents other companies from using their invention illegally", 即 Aquaflow 需要受到专利的保护, 可知填 patent。

27 题干问 "什么帮助藻类产生和保存能量", 初步判断需填写一个名词。重点词 create、reserve energy。根据 G 段第二句 "Algae are the … produce and store energy by the process of photosynthesis", produce and store energy 对应 create and reserve energy, 故填 Photosynthesis。

译文 | 水产品: 新西兰的藻类生物柴油

A 新西兰 Aquaflow 生物经济公司生产了世界上第一批野生藻类生物柴油。能源和气候变化问题部长戴维·帕克 (David Parker) 在惠灵顿进行了成功的试驾。这位部长自己用 Aquaflow B5 混合生物柴油给一辆柴油驱动的路虎车加了油。随后, 他驾驶着这辆车在议会大厦的前院周围转了一圈, 到场的有宾客、媒体、公众, 甚至还有他的绿党联合领导人珍妮特·菲茨西蒙斯 (Jeanette Fitzsimons)。Aquaflow 生物经济公司总部位于马尔伯勒, 2006 年 5 月, 该公司首次宣布从当地污水池中提取的微藻中生产出了世界上第一批生物柴油燃料。

B Aquaflow 生物经济公司的发言人巴里·利 (Barrie Leay) 说: "我们相信我们是世界上第一家使用野生藻类生物燃料驱动车辆的公司。此外, 这项测试会让业内人士感到意外, 因为他们预测这项突破将在遥远的未来发生。" 他还表示, 公司花了将近一年的时间才研发出这种燃料, 这种燃料对新西兰人和相信这种环保技术潜力的团队来说, 将是一次绝佳的机会。

C 基于藻类的生物柴油有望成为新西兰汽车的一种经济的和更清洁的替代燃料。然而, 除了作为汽车、轮船和公共汽车的燃料, 它还可以用来取暖和发电。毫无疑问, 全球每年对这些环保燃料的需求量都在数十亿升。好在藻类资源丰富, 因为它是在富含营养的废水中自然产生的, 比如在污水管理系统 (EMS) 的沉淀池中产生一样。它既是本土的, 又是可再生的, 还能产生许多有益的副产品。

D　这一切都始于 Aquaflow 生物经济公司去年与马尔伯勒区议会达成的一项开始试点项目的协议，项目旨在从他们位于布伦海姆的污水管理系统（EMS）沉淀池中提取藻类。通过使用这些池塘的主要污染物作为燃料原料，该公司还帮助了委员会的清理排水的生物降解程序。即使是奶农和食品加工单位也可以采用同样的方法从废水中获得重大好处。

E　生物燃料是与矿物柴油混合，而不是以原始形式被使用的。它们还有助于达到政府的 B5 目标，即 5% 的混合。最终，随着生物燃料产量的增加，这一比例有望扩大。与此同时，Aquaflow 生物经济公司计划在明年将其产能提高到 100 万升。该公司还将在圣诞节前为潜在投资者发布招股说明书。12 月 11 日在梅西大学惠灵顿校区的试驾可能是吸引更多投资者的主要亮点。

F　除了生物燃料，藻类已经被用作肥料、牲畜饲料和土壤改良剂。水生和微生物种都可以在池塘和透明池中培育以处理废水。这个过程被称为藻类养殖，并且在大规模实践时，它能成为水产养殖的一个亮点。

G　更重要的是，Aquaflow 的生产受一项临时专利的制约，这个专利可防止其他公司非法使用他们的发明。藻类是最简单的通过光合作用产生和储存能量的植物有机体。藻类都富含脂类和可燃元素，Aquaflow 生物经济公司正在努力以更经济的方式来提取这些元素。此外，虽然藻类善于吸取污水中的所有营养物质，但过多的藻类可能会产生令人难以忍受的臭味和水色变化。因此，对委员会来说，与该公司的合作是处置和清理藻类的极好的替代方式。

H　天然海藻也是重要的食物来源，因为除了含有碘、铁、钾、镁、钙等之外，它们还含有丰富的维生素 B2（核黄素）、B6（吡哆醇）、B3（烟酸）和维生素 C。商业化生产的藻类和蓝藻也被作为保健品销售，螺旋藻、小球藻和杜氏藻（一种维生素 c 补充剂）就是突出的例子。此外，可能会让你很惊讶的是，藻类是许多国家的民族食品。日本人食用 20 种以上藻类，而中国人食用的藻类食物超过 70 种。藻类的天然色素也被用作化学染料的环保替代品。

I　培育藻类最值得注意的一点是，它们既不需要任何特殊护理，也不会与粮食作物争夺土地、化学品和肥料等资源。所有藻类生长所必需的都是在自然中大量存在的物质，从废水到免费的太阳能，投入和过程都是可持续的，藻类的使用也是可持续的。

Passage 3

Reading Keys,
Questions 28 – 40

28	B	33	TRUE	38	C
29	C	34	TRUE	39	B
30	A	35	NOT GIVEN	40	C
31	A	36	FALSE		
32	FALSE	37	B		

■ 思路解析

Questions 28 – 31　※题目类型：人名配对题

28　公司认为所有改进过的新产品比老产品更容易被消费者接受，重点词为 new products with improvements，由第三段第三、四句"Companies also assume that consumers will by default embrace new products… Communications scholar Everett Rogers hypothesised this theory…"可知 Everett Rogers 提出理论——公司认为消费者会默认接受提供增值价值的新产品，new products that offer incremental value 与 new products with improvements 对应，故选 B。

29　产品变糟的特点比同等量的改善的特点更能影响消费者，重点词是 worsened、influence、enhanced，第四段最后一句提到 Kahneman 和 Amos Tversky 得出了功能的退化对购物者的影响比类似程度的改善大得多，其中 worsened 对应原文 deteriorating，influence 对应原文 impact，enhanced 对应原文 improvement，故选 C。

30　使用了一个特殊词语来描述比起他们可能获得的东西人们更珍惜他们已经拥有的东西的现象，由第六段前两句话"This loss aversion prompts people to value products they already own more than those they do not. Behaviour economist Richard Thaler referred to this as the 'endowment effect'."可知 Richard Thaler 把这种现象叫做 endowment effect（禀赋效应），故选 A。

31　做了一个实验来衡量人们赋予他们拥有的物品的价值和他们没有的物品的价值，重点词为 an experiment，第六段提到 Thaler 做了一个实验（Thaler conducted an experiment… "Buyers" were willing to pay on average just $3.12.），表明卖家（物品拥有者）对杯子的平均估价高于买家（非拥有者），也就是说人们对已经拥有的物品估价更高，对没有的物品估价更低，故选 A。

Questions 32 – 36　※题目类型：正误判断题

32　题目说 Kahneman 和 Tversky 认为物品的价值对消费者来说是客观的，重点词为 Kahneman 和 Tversky，根据人名定位到第四段，由 "First, people tend to value how attractive a new item is based on its subjective or perceived value." 可知物品的价值基于人们对它的主观价值和感知价值，objective 和 subjective or perceived 矛盾，故 FALSE。

33　题目说根据 Kahneman 和 Tversky 的看法，人们倾向于将一件新物品和他们熟知的物品做比较。重点词为 Kahneman 和 Tversky 以及 a new item、the ones they know well，根据 Kahneman 和 Tversky 定位到第四段 "Second, consumers consider a new product relative to one they already own or are familiar with." 可知消费者认为新产品是相对于他们已经拥有或熟悉的产品而言的，即会把新产品和已知产品进行比较，故 TRUE。

34　题目说对 Knetsch 的研究的第一组参与者来说，咖啡杯和巧克力棒的价值有很小的区别，重点词为 Knetsch's study，根据人名定位到第七段，该段最后一句 "The choices were nearly split evenly, with 56% of students opting for a mug and another 44% for a chocolate bar." 说差不多平分，56% 的学生选择了杯子，44% 的学生选择了巧克力棒，选择咖啡杯和巧克力棒的人数几乎差不多，故两者价值区别很小，故 TRUE。

35　题目说 Knetsch 的第二组实验参与者在实验之后会被提供巧克力，重点词为 the second group of Knetsch's experiment，第八段第一句 "Group two had no choice in the matter and were given a coffee mug, and the third group were similarly given just a chocolate bar." 未提及实验之后是否会给第二组参与者巧克力，故 NOT GIVEN。

36　题目说大多数人都知道他们的购买偏见，重点词为 the majority of people，由最后一段倒数第三句 "The most notable takeaway from the psychological experiments is how oblivious most people are to their behaviours." 可知大多数人都未察觉到自己的购买行为，oblivious 与 are aware of 矛盾，故 FALSE。

Questions 37 – 40　※题目类型：单选题

37　题干意思为即使新产品是对现有产品改进后的产品，会怎么样，重点词为 a new product，第一段主要围绕 new products 展开，由 "Even when businesses spend billions of dollars investing in new products, the odds are still stacked against them. For example a recent study…" 可知，即使企业花费数十亿美元投资于新产品，成功的机会依然渺茫，且研究发现 40% 到 90% 的新产品都失败了，也就意味着新产品仍然很可能不会被消费者所接受，故选 B。

38　题干问从消费者的角度来看，新产品的关键弱点可能与什么有关，重点词为 weakness 和 consumer's perspective，第二段第四句 "New products may be at a disadvantage as they require consumers to change some forms of behaviour and that comes with a cost." 说因为新产品要求消费者改变行为方式，因此对新产品不利，change some forms of behaviour 和 C 选项中的 behavioural change 对应，故选 C。

39　题目问作者从 Thaler 的实验中得出什么观点，从第六段第一句 This loss aversion prompts people to value products they already own more than those they do not 可知，对损失的厌恶促使人们更重视已经拥有的产品，实验结果也是卖方出价比买方要高，关键词是 value... more than...，与 B 选项中 place a greater value 对应，故选 B。

40　题目问我们能从 Knetsch 的实验结果知道什么，由最后一段 "Surprisingly, only 11% of group two participants wanted to trade for a chocolate bar and only 10% of group three participants wanted a coffee mug instead... a consumer feels a painful loss when they are giving up a product they have in their hands" 可知，实验结果是只有极少数人愿意用自己已有的商品去换别的商品，消费者在放弃已有商品时会感到一种令人痛苦的损失，即很少有人会愿意放弃对已有商品的所有权，故选 C。

译文 ｜ 接受新产品的心理

企业界竞争非常激烈，企业要么被迫创新，要么落后于竞争对手。即使企业花费数十亿美元投资于新产品，成功的机会依然渺茫。以最近的一项研究为例，该研究发现 40% 到 90% 的新产品都失败了。希望在美国销售包装商品的公司每年向消费者推出 3 万件新产品，失败率至少为 70%。大多数产品不能在商店的货架上停留超过 12 个月。20 多年来，失败率一直保持不变。根据另一项研究，即使是那些获得先发优势的公司最终也被挤出了市场。

专家们继续研究的问题是，为什么好产品无法成功。毕竟，能够为终极用户提供更多好处的产品应该受到那些愿意花钱的消费者的欢迎。这个问题的答案可以在心理学中找到。新产品可能处于不利地位，因为它要求消费者改变某种行为方式，而这是要付出代价的。以一款更先进的新智能手机为例，它是消费者想要的东西，但当消费者从一个服务提供商切换到另一个服务提供商时，他们需要支付罚金。如果消费者需要自学如何使用新技术，那么他们需要付出时间成本。

对一家公司来说，量化这些成本可能很容易，但要量化与更换手机供应商或学习新技术相关的心理成本，即使不是不可能，但也是很困难的。消费者会对他们心理上的不理性行为感到内疚，因为他们高估了自己现在所用的产品的好处。公司还认为，消费者会默认接受提供增值价值的新产品，而且单这一点就足以让他们购买产品。传播学学者埃弗雷特·罗杰斯（Everett Rogers）在20世纪60年代提出了这一理论，并称之为"相对优势"概念，他认为，这是消费者购买新产品最重要的驱动力。这一概念背后的理论有一个重大缺陷，因为它再一次忽视了影响决策的心理偏见。

在2002年，心理学家丹尼尔·卡尼曼（Daniel Kahneman）探究了消费者为什么以及何时会远离理性的经济行为。卡尼曼和心理学家阿莫斯·特沃斯基发现，人类对不同选择的反应有四种不同的方式。首先，人们倾向于根据一件新物品的主观价值或感知价值来评价它的吸引力。其次，消费者认为新产品是相对于他们已经拥有或熟悉的产品而言的。第三，消费者会关注某一产品相对于他们已有的同类产品的改进。最后，也是最重要的一点，功能的退化对购物者的影响要比类似程度的改善大得多。

这些特征在很大程度上已经通过多次调查和研究得到了证实。在一项研究中，参与者被告知他们可以接受一种赌博方式，即有50%的机会赢100美元，也有50%的机会输同样多的钱。不用说，很少有人会想参与一个相当于抛硬币的提议，因为他们想要处于优势地位。然后，研究人员改变了条件，让参与者赢100美元的可能性比输100美元的大一点点。直到赢得100美元的可能性比输掉100美元的可能性高出两到三倍，大多数参与者才放心地下了赌注。

这种对损失的厌恶促使人们重视自己已经拥有的产品，而不是没有拥有的产品。行为经济学家理查德·塞勒（Richard Thaler）将此称为"禀赋效应"。塞勒做了一个实验，他给一组人一些咖啡杯，问他们愿意卖多少钱（价钱从25美分到9.25美元不等）。另一组被问及他们是愿意接受咖啡杯还是现金。在第一次试验中，杯子的"卖家"对杯子的平均估价为7.12美元，而"买家"平均只愿意支付3.12美元。在随后的试验中，"卖家"对杯子的估价为7美元，而买家将购买杯子的价格平均提高到3.5美元。

塞勒的发现与经济学家杰克·克耐奇（Jack Knetsch）的一项类似研究结果一致。克耐奇发现，90%的受访者认为放弃已经拥有的东西是一种让人感到痛苦的损失。这些数据来自一项由三组学生组成的研究，第一组的参与者被要求在咖啡杯和巧克力棒之间做出选择，巧克力棒在商店里的价格和咖啡杯差不多。56%的学生选择了杯子，44%的学生选择了巧克力棒。

第二组没有选择，只给了他们一个咖啡杯，第三组同样也只给了一个巧克力棒。在那时，第二组参与者被问及他们是否想要用咖啡杯换巧克力棒，而第三组参与者被给予了一个类似的选择，即用巧克力棒换咖啡杯。令人惊讶的是，第二组中只有11%的参与者想要换巧克力棒，第三组中只有10%的参与者想要换咖啡杯。研究人员认为，研究结果足以得出这样的结论：当消费者放弃手中的产品时，他们会感到令人痛苦的损失。心理学实验中最值得注意的结论是，大多数人未察觉到自己的行为。即使能证明他们的行为不理性，人们也会表现出震惊和轻微的戒备。所有的实验都证明了这些行为特征是一致的。

Writing

◼ Task 1

审　题

图表描述在 2 周的时间内，在澳大利亚参与不同活动的男孩和女孩（年龄为 5 ~ 14 岁）的比重。

图表类型

柱状图

分析思路

先对比图中不同活动参与度的最大值和最小值。可以很快看出，最受欢迎的为 Watching TV，而 Skateboarding/Rollerblading 和 Arts and Crafts 相对小众一些；接着对参加同一活动的男孩、女孩的比例进行对比。从图中可以看出 Watching TV 中男孩和女孩百分比几乎一致；Skateboarding/Rollerblading，Cycling 和 Computer Games 的数据都是男孩参与度大于女孩；唯有 Arts and Crafts 中女孩的百分比大于男孩。

参考写作结构

首　段：概述图表信息/改述题目
综述段：描述柱状图中最明显的特点和规律
主体段：描述和对比柱状图中细节，可从最大值往最小值开始描述；注意凸显出数据中有特
　　　　点的信息，如两值相同和数据反超等

参考范文⊖

The bar graph provides information about the proportion of Australian boys and girls in the 5 to 14 age bracket who take part in different pastimes over two weeks.

Overall, nearly all these youngsters watch TV, which is the only option being equally popular with both boys and girls. In contrast, computer games and outdoor exercise

---

⊖ 范文中加色字为高分表达。

appeal more to boys whereas girls have a preference for arts and crafts.

As mentioned, nearly 100% of both genders watch TV every fortnight. Playing computer games is the second most popular option, with 80% of boys and just over 60% of girls spending time doing this activity.

This gender gap is also reflected in physical activities including cycling, skateboarding and rollerblading in which the percentage of boys consistently exceeds that of girls by nearly 20%. Only half as many girls as boys participate in skateboarding or rollerblading.

The only pastime which is significantly more popular with girls is arts and crafts. Half of the girls invest their time in these fields, compared to only about 30% of the boys. In fact, of the five activities shown in the graph, doing arts and crafts is the least popular leisure activity among Australian boys aged between 5 and 14.

Overall: 7.5

Task 2

审　　题

越来越多的人使用电脑和电子设备来获取信息，因此纸质书、杂志和报纸已经没有必要。对于这一观点你在多大程度上同意或不同意？

讨论对象

使用电脑和电子设备来获取信息和通过纸质媒体获取信息

写作观点选择

完全同意/部分同意（如同意电脑等电子设备的确越来越盛行，但不同意纸质书的出版物没有必要）/完全不同意

写作论据准备

通过电脑等设备获取信息：

◇ 便利的 convenient
◇ 信息最新的 up-to-date
◇ 提供有效信息的 informative

◇ 省时省力 save time and effort
◇ 节省空间 save space
◇ 环保 eco-friendly

通过纸质书、杂志、报纸获取信息：

◇ 内容真实可靠 authentic and reliable

◇ 免受干扰 free from distraction

◇ 做笔记 make notes

◇ 可收集的 collectible

◇ 有利于印刷业、出版业的发展，促进就业 conducive to the development of printing and publishing industry, promote employment

参考写作结构

首　　段：引出讨论对象 + 表明观点（同意或不同意及其程度）

主体段1：同意（不同意）的论点 + 论据

主体段2：对立观点的部分合理性 + 论据

末　　段：重申观点

参考范文[⊖]

With the increasing popularity of new electronic media, getting information through various electronic devices has become the mainstream. While traditional printed books and newspapers seem less appealing and unnecessary to many people, I believe they still play a part in acquiring knowledge.

It is true that nowadays many people are accustomed to using computers and other digital media devices for their convenience and timeliness. People can find the information they want at the touch of a key or screen instead of flipping through many books, which can save much time and efforts. Compared with the content on print media, what people access on electronic media is always up-to-date, so they can be updated on the latest information and news reports.

However, print media still enjoys some edges that digital media may not have. One of its advantages is that what is written in books or newspapers is usually authentic and reliable. For example, to report a piece of news in paper, journalists often spend more time than those online bloggers in interviewing various relevant parties so that the report is comprehensive and objective; before finalising the draft, editors need to proofread the writing for several times, ensuring that every word and even punctuation is ready to be published. These rigorous steps greatly improve the reliability of newspapers and other printed materials.

⊖ 范文中加色字为高分表达。

Another advantage of reading printed books or magazines is that it will keep the readers more focused and absorbed for there are no distractions. Instead, reading on an electronic device, especially a mobile phone, can be easily interrupted by advertisements or notifications of new messages, all of which can distract the reader and reduce his reading efficiency.

In conclusion, it is inevitable that more people will access information through computers or other devices, but it does not mean that print media has become redundant. I believe both have their own advantages and they are complementary, so print media will never die out.

Overall: 7. 5

Speaking

Part 1 | Break

Do you prefer a long break or several short breaks?

I prefer several short breaks over a long break. I've tried out both methods and found that I'm more productive when I take short breaks regularly. When I take a long break after hours of studying, even if I know I have some more hours of studying to come, I feel discouraged. On the other hand, when I can look forward to the next 5-minute break, studying is a piece of cake.

高分表达

◇ try out 尝试

◇ productive /prə'dʌktɪv/ a. 高产出率的

◇ discouraged /dɪs'kʌrɪdʒd/ a. 灰心的

◇ on the other hand 另一方面

◇ look forward to 盼望

◇ a piece of cake 小菜一碟

What do you usually do during a break?

During a break, I usually hit the sack! After a 10-minute power nap, I feel refreshed and motivated to continue studying, even if I still have hours to go. I've even pulled a few all-nighters with this method and went to school the next day feeling fit as a fiddle.

高分表达

◇ hit the sack 睡觉

◇ power nap 恢复精力的小睡

◇ refreshed /rɪ'freʃt/ a. 恢复精神的

◇ motivated /'məʊtɪveɪtɪd/ a. 有积极性的

◇ all-nighter /ɔːl 'naɪtə(r)/ n. 通宵的活动

◇ fit as a fiddle 非常健康

Why do you need to take a break?

Sometimes I have my head in the clouds. I feel myself drifting off mentally again and again to a point where I'm just daydreaming. That's when I know I need to take a break. If I continue "studying" like this, I can't memorise anything I read, let alone retain it later.

高分表达

◇ have one's head in the clouds 心不在焉

◇ drift off 迷迷糊糊地睡去

◇ daydream /'deɪdriːm/ *v.* 做白日梦

◇ memorise /'meməraɪz/ *v.* 熟记

◇ let alone 更不必说

◇ retain /rɪ'teɪn/ *v.* 保持

How often do you take a break?

I use the Pomodoro technique to time my breaks. I take a five-minute break every 25 minutes and a 15-minute break every one and half hours — during which I take a power nap. For the past five years, I've tried many techniques, and I found the Pomorodo technique to be exactly my cup of tea.

高分表达

◇ time /taɪm/ *v.* 计时

◇ take a power nap 打个盹

◇ my cup of tea 符合我的喜好

Part 2

Describe an occasion when you could not use your mobile phone.

You should say:

> **when it was**
>
> **where it was**
>
> **why you could not use your mobile phone**

and how you felt about it.

You will have to talk about the topic for one to two minutes. You have one minute to think about what you are going to say. You can make some notes to help you if you wish.

I was put into a new class last semester. I didn't know any student nor the teacher. Even though I became familiar with all of them after some weeks, I still missed my old classmates a lot. When the teacher wasn't looking, I always took my phone out of my pocket and sent a text to our group chat to see how they were doing. It put a smile on my face to hear from them.

One day, the conversation was particularly exciting and I couldn't put the phone down for a minute. I threw caution to the wind and continued texting under the table, even when the teacher was looking at me. There wasn't a snowball's chance in hell she wouldn't see me, but I didn't care because I needed to give my two cents in the group chat. Of course, she caught me and took my phone away. From that day on, she had me put my phone on her table every time I entered the classroom and take it back when I left.

At first, I felt sad and mistreated. But having my phone taken away was a blessing in disguise because after some weeks I grew closer to my new classmates and we got along really well! Once I could have my phone on me again, I didn't even want to use it in class anymore.

高分表达

- ◇ become familiar with 熟悉
- ◇ put a smile on one's face 让……面带笑容
- ◇ throw caution to the wind 不顾一切
- ◇ a snowball's chance in hell 毫无机会
- ◇ give one's two cents 分享意见
- ◇ mistreated /mɪs'triːtɪd/ a. 受到不公平对待的
- ◇ a blessing in disguise 因祸得福
- ◇ get along 与……和睦相处

Part 3

Do you think it's necessary to have laws on the use of mobile phones?

I don't think there is a need to do so. Institutions and companies should be able to make up their own rules and decide when the use of mobile phones is appropriate and when it isn't. Regulating it by law is barking up the wrong tree. However, we have to educate everyone

— especially the youth — about the dangers of excessive mobile phone use. Nowadays, many people don't know when it's acceptable to take a call. So, if we can educate them properly, we don't need laws.

高分表达

- ◇ appropriate /ə'prəuprɪət/ *a.* 合适的
- ◇ regulate /'regjuleɪt/ *v.* 控制
- ◇ bark up the wrong tree 弄错了目标
- ◇ excessive mobile phone use 过度使用手机
- ◇ acceptable /ək'septəbl/ *a.* 可接受的

What do you think of children having mobile phones?

It depends on different factors whether children should have mobile phones or not. This is not a black and white question. For example, I got my first mobile phone from my parents when I was just 12 years old. For safety reasons, it served as a lifeline between me and my parents. They could contact me wherever I went. On the other hand, my addiction to games and texting kept growing because of the phone.

高分表达

- ◇ a black and white question 非黑即白的问题
- ◇ lifeline/'laɪf,laɪn/ *n.* 救生索
- ◇ addiction /ə'dɪkʃ(ə)n/ *n.* 上瘾
- ◇ texting /'tekstɪŋ/ *n.* 发信息

At what age should children have mobile phones?

I don't think we should declare an age limit for mobile phones. Children should have mobile phones whenever it's essential for their safety. Being able to call someone in case of an emergency is very important. What parents and teachers worry about is that children are playing video games, watching videos, and chatting all night long. That's why we shouldn't buy them the newest phone that costs an arm and a leg. Children don't need all these features. A simple phone that works for calls and messages is enough.

高分表达

◇ age limit 年龄限制

◇ essential /ɪˈsenʃl/ *a.* 至关重要的

◇ in case of an emergency 在紧急情况下

◇ all night long 一整晚

◇ cost an arm and a leg 价格昂贵

◇ feature/ˈfiːtʃə/ *n.* 功能

Are people politer now than in the past?

Although we hear many people complain about today's youth, I think the general level of politeness hasn't changed. No matter how developed a country is, there will always be rude people whose parents failed to teach them manners, and there will always be kind-hearted ones who are naturally polite. That's how it always has been and how it always will be.

高分表达

◇ level of politeness 礼貌的程度

◇ fail to 未能

◇ manners /ˈmænə(r)z/ *n.* 礼貌

◇ kind-hearted /kaɪndˈhɑː tɪd/ *a.* 善良的

Test 4

Listening / 209

Reading / 223

Writing / 237

Speaking / 240

Listening

Part 1

Listening Keys,
Questions 1 – 10

1	rehearsal(s)	6	dinner
2	male	7	25
3	costumes	8	16
4	Tuesday	9	modern
5	August	10	hospital

JANE: Good morning, Green Street Drama Society, Jane speaking. How may I help you?

JAMES: Oh, hi Jane. My name is James. I've just moved into the area and I'm thinking about joining your group. My friend Arthur — Arthur Jones — is one of your members and he recommended that I join.

JANE: Oh, that's great. James, we're always looking for new members. Just to give you a bit of background, our amateur drama society has been running since 1976 and we currently have 80 active members, so it's a wonderful part of the community. Do you know where we are?

JAMES: Yes, I think I have seen it — it's on the university side of the river near the main Post Office… If I remember correctly, it's on Green Street.

JANE: Yes, that's right, Number 117 Green Street is our postal address. If you want to come and check out the rehearsals, then you should come to The Club House. ❶ It's on the same road, just before the Post Office.

JAMES: OK, got that. So what kind of things can I help out with?

Audioscripts

1 此题定位词为 the club house，根据空格前 for holding 可知答案为名词，原文意思为如果你想看彩排就去 the club house，即 the club house 为进行彩排的场所，故填 rehearsal(s)。

209

2 此题定位词为 actors，填空处后为 singers，可预判答案很可能为形容词，在听到 actors 后接着出现了 male singers，故填 male。

3 此题定位词为 Errands 和 props，题干 taking care of 包含了去拿道具、戏服等工作，故填 costumes。

4 此题定位词为 at 7 pm，可判断答案为时间相关词，注意提到了 Thursdays，但是由 used to 可知是过去这样做而不是现在，now 后才为答案，each 与 every 为同义替换，故填 Tuesday。

5 此题定位词为 Summer holiday，填空处前面为介词 in，可猜测答案与时间相关，有可能表月份，summer break 与 summer holiday 对应，故填 August。

JANE: We are actually currently looking for actors, oh, and male singers. ❷ We already have 3 female members in the group.

JAMES: That sounds interesting, but I am afraid that I don't have any experience in acting.

JANE: Oh, that's OK. No experience is needed, because we will give you the necessary training. We are thinking of staging Hairspray as our musical for next year. Are you more interested in acting, or singing?

JAMES: Well, I would like to do acting. Most recently my friend played the role of Harry Bright in *Mama Mia*! That was with the Footlight Players in Brighton, it was great fun.

JANE: That's great. Oh right, we also need people to lend a hand by running errands from time to time, mainly picking up props and costumes. ❸ Can you drive?

JAMES: Yes, I've got a full licence and I have my own car, that won't be a problem.

JANE: Fantastic. Hm... what else...?

JAMES: Oh, yes. I nearly forgot. When are your meetings held? On Thursdays?

JANE: No, we used to have them on Thursdays, now we meet on each Tuesday at 7 pm. ❹

JAMES: Oh, I thought my friend Arthur said Thursdays...

JANE: Yes, that was actually for last year. And we usually close for our summer break for a few weeks in August. ❺ So our first meeting isn't until the 6th September.

JAMES: Okay, I will keep that in mind.

JAMES: How much does it cost to join?

JANE: Let me just double check… Here it is. It is 60 pounds. … I can also tell you that with the membership comes a club dinner which we usually hold just before we close for the summer. ❻

JAMES: Oh, and do you have any concessional rates?

JANE: For those who are unemployed or retired, it's only 25 pounds. ❼ Last month, there was a discount for retirees, the price was only 15 pounds, but now it's gone back to the original price.

JAMES: I'm working so that doesn't apply to me. I was thinking more about my kids. Just to check, is this an adults-only drama society, or are children able to join?

JANE: Unfortunately, children can't join at this stage, we have an age limit of 16. ❽ But they can join the local children's drama club. Would you like their contact number?

JAMES: Yes please, that would be useful. I have twin girls who are twelve and they really enjoy drama so I was hoping there would be a club for them.

JANE: That's right, get them on the stage when they're young! The contact person is Maria George and her number is 564 73218.

JAMES: That's great, thanks for that information. So, what types of plays do you mainly put on?

JANE: It's mostly modern plays, ❾ we don't really do classical stuff, like Shakespeare or Moliere.

6　此题定位词为 60 pound fee，需要注意听与 60 pound fee 相关的信息，由内容可知会费里包括晚餐，故填 dinner。

7　此题定位词为 jobless or retired people，填空处后为 pounds，可知答案为数字，先提到了数字 25，时态是一般现在时，可确定为答案为 25，后面接着提到了数字 15，但是是过去的状态，所以填 25。

8　此题定位词为 Minimum age，即最小年龄，可确定填数字，由文中可知孩子不能参加，接着说出了年龄限制是 16 岁，故填 16。

9　此题定位词为 Generally perform，即通常表演什么，mostly 和 Generally 对应，虽然后面提到了 classical stuff，但表达的意思是否定的，故填 modern。

JAMES: I see. Do you organise any events on special days or occasions?

JANE: We do a Christmas Charity Performance each year, with the money going to a children's hospital. ❿

JAMES: That sounds like fun. I hope I can be a part of that.

JANE: Well we hope so, too, and I look forward to meeting you soon. Would you like to come along in September?

JAMES: Yes, that would be great for me.

JANE: We look forward to meeting you then, James.

JAMES: Thanks Jane, see you then.

10 此题定位词为 Christmas charity，填空处前面为 children's，可推测答案为名词，由文中信息可知钱用于儿童医院，故填 hospital。

Part 2

Listening Keys,
Questions 11–20

11	A	16	C
12	B	17	E
13	C	18	A
14	B	19	D
15	A	20	B

Audioscripts

Good day everyone! Welcome to the Melbourne Zoo! My name's Mark, and I'd like to welcome you today. If you have a moment, I'd like to give you some information about our zoo before you enter. Please feel free to ask me any questions at the end of my talk.

As you know, it's November now, and that means longer days. I have some good news for you. Anyone who hates getting up early in the morning can now enter the zoo after dinner! Because of the time of year, we are offering a two-hour mini-tour after 7 pm. Seeing the animals at a different time of day will be a fascinating experience for many of you and I encourage you to sign up. ⓫ Unfortunately, due to a fire last month, we no longer allow bonfire nights. By the way, we have been planning two parties for Christmas next month, we'll post the details on our website, it should be a lot of fun.

So let me tell you a little about our residents here at the zoo. Despite what was recently reported in the media, the most popular animal around here is not the kangaroo or even the sheepdog. No, our star animal here is without a doubt, the koala. ⓬They are sedentary creatures and can sleep for up to twenty hours a day, so you'll have to keep an eye out for them. You should be able to spot some of them in the treetops, hiding behind branches. But, if you're lucky, you might see one run across your path.

Of course, we do have kangaroos. They are truly fascinating creatures. It might interest you to know that they are the only large animals that use hopping as a means of locomotion. They are generally very friendly, and while we have no problems with people feeding them, we always tell our guests that it's important to stand with an upright posture when giving them food. ⓭ The kangaroos may interpret you bending over as a sign of aggression, so please be careful. Also, no matter how cute the babies are, any physical contact should be avoided. The adults are quite protective of their young while they are still in the pouch, so please refrain from the urge to give them a pat. They aren't greedy animals, and will generally stop eating once they are full. So, if you have some extra food, you might need to find another one to feed.

As you may have heard, our wild dog pen is temporarily

11 此题定位词为 November，原文说现在晚上 7 点后提供两个小时的迷你旅游，后面内容都为干扰信息，由 Unfortunately 可判断其后面的内容不是答案，故选 A。

12 此题定位词为 most popular，原文提到 "the most popular animal around here is not ..."，由 not 可知 kangaroo 和 sheepdog 不是答案，由 is without a doubt 可知其后面提到的 koala 才是最受欢迎的，故选 B。

13 此题定位词为 key，原文说给它们食物时，保持直立的姿势是很重要的，important 和 key 为同义替换，standing up straight 和 stand with an upright posture 为同义替换，故选 C。

14 此题定位词为 wild dog area，原文说现在正在修复围墙，fixing the fences 和 enclosure is under repair 对应，故选 B。

15 此题定位词为 discount tickets 和 this year，需要注意时间信息，原文说网站目前正在维护中，所以今年的优惠券只在礼品店附近的咖啡厅有售，注意 gift shop 是 café 位置的参照物，故选 A。

16 此题定位词为 Arena，原文提到 Arena 后要注意听后面的内容，原文说为了到那里，需要过桥，一直走到路的尽头，然后发现它在右边，故选 C。

17 此题定位词为 Educational hall，原文说在卫生间的西边，在图中找到 toilet，其西边为 E，故选 E。

18 此题定位词为 Picnic spot，原文中提到的 having a picnic 和 a great spot 与 Picnic spot 对应，原文接着说它是环绕植物园的区域，也正对着河，在图中找到植物园（botanic garden），符合特点的只有 A。

closed, but it should reopen soon. You'll be happy to know that our dogs are all fine and in good health, and I think they are quite excited about their new home. Right now, we are fixing the fences. They are wild animals after all, and we need to consider public safety before opening the exhibit. But please come back to see them when we are finished. ⑭

Speaking of return visits, if you enjoy our zoo and want to come back, you may be interested in getting a discount ticket. We used to sell them at the entrance of the zoo as well as on our website, but the website is currently under maintenance, so the coupons are available only at the café near the gift shop for this year. ⑮So, if you're interested, make your way over there once you are ready. Be informed, there are a lot of tourists around today, so the earlier, the better.

Now, if I can bring your attention to the map of our zoo, I'll provide a brief description of the grounds so that no one gets lost. If you'd like to see some of our animals up close, then you should visit one of our shows in the Arena. We have a show every half hour, so you're sure to see something. We are at the entrance, to get there, cross the bridge and go straight to the end of the path and you'll find it to your right. ⑯For those who are looking for a quieter place to learn about the history of our zoo, in the north of the zoo, we have an educational hall ready for you. It's easy to find, just to the west of the toilets. ⑰

With such beautiful weather right now, I know many of you would love to spend the afternoon having a picnic. There is a great spot for you in the zoo. It's the area surrounding the botanic garden and it's also facing the river. The view is fantastic there! ⑱ Some of you may recall that our photo printing site was in the northeastern corner of the zoo. It has now been moved to the building next to the bridge. ❶❾ Finally, I'm sure you've noticed that it's quite warm today. If you are not up for walking, don't worry. We have bike sheds at different locations across the zoo and the bikes are free for our guests, so just grab one and take it for a ride. Once you've got your bike, it's only a 5-minute ride to the gift shop and the exit is just beside it. You can't miss it. ❷⓿Please note that cycling is only permitted on the designated paths.

Alright, that's the end of my talk. I hope you have a great time visiting all the animals. Take as many pictures as you like, and don't forget to share them with your friends. Now, does anyone have any questions?

19 此题定位词为 Photo printing shop，虽然前面提到了 photo printing site was in the northeastern corner of the zoo，但需要注意是一般过去式，所以不是答案出处，接着听到 It has now been moved…，可知换了位置，现在位于桥旁边，故选 D。

20 此题定位词为 Gift shop，原文说骑自行车 5 分钟就能到礼品店，出口就在礼品店旁边，在图中找到出口（exit），需要通过自行车车道，且位于出口旁边的只有 B，故选 B。

Part 3

Listening Keys,
Question 21 –30

🔑

21	B	26	A
22	B	27	E
23	C	28	D
24	C	29	A
25	A	30	B

MR WHITE: Hello, Natasha. Come on in. Sit down.

NATASHA: Thanks, Mr. White. Did you manage to look over the draft of my field trip report?

MR WHITE: Yes, and I have a few observations and some things I would like to see revised.

NATASHA: I see. Feedback is always appreciated, positive or negative.

Audioscripts

MR WHITE: May I ask, what was your motivation in completing this report? If you want extra credit to go towards your final grade, I'm afraid it doesn't work like that.

NATASHA: Not at all. I wasn't sure which aspect of science I wanted to study and thought this might help me focus. After this field trip, I've realised that geology is a field I would love to be involved in, and I've signed up for a course next term. ㉑ And, actually, having worked on the draft, I've learned that I need practice at writing reports like these!

MR WHITE: I can't argue with that. Geology is one of my favourite subjects, too, but I don't advise using this report as a basis for any further assignments. The details you've included are informative, though your organisation is relatively poor.

NATASHA: I will take that down. How do you feel about the introduction?

MR WHITE: It's not bad at all, but you need to follow it through in the main part of the essay. The school website has many essay templates you can use, including the ones for a scientific report, which is what you need here. I'd like you to download one and revise accordingly. ㉒ Can you do that?

NATASHA: Yes. And I am thinking about adding more details to make the report more convincing. Do you have any advice?

MR WHITE: Well, actually, I don't think it's necessary to do that. Your choice of survey site was an interesting one. Was there a reason you chose this particular site? We have a map in the lab which is marked with all the sites in the local area that are geologically and geographically noteworthy. But yours wasn't one of them.

NATASHA: Knowing they had been repeatedly studied by geography students, I wanted to try somewhere different. I

---

21 此题定位词为 Why 和 Natasha，注意 Natasha 说话的内容，她说她不确定想学哪方面的科学，认为写这个报告可能会帮到她，也就是帮她决定学什么科目，故选 B。

22 此题定位词为 Mr. White advise，注意 Mr. White 说话的内容，他说学校网站上有很多可以使用的论文模板，建议下载一个，建议与使用模板相关，故选 B。

believe every place is geologically unique, so I closed my eyes and stabbed the map, then looked for the nearest open site. ㉓ Fortunately, it was easily accessible.

MR WHITE: Interesting. What did you hope to gain from your field trip? Surprisingly, the grasses in the area you chose are quite dense though the soil is somewhat sandy — were you thinking of finding out any special properties in the soil that may cause this?

NATASHA: Not particularly. I'm very interested in the elements that make up different soil types and the dunes have always captured my interest, because of the sand content. ㉔ As an added bonus, I was also able to try out a number of the soil-testing techniques you've been coaching us in.

MR WHITE: I noticed you've also incorporated some of your fellow-students' data in your report.

NATASHA: Yes, in an effort to make my own findings more accurate, I thought it is wise to get a broader view by merging their data with mine. ㉕

MR WHITE: Good idea. Your report is reasonably comprehensive. Incorporating others' findings like this also enables you to compare your methods with other people's.

NATASHA: Yes, I thought that would be beneficial.

MR WHITE: I note that you've included quite a detailed map of the site. How did you go about drawing that? I'm assuming you took photographs and used a graphics program?

NATASHA: I took a satellite image with me to the viewing platform at the dune's Visitor Centre. I can see the whole area from up there! Then I marked in the details I could see. ㉖ Some of my classmates just copied the local map with

23 此题定位词为 Natasha 和 the field trip site，原文中听到 so 后应该可确定答案就是其后面的内容，她说她是闭上眼睛，随便在地图上找的一个地点，故选 C。

24 此题定位词为 main aim，需要注意听 Natasha 说话的内容，由 Not particularly 可确定前面说的内容不是答案，答案在 Not particularly 的后面，她说她对构成不同土壤类型的元素非常感兴趣，一直对沙丘很感兴趣，elements that make up different soil types 和 soil content 对应，故选 C。

25 此题定位词为 data from other students，原文说为了使她自己的发现更准确，所以将其他学生的数据与她的数据合并，more accurate 和 more reliable 对应，故选 A。

26 此题定位词为 a detailed map，原文说她带着一张卫星图片来到了沙丘游客中心的观景台，并在能看到的细节上都做了标记，即她进行了仔细观察，这里重点是理解听力原文意思，进行归纳，故选 A。

tracing paper, but I didn't feel it was detailed enough.

MR WHITE: What equipment did you use to survey the site?

NATASHA: I predominantly used the soil pH test kit you recommended but it's quite technical and I found it difficult to use. There were so many buttons and I didn't know which ones to click! ㉗

MR WHITE: Hmm, it is somewhat complex since it's quite professional, but a bit of training would help. Now, your data collection sheet has some issues.

NATASHA: I know. It's a bit disorganised, isn't it?㉘ What should I do?

MR WHITE: Begin with the main topic, then put all the variables that you need in separate columns, and use a fresh line for each sample.

NATASHA: OK, I'll do that. I thought my literature review was good though — clear and comprehensive.

MR WHITE: It didn't really give a full picture and you neglected some parts which are important. ㉙ I recommend you gather a greater selection of materials. There are some excellent books and papers I can recommend to you on the subject.

NATASHA: Oh, that would be very helpful. Um, how do you feel about my notes based on conversations with local residents? You know, about their experience of growing different plants in similar soil types?

MR WHITE: It's always a good idea to incorporate some real-world experiences in a report like yours.

27 此题定位词为 The test kit，Natasha 说她觉得检测工具很专业，但是发现它很难用，difficult 和 complicated 为同义替换，故选 E。

28 此题定位词为 Data collecting sheet，disorganised 和 poorly organised 为同义替换，故选 D。

29 此题定位词为 Literature Review，原文说文献评论并没有给出完整的内容，并且忽略了一些重要的部分，表示行文发展不充分，对应 inadequately developed，故选 A。

NATASHA: I wasn't sure whether it's redundant, but I learned a lot.

MR WHITE: It's an established research method.

NATASHA: It took a long time, though. **㉚** Next time I should limit the number of questions I ask, or get someone to help transcribe the recordings.

MR WHITE: (*laughs*) You'll be asking for a research assistant next!

30 此题定位词为 Interviews，对应原文中 conversations with local residents。另外，Natasha 虽然提到了 redundant，但由 wasn't sure 判断可知并不确定，所以不可选，后面接着说花费很多时间，takes a long time 和 time-consuming 为同义替换，故选 B。

Part 4

Listening Keys,
Questions 31 – 40

31	monkey(s)	36	source
32	chemical	37	accurate
33	chocolate	38	childhood
34	orange	39	irritable
35	fear	40	spices

As you know, humans have five senses — we can taste our favourite foods, hear our favourite songs, see a beautiful landscape, feel the soft breeze on our skin, and smell the things around us. Today we are going to talk about sense of smell.

Audioscripts

Many people believe that the sense of smell is not as important as seeing or hearing. But it actually plays a key role in our enjoyment of many things, and subconsciously even affects our attraction to another person. Scientists estimate humans can distinguish perhaps billions of distinct scents. Sense of smell is common to all land animals, although it is more developed in some than in others.

31 此题定位词为 Less developed，根据填空处前有 in，可推测答案很可能为名词，原文说猴子的嗅觉并不像我们想象的那么灵敏，we would imagine 和 people generally think 对应，故填 monkey(s)。

32 此题定位词为 distinguish，即区别什么气味和其他气味，原文说某些灵长类动物能够探测到化学气味，并能将其与其他气味进行区分，故填 chemical。

33 此题定位词为 common aromas，因为有 like，需要注意听举例内容，原文说我们能识别出我们熟悉的气味，比如巧克力的香味，scents we are familiar with 与 common aromas 对应，故填 chocolate。

34 此题定位词为 in a club 和 positive feelings，需要注意听举例内容，原文说例如，夜总会里的橘子味可以使人高兴和兴奋，happy and excited 对应 positive feelings，故填 orange。

35 此题定位词为 sweat，原文说一些科学家认为，我们可以通过闻另一个人汗液中的荷尔蒙分子来发现他们的恐惧，detect 与 being aware of 对应，故填 fear。

Previously, I conducted some research into the sense of smell of various animals. Curiously, monkeys' sense of smell is not as strong as we would imagine. **31**Many other animals have a stronger sense of smell. Interestingly though, certain primate species are able to detect chemical odours, differentiating the abundance of other scents around them. **32**Many creatures have this ability, including humans. In fact, even machines can detect certain smells. For example, scientists and technologists created detectors to sniff out things like smoke and paint fumes.

As for us human beings, we can all recognise scents we are familiar with, things we smell every day, such as the aroma of chocolate. **33** But our noses can make out subtler scents also. Research shows that different scents can pass different messages to humans, affecting their emotions and feelings subconsciously. The smell of orange in a nightclub, for example, can make people happy and excited. **34**

Accordingly, the use of some scents in nightclubs is being trialled both to satisfy party-goers and entice people in. Some smells are instrumental in this, as it has been discovered that people are easily influenced when they are exposed to these scents. So we can see that scent really does play an important part in our lives.

Researchers have noted that subconsciously we rate a person's attractiveness based on smell. We are more drawn to people we think smell good, whether we know it or not. Interestingly, some scientists even believe we can detect fear in another person, by smelling the hormone molecules in their sweat! **35**

As humans, we don't use our sense of smell as liberally as people did in the past. These days, we cover unpleasant smells with deodorant and air freshener, but really, these odours we find offensive are important to us, and can protect us. For instance, when we smell chicken that has been too long in the fridge, we are less likely to eat it, and therefore save ourselves from becoming sick. Unfortunately, with the covering up of these scents, humans nowadays often cannot pinpoint the source of the smell, potentially exposing ourselves to harm. **36**

Our sense of smell is extremely important, and it works with other senses. Because our senses of taste, touch, sight and hearing are not always accurate, our nose can help us experience the world around us better. **37** For instance, if it is dark and we are not able to see, our sense of smell still operates no matter what.

As a researcher, I'm very interested in the memories certain aromas can evoke in us. We have all at one time or other experienced flashbacks to bring back our childhood when exposed to certain aromas. **38** As an example, whenever someone smells freshly cut grass, they might be immediately taken back to the good old days at their grandparents' home.

Another reason why smell may be important to humans is that we can often detect emotions of a person due to their smell. This may subconsciously affect how we react to people, and how we treat them when they are perhaps irritable or if they suffer depression. **39** There is ongoing research into whether we can detect emotions in a person just by smell. The results should be very interesting.

Those who have a strongly developed sense of smell may have career opportunities open to them. Many jobs require a sense of smell, such as coffee-roasters. Those who can tell the subtle

36 此题定位词为 dangerous，原文说由于有些气味被掩盖了，如今人类往往无法确定气味的来源，这可能会使我们自己受到伤害，pinpoint 和 detect 对应，exposing ourselves to harm 与 dangerous 对应，故填 source。

37 此题定位词为 Other senses，原文说我们的味觉、触觉、视觉和听觉并不总是准确的，鼻子可以帮助我们更好地体验周围的世界，"senses of taste, touch, sight and hearing" 与 Other senses 对应，故填 accurate。

38 此题定位词为 recalling experiences，原文说当我们置身于特定的香味中时，我们都有过一次或多次回忆童年时光的经历，experienced flashbacks 与 recalling experience 对应，故填 childhood。

39 此题定位词为 depressed，需要注意答案与 depressed 为并列关系，原文说可能会在潜意识里影响我们对他人的反应，以及影响我们在他人可能易怒或抑郁时如何对待他们，故填 irritable。

40 此题定位词为 sellers，在听到 coffee roasters 后要注意答案即将出现，原文说那些能分辨出香料细微差别的人，就能成为这些商品的优秀销售人员。salespeople 和 sellers 为同义替换，故填 spices。

differences in spices, for example, could make good salespeople for stores selling these goods. ④⓪

So we can see, rather than being a tool merely for gaining a little more enjoyment out of life, the sense of smell is also a useful one, even vital.

Reading

Passage 1 Reading Keys, Questions 1 – 13	1	C	6	B	10	hormonal standards
	2	B	7	C	11	emotional
	3	D	8	B	12	resilience
	4	A	9	psychological injury	13	procrastination
	5	C				

■ 思路解析

Questions 1 – 5 ※题目类型：人名配对题

1 题目陈述为"应对机制会根据个人情况变化"，重点词为 individual's condition，首先在原文中划出题目中的人名，逐一对他们的观点进行分析。发现 F 段中 Jan Elsner 提出没有一种方法是适用于所有人的（She also suggests that there is no one-size-fits-all approach …），也就是说处理压力的方法应该根据个人情况决定，故选 C。

2 题目陈述为"花时间体验大自然能很好地缓解压力"，重点词为 Spending time in nature，需要在文中找与 nature 相关的内容，E 段 Vanessa Stoykov 说为了放松和整理她的思绪，只要有可能，她就会定期去山上旅行（To unwind and unclutter her mind, she makes regular trips to the mountains whenever possible.），makes regular trips to the mountains 即 spending time in nature，故选 B。

3 题目陈述为"人们需要对他们的生活节奏保持一个现实的期望"，重点词为 a realistic expectation，I 段 Gal Zauberman 和 John Lynch 认为在未来几周或一个月内，人们将会像他们现在一样忙碌（…a person will be simply as busy as he or she is right now），该段后半部分提到人们认为他们将来会有更多的空闲时间（we generally perceive that there will be more "surplus" time in the future than in the present），意味着人们对将来是否忙碌怀有不现实的期待，故选 D。

4 题目陈述为"为了应对压力，有时需要改变目前的安排"，重点词为 amend the current arrangements，D 段 Neil Plumridge 说为了应对压力，他会确定需要改变什么并采取行动

（identifies what needs to be changed and does something），be changed 与 amend 对应，故选 A。

5　题目陈述为"冥想是处理压力的一种常见方法"，重点词为 Meditation，G 段 Jan Elsner 说她的大多数企业客户依靠瑜伽和冥想来处理他们的不良压力（most of her corporate clients rely on yoga and meditation to...），并认为冥想和瑜伽都可以帮助重新设置大脑和身体的反应（Both meditation and yoga can help you reconfigure your mind and body's reaction），故选 C。

Questions 6 – 8　※题目类型：单选题

6　题目问员工不健康的主要原因是什么，C 段第一句"any person can understand that being too engrossed in work can ultimately take a toll on one's health and it is the main reason behind their health problems ... and mental well-being"，表达过于投入（too engrossed）工作最终会对健康产生负面影响，而且是其主要原因，与 B 表意一致，故选 B。

7　题目问作者提到积极心理学是想指出什么，G 段中提到积极心理学可以有效帮助人们在对抗压力的过程中建立对压力的适应力（effective in building one's resilience to deal with stress over time），而且"好的"压力还具有累积性，即通过正确的心态（right mentality）去处理压力可以提升我们对压力的应对能力，故选 C。

8　题目问 I 段中作者提出了什么观点，文中 I 段倒数第三句 view future time investments with relative clumsiness 指出人们相对笨拙地看待未来时间投入，I 段倒数第二句"there will be more 'surplus' time in the future than in the present"认为将来会比现在有更多的"剩余"时间，即人们对于将来的可利用时间量的评估缺乏客观性，故选 B。

Questions 9 – 13　※题目类型：摘要填空题

9　根据报告，由压力引起的什么可能占所有保险索赔成本的四分之一以上，填空处很可能为名词或名词短语，重点词为 over a quarter 和 insurance claims，需要在文中找数字类表达，C 段出现了 27%（over a quarter），且内容和 insurance claims 相关，故在该段找答案，根据"Another 2003-2004 report... claims for psychological injury accounted for 7% of all claims but their costs took up approximately 27%..."可知心理伤害索赔的成本约占所有保险索赔成本的 27%，故填 psychological injury。

10，11　题干问尽管科学家可以用什么来量化压力水平，但是这些测量只能帮助识别压力，而不能帮助我们识别或修复压力对精神或什么的影响，重点词为 stress levels 和 intellectual，

F 段最后一句 "While a psychologist may consider hormonal standards to… it is hard to gauge if the same level of stress is having an equal (emotional or cognitive) impact on…" 说虽然心理学家可能会根据激素水平来判断病人是否有压力，但很难判断相同的压力水平对任何两个人是否有相同的（情感或认知）影响，故第 10 题填 hormonal standards，gauge 和 determine 对应，intellectual 和 cognitive 对应，故第 11 题填 emotional。

12　题干问积极心理学家试图通过冥想等练习来帮助人们增强个人对压力的什么，填空处很可能填名词或名词短语，重点词为 Positive psychologists 和 meditation，G 段提到了 positive psychology 和 meditation，故在该段找答案，该段主要写冥想和瑜伽能够帮助人们有效应对压力，且能有效建立一个人应对压力的适应力，由 "…but is effective in building one's resilience to deal with stress over time" 可知填 resilience。

13　题干问 over-commitments 这个问题和什么有关联，由前面的 over-commitments 可定位至 H 段后半部分 "Over-commitments like these are stress incubators."，stress incubator 指压力孵化器，和题干 "After all, it is well known… stress increases（压力增加）" 相对应。Neil Plumridge 进一步用拖延症来解释，题干 be related to 对应原文 "He… with reference to procrastination…"，故填 procrastination。

译文 ｜ 工作场所的压力

A　如果花点时间去观察多忙碌才算是太忙，有人会认为这类似于错过享受一顿漫长的午餐；还有人可能会把它比作错过全部的午餐。对一些人来说，一个月不能请一次病假就是太忙了。然而，对另一群人来说，即使是在周末，白天黑夜都要保持专注是一种常态。值得注意的是，对于大多数高管来说，他们的工作节奏可能是非常繁忙的，甚至说是疯狂的。管理咨询公司科尔尼（AT Kearney）副总裁、亚太区电信主管尼尔·普拉姆里奇（Neil Plumridge）表示，他每周的工作时长在 45 小时至 80 小时之间波动。

B　普拉姆里奇使用三个标度来衡量他的工作量：它们是日程安排、睡眠和家庭。当他不得不连续地重新安排他的会见时，他就知道他有很多事情要做；以及当他连续三个晚上睡眠不足 6 小时的时候。他没有时间和家人在一起，他有个三岁的女儿，还有一个尚未出生且有望在 10 月份出世的女儿。每当普拉姆里奇错过一个结婚周年纪念日，就意味着事情出了问题。

C　不管过度忙碌这个概念是多么主观的事情，每个人都可以理解太过于专注于工作最终会对一个人的健康造成损害，而且它是造成健康问题的主要原因。明显的症状包括紊乱的睡眠，以及身体和精神状态下降。事实上，根据国家工人补偿协会数据，与其他工伤相比，压力导致职场中损失的时间最多。这种结果的代价相当昂贵，员工因压力而休假的平均时间为 16.6 周。联邦政府保险公司 Comcare 在 2003—2004 年度报告中称，心理伤害索赔占所有索赔的 7%，但其成本约占 27%，高于平均水平。

D 专家表示，不管是打高尔夫球、做按摩还是游泳，休息都不足以缓解压力；相反，人们有必要重新评估自己的工作量。例如，为了应对压力，尼尔·普拉姆里奇（Neil Plumridge）会找出需要改变的地方，并采取行动，比如为一项任务或项目留出额外的资源；或者延长期限，或者只是重新调整最后的期望，这可能需要很多天的时间。他的同事们帮了大忙，因为他们在商业困境中互相指点。有另外一个人来审视问题总是有益的。

E 但是压力的问题并不局限于大公司内。凡妮莎·斯托伊科夫（Vanessa Stoykov）经营着自己的广告和公关公司，她在服务金融和专业公司领域拥有丰富的经验，而她也是压力的受害者。她的品牌 Evolution media 增长如此之快，以至于在去年她刚生完第一个孩子后，品牌就登上了 BRW 增长最快企业 100 强榜单。在经营自己的生意时，常常会有这样的时刻：在同时应付各种各样的活动中，一个人的脑袋感觉像快要爆炸一样。为了放松和整理她的思绪，只要可能，她就会定期去山上旅行。这些短期的缓解对她是有帮助的，因为她的公司在不断地运转：雇佣新员工，培训他们，引导他们了解工作文化、客户，等等。

F 墨尔本专门从事高管培训的心理学家简·埃尔斯纳（Jan Elsner）提供了缓解这种压力状况的建议。她指出，高级管理人员和商业人士通常会在高要求的工作投入中成长。她还建议说，没有一种万能的方法，因为有些人可能在有急性压力时表现最好，而另一些人可能更喜欢一种持续的压力水平以获得最佳表现。虽然心理学家可能会考虑激素水平来判断病人是否有压力，但很难判断相同的压力水平对任何两个人或者他们的经历是否有同等的（情感的或认知的）影响。

G 埃尔斯纳的实践围绕着一种被称为积极心理学的思想流派，根据这种思想流派，对一项事业感到积极、投入、有挑战性或有贡献性不会减少一个人的压力，但可以在一段时间内有效地建立一个人应对压力的韧性。因此，好的压力带来的感觉是以勇气和意愿面对这一切，好压力与不良压力同样具有积累性。她还透露，她的大多数企业客户依靠瑜伽和冥想来控制他们的不良压力。埃尔斯纳还提到了一项研究，该研究得出的结论是，冥想能够改变大脑的生物化学结构，重新连接大脑和身体，从而对压力做出不同的反应。冥想和瑜伽都可以帮助你重新配置你的思想和身体的反应，如果人们掌握了它，就能完全控制压力。

H 回到尼尔·普拉姆里奇，他断定我们不切实际的目标设置会使我们陷入压力。例如，当一个人意识到他一天只可以完成一个任务的时候，却承诺一个客户明天他将交付任务 A，然后承诺另一个客户明天将交付任务 B，而他也为了兑现他的话使自己承受极端压力。

事实上，他可以很容易地告诉其中一个客户给他更多的时间。像这样的过度承诺是压力孵化器。普拉姆里奇进一步以拖延症来解释这一现象——工作扩张到填满所有可用的时间。有研究表明，许多人可能天生就会这么做。

发表在《实验心理学杂志》2月版上的另一项研究发现，我们大多数人倾向于认为我们将来不会比现在忙碌。不过，该报告的作者、北卡罗来纳大学（University of North Carolina）的盖尔·扎伯曼（Gal Zauberman）教授和杜克大学（Duke University）的约翰·林奇（John Lynch）教授认为，这是一种谬误。他们明确表示，平均而言，一个人在未来几周或一个月内，将会像现在一样忙碌。但在日常生活中，事情就有点不同了。很多人过早地对一些任务做出承诺，而如果他们必须立即着手这些任务的话，他们则会避免这样做。换句话说，这意味着人们通常相对笨拙地看待未来时间投入。有趣的是，我们普遍认为未来的"剩余"时间会比现在更多。虽然这是一个值得思考的问题，但研究人员认为，造成压力的一个主要原因是，我们低估了完成一项预期任务所需的时间，并且未能有效地衡量我们未来的时间竞争。

Passage 2

Reading Keys,
Questions 14 –27

14	Elephantidae	19	Pleistocene epoch	23	C
15	gestation	20	geographic range	24	B
16	universal consensus	21	A	25	C
17	archaeological records	22	B	26	B
18	empirical			27	A

思路解析

Questions 14 –20　※题目类型：摘要填空题

14　题干问作为什么的一员，猛犸象与现代大象关系密切，此处为介绍性内容，在A段开头寻找答案，重点词为 modern elephants，由 "These species belonged to the Elephantidae family... the current elephant species and their antecedents." 可知猛犸象属于象科，modern elephants 和 current elephant species 为同义替换关系，故填 Elephantidae。

Test 4

15 题干问它们体型庞大，高度社会化，并且有很长的什么期，重点词为 large、social 和 their young，A 段第三句提到猛犸象体型大的特点（mammoths had a reputation for being huge），最后一句提到猛犸象群体存在社会结构（These mammoth species almost certainly had social structures），可猜测答案很可能在 A 段中间部分，由 mammoths most likely had twenty-two months of gestation before culminating in the birth of one calf 可知在小象出生前，猛犸象可能有 22 个月的妊娠期，其中 calf 即 their young，twenty-two months 和 long periods 对应，故填 gestation。

16 题干说加州大学的一名研究人员认为，人类的猎杀是猛犸象灭绝的原因，但是这一观点并没有什么，重点词为 A researcher from the University of California，B 段倒数第二句提到了加州大学的 John Alroy，与 A researcher from the University of California 对应，需要在后文中找答案，C 段主要说 Alroy 的假设，D 段第一句 "The assessment by Alroy does not have universal consensus though." 说 Alroy 的观点并没有得到普遍认同，故填 universal consensus。

17 题干问什么没有提供人类杀死猛犸象的证据，根据 MacPhee 在 D 段中找答案，该段第三句 "Ross MacPhee, a mammologist... archaeological records that only contain a handful of stone tools embedded in the bones of mammoths..." 说 Ross MacPhee 指出考古记录只包含少量的证据，不足以证明人类杀死了猛犸象，故填 archaeological records。

18 题干说另一种观点认为疾病可能导致了猛犸象的死亡，但是没有什么证据来支持这一观点，填空处很可能填名词或名词短语，重点词为 disease，E 段提到 MacPhee 认为是致命的疾病导致了猛犸象的灭亡（The recurrent lethal disease outbreaks would quickly lead to extinction.），但是他没有任何经验证据来支持他的假设（MacPhee does not present any empirical evidence to support his hypothesis.），故填 empirical。

19 题干说一位古生物学家指出什么时代可能是导致猛犸象灭绝的原因，重点词为 A paleontologist 和 era，根据顺序原则定位到 F 段，该段第三句 "Pleistocene epoch era was characterised by significant climatic instability as Russell Graham, a paleontologist, explains." 说 Russell Graham 认为更新世时期气候不稳定是一个原因，故填 Pleistocene epoch。

20 题干说大型动物群可能无法适应变化的环境，而这种变化减少了他们的什么。重点词为 megafauna、changing environment、reduced。由 F 段 "However, the intensifying harsh

environment may have been too much for megafauna and caused their geographic range to diminish." 可知过于恶劣的环境使得大型动物吃不消，同时导致他们的地理分布范围减少。have been too much for 对应题干 may not have been able to adapt，reduced 是 diminish 的同义替换，故填 geographic range。

Questions 21–27 ※题目类型：人名配对题

21 题目说可以通过测量人类猎杀的速率和人口的稳定增长来计算灭绝速度，重点词为 hunting 和 population，需要在文中找与人类相关的内容，C 段提到了人类捕杀哺乳动物，且有相关数字，故定位在该段，该段前半部分主要讲根据人口数量和其增长速度，可以计算出人类每年捕杀的哺乳动物的数量以及动物种群的灭绝速度（Assuming there were 100 human beings at the beginning with a population growth of 2% per year，Alroy found that... within 1,000 years.），这一假设是 Alroy 提出的，故选 A。

22 题目说应该分析已经灭绝的哺乳动物的尸体来寻找疾病的迹象，重点词为 analyse the bodies 和 disease，E 段提到 MacPhee 认为是致命的疾病导致了猛犸象的灭亡，而且他认为对猛犸象的 DNA 和组织分析能帮助发现致命的微生物（MacPhee is confident that DNA and tissue analyses... reveal the deadly microbes.），DNA and tissue analyses 与 analyse the bodies 对应，deadly microbes 和 disease 对应，故选 B。

23 题目说有些物种可以在更具挑战性的环境中茁壮成长，重点词为 more challenging environments，F 段提到 Russell Graham 认为气候环境对一些物种的生存产生了影响，一些动物能在恶劣的环境下抓住机会并茁壮成长，但一些巨型动物的数量却会减少（Some animals seized the opportunities and flourished... hash environment may have been too much for megafauna and caused their geographic range to diminish.），harsh environment 和 more challenging environments 对应，故选 C。

24 题目说如果猛犸象被大范围猎杀，我们将会在它们的遗骸附近看到石器，重点词为 stone tools 和 mammoth remains，D 段 MacPhee 发现在猛犸象的骨头中有一些石器（Ross MacPhee, a mammologist... a handful of stone tools embedded in the bones of mammoths...），the bones of mammoths 和 mammoth remains 对应，故选 B。

25 题目说不管有没有人类活动，猛犸象注定要灭绝，F 段最后两句"...can be traced to human hunters in the period of extreme cold, the Ice Age. However, Graham believes that changing climate scenarios could predict with accuracy that these species would still become extinct eventually.", Graham 认为变化的气候可以准确预测猛犸象最终仍然会灭绝（不管有没有人类活动的影响），故选 C。

26 题目说人类可能带来了可以杀死猛犸象的寄生虫，重点词为 parasites，E 段第二句"His suggestion is that people likely initiated very lethal diseases, probably through parasites or the dogs…"说 MacPhee 认为人类可能通过寄生虫或狗引发致命的疾病导致猛犸象的死亡，故选 B。

27 题目说猛犸象因为其养育后代的方式而变得脆弱，重点词为 vulnerable 和 the way they raised their young，C 段最后一句"In particular, large mammals are susceptible to pressure because… their offspring need protracted care."表明猛犸象（大型哺乳动物）因为其妊娠期长，且它们的后代需要更长时间的照顾，所以容易受到影响，susceptible 和 vulnerable 为同义替换关系，这一观点由 Alroy 提出，故选 A。

■ 译文 | 猛犸象灭绝

A 猛犸象以长而弯曲的象牙为特征，而北部品种以长毛覆盖为特征。这些物种属于象科，而象科也包括当前大象品种的两类及其祖先。和它们的近亲相似，猛犸象以体型庞大著称。这些物种中最大的一种，肩部高度可达 4 米，重达 8 吨。体型异常巨大的雄性猛犸象体重可达 12 吨以上。然而，在大多数情况下，猛犸象的体型只有现在的亚洲象那么大。在大约六个月大的时候，一副小象牙第一次出现，后来被一副持久的象牙所取代。新长出的象牙大约每年生长一到六英寸。对当前大象物种的研究表明，猛犸象很可能需要 22 个月的妊娠期生产一头小象。几乎可以肯定的是，这些猛犸象的社会结构与现在的亚洲象和非洲象很相似，它们都是由雌性象群和母象首领组成，而雄性象在成年后则过着独居生活或形成松散的群体。

B 很难想象，如今处于现代化、城市化和汽车的时代的北美曾经是猛犸象、奶牛般大小的地懒、熊一般大小的海狸、骆驼以及其他猛兽的家园。大约 11000 年前，这些巨大的哺乳动物灭绝了，它们总共大约 70 个物种。这些物种灭绝的时间段差不多与人类来到美洲大陆和引发了灭绝理论的剧烈气候变化因素相一致。尽管经过多年的科学研究，物种灭绝确切的原因仍不清楚。最近的一些发现支持了一种有争议的假设，即人类的猎杀导致了巨型动物的灭绝。过度捕杀模型产生于 20 世纪 60 年代，当时保罗·S·马丁（Paul S. Martin）在亚利桑那大学（Arizona University）提出了这个议题。从那时起，该模型的批评者提出，没有证据支持早期美洲人将动物猎杀到灭绝的程度。然而，加利福尼亚大学的古生态学家约翰·阿尔罗伊（John Alroy）在脊椎动物古生物学年度会议上认为，狩猎导致的物种灭绝是可信的且不可避免的。通过计算机模拟，他证明了即使是普通的捕猎量也足以消灭这些动物。

C 假设一开始有100个人，人口以每年2%的速度增长，阿尔罗伊发现一个50人的群体每年可以杀死15到20只哺乳动物，所以人类可以在1000年内消灭所有的动物种群。特别是大型哺乳动物备受（被捕猎灭绝的）压力，因为与小型哺乳动物相比，它们的妊娠期更长，它们的后代需要更长时间的照顾。

D 不过，阿尔罗伊的看法并没有获得普遍同意。首先，这个结果在一定程度上取决于灭绝动物的估计数量，而这种估计是不可靠的。罗斯·麦卡菲（Ross MacPhee）是来自纽约自然历史博物馆的哺乳动物学家，他尖锐批判了阿尔罗伊的发现，他通过调用相关的考古记录，发现其中只包含少量的石器嵌在猛犸象的骨骼上，且没有一个（骨骼）是公认的来自其他巨型动物的尸体。这与狩猎导致哺乳动物灭绝的预期相反。某些动物种类的活动范围很广，其中一个例子就是生活在北至育空（Yukon）和南至墨西哥的巨大的地懒。这一范围本身就不太可能让这个物种被屠杀到灭绝的程度。

E 麦卡菲的论点是，人类最有可能对猛犸象和其他同期物种的灭绝负有责任，尽管人类没有直接导致这些物种的灭绝。麦卡菲的意见是，人们可能引发了非常致命的疾病，通过寄生虫或狗广泛传播到新生物圈中免疫力低下的物种中。他的理论与保罗·马丁的过度捕杀模型相似，即大型哺乳动物的数量将很难恢复。反复发生的致命疾病暴发很快导致灭绝。麦卡菲没有提供任何实验证据来支持他的假设，此外，也很难找到证据，因为致命的疾病会很快杀死这些动物，而不会在骨头上留下痕迹。然而，麦卡菲相信，通过对最后的猛犸象种群的 DNA 和组织分析，可以发现致命的微生物。

F 另一个关于北美猛犸象灭绝原因的提议与人类无关。新提议的支持者将灭绝归咎于天气。正如古生物学家拉塞尔·格雷厄姆（Russell Graham）所解释的那样，更新世时期以显著的气候不稳定性为特征。恶劣的天气导致一些栖息地消失，一些形成群落的物种被迫分开。一些动物抓住了机会并茁壮成长，然而，日益加剧的严酷环境可能对巨型动物来说太难以承受了，导致了它们的地理范围缩小。这对那些需要更大空间才能生存的巨型动物来说意味着厄运。尽管有相当数量的种群在更新世幸存下来，但正如格雷厄姆所说，新仙女木时期（即长达 1300 年的气候强变冷时期）的出现对它们来说实在是太难以承受了。阿尔罗伊确信巨型生物的灭亡可以追究到极度寒冷的冰河时代的人类猎人。然而，格雷厄姆认为，不断变化的气候可以准确地预测到：这些物种最终还是会灭绝。

Passage 3

Reading Keys,
Questions 28 – 40

🔑

28	understand	
29	conveying	
30	involuntary	
31&32	*IN EITHER ORDER*	
	disgust fear	

33 E	38 B
34 B	39&40
35 H	*IN EITHER ORDER*
36 D	B D
37 F	

■ 思路解析

Questions 28 – 32 ※题目类型：摘要填空题

28 根据 It is not difficult to 可知填空处为动词，大意为如果仔细观察人们的面部表情，就不难……他们的情绪，section A 第二句 "… is easy for anyone paying attention to understand" 表明任何一个注意他人表情的人都很容易理解他人的情绪，not difficult 是 easy 的同义替换，watch carefully 是 pay attention 的同义替换，故填 understand。

29 根据 a method of 可知填空处为动词 ing 形式，大意为这是因为表情是一种向他人……情感的方式。section A 倒数第二句 "… and a way of conveying information" 中 a way of 和题目中 a method of 为同义替换关系，故填 conveying。

30 根据 they are usually 可知填空处很可能为形容词，大意为即使试图隐藏感受，面部表情仍然可能显示出真相，因为它们通常是……，section B 第一部分第二句 "Facial expressions are very much tied to emotion and are more often than not involuntary." 表明面部表情通常是不由自主的，后文接着举例，一个悲伤的人就算试图表现得很快乐，他的真实感受还是会通过面部表情流露出来，和题目意思相符，故填 involuntary。

31，32 题目大意为有些情绪比其他情绪更难分辨，例如，人们通常很难区分……和……，很明显 31 和 32 所填词为并列关系，section C 第一部分第一、二句 "Not all emotions are easy to understand… of disgust and fear are difficult to tell apart." 大意为并不是所有的情绪都容易解读，厌恶和恐惧就很难区分，tell apart 和 tell the difference 为同义替换，故填 disgust、fear。

Questions 33–38　※题目类型：段落细节配对题

33　题干意思为"两个关于人类面部可表达的情感范围理论的对立"，重点词为 contradiction、range of emotions。由 section E 中 "Charles Darwin… thought at the time that a human face could show just a few emotions… Duchenne who argued… at least 60 different emotions." 可知双方对人类面部可以表达多少种情感有不同的看法，数量 60 对应题干中的 the range of emotions，且原文中 "This theory contradicted…" 帮助定位 section E，故选 E。

34　题干意思为"对不由自主的面部表情会导致尴尬的解释"，重点词为 involuntary 和 embarrassment，section B 第二部分第一、二两句 "This nature of facial expressions… lead to embarrassing social situations." 表明不由自主的面部表情有时会导致令人尴尬的社交情况，接着对这一观点进行了举例说明（For example…），embarrassment 和 embarrassing 为同义替换，故选 B。

35　题干意思为"提及社会因素导致表达情感产生的文化差异"，重点词为 social factors、cultural difference。section H 最后一部分 "Findings on contempt… the expressions of contempt and other social emotions vary across cultures"，有初步证据表明鄙视和其他带有社会成分的情感在不同文化中表达方式不同，与题干意思相符，故选 H。

36　题干意思为"仅依靠单一的身体暗示可能错误判断一个人的情绪的原因"，重点词为 a single physical cue 和 wrong，section D 前半部分主要说虽然能通过快速眨眼这一特点来判断人们是否说谎，但也有说谎者并不表现出快速眨眼的特征，然后接着总结 "As such, non-verbal traits… focusing on only one cue is reckless."，也就是说只关注一个线索来进行判断是鲁莽的，其中 only one 和 a single 对应，reckless 和 wrong 对应，故选 D。

37　题干意思为"提及一个实验说明地理位置对于人们理解面部表情没有影响的具体例子"，关键词 geographical location、facial expressions。section F 第二部分第一句 "Isolated people from the South Fore region of New Guinea… identify the accurate facial expressions at the same rate as the non-isolated control group"，该试验证明偏远地区（新几内亚的 South Fore 地区）和非偏远地区的人可以相同的速度准确识别出面部表情，即在这个具体试验（事例）中，地理位置（偏远与否）并未使参与试验的人对面部表情的理解产生差异，故选 F。

38　题干意思为"一个关于面部表情的常见的错误假设"，重点词为 a common mistaken assumption，section B 第一部分第一句 "A major misconception when discussing facial expressions is to assume that they are voluntary. " 说当人们讨论面部表情时，他们对面部表情的一个主要的误解就是认为这些表情是自发的。a major misconception 和 a common mistaken assumption 对应，故选 B。

Questions 39 – 40 ※题目类型：多选题

39，40 题目问以下哪两个观点出现在埃克曼在新几内亚的研究中，根据 Ekman's studies in New Guinea 定位到 section F 和 section G，由 section F " In the 1960s, studies by scientist Paul Ekman supported Darwin's stance to a large degree. " 可知 Ekman 的研究在很大程度上支持了达尔文的立场，即他的研究认为达尔文的看法在很大程度上是正确的，故选 B；由 section G " Ekman had found that the participants across the five geographically dispersed locations had similar facial expressions for emotions. " 可知 Ekman 发现在五个分散的地理位置上的参与者对于情绪都有相似的面部表情，即许多情感的表达在不同的文化中似乎是相同的，similar 和 appears to be the same 对应，故选 D。

▌ 译文 │ 面部表情

A 面部表情最好被定义为面部肌肉的一个或多个动作或位置。它通常可以用来表达一个人的情绪状态，而且对任何人来说，只要注意了别人的面部表情就很容易理解。著名作家查尔斯·狄更斯曾说过："一个人的面部表情通常有助于传达他的思想，或相当于他的言语。"面部表情也是一种非语言交流的形式，是传递信息的一种方式。这并不是人类所独有的，因为许多动物的面部表情都很容易理解。

B 当讨论面部表情时，人们对它的一个主要的误解就是认为它们是自发的。面部表情与情绪密切相关，而且往往是不由自主的。一个悲伤的人可能会试图竭力传达相反的信息，并向外部世界宣告他们实际上是快乐的。但他们最终可能会不由自主地流露出自己的真实感受，尽管他们试图用完全相反的方式来表达自己的感受。

   面部表情的这一性质并不只体现在一个人对自己的感觉上。有时它会导致令人尴尬的社交情景。例如，一个人可以通过一个简短的厌恶表情，不由自主地传达出他们觉得刚刚遇到的人没有吸引力的信息。他们可能想表现出一种不那么无礼的表情，但他们就是忍不住要表现出他们的真实感受。

C 并不是所有的情绪都容易理解。事实正好相反，因为厌恶和恐惧的感觉是很难区分的。原因很简单：脸部的活动范围很小，厌恶和恐惧之间的区别可以分解为面部特征相对应位置的极小差别。

有时候，一个人的脸可以表达一种中性的情绪——就像通常情况下，一切都很正常，没有压力时的情绪。然而，一个中性的面部表情的特点可能与一个有特定情绪的面部表情特点非常相似。一个人看着自己的新同事或朋友，可能会猜测他们很难过，但事实上他们并不难过，像这样的情况每天都在发生，而且经常发生。

D 一个人的眼睛也可以显示出他们在任何时候的感受。威廉·莎士比亚曾经说过，"眼睛是心灵的窗户"，这句话是有道理的。波士顿学院的教授乔·特切发现了眨眼和压力之间的关系。他解释说，快速眨眼与不愉快的感觉有关，尤其是在说谎者中能体现出来。

然而，这个理论的关键是这个人需要对撒谎感到内疚。从撒谎中获得快乐的人，比如精神病患者，不会表现出类似的快速眨眼的特征。因此，非语言特征和线索是多样化的，只关注一个线索是草率的。

扑克玩家中，专家级玩家以判断他人的面部特征而闻名。一个扑克新手如果在打牌时虚张声势，他很可能会在桌上放筹码时眨眼。专业的面部表情解读者会毫不犹豫地利用他的优势来赢一手。同样，对于一个扑克新手来说，仅仅需要一纳秒的时间，他就可以直观地告诉周围人他手里拿着的是好牌。扑克高手会立即收手，避免落入潜在的陷阱。

E 查尔斯·达尔文在《人与动物的情感表达》一书中指出，各个年龄段的人和动物都是通过类似的行为来表达情感的。他还认为，一个人的脸只可以表现出一些情绪。这一理论与法国医生 Guillaume-Benjamin-Amand Duchenne 的观点相矛盾，他认为人类至少可以表达 60 种不同的情绪。

F 在 20 世纪 60 年代，科学家保罗·埃克曼的研究在很大程度上支持了达尔文的立场。埃克曼对来自新几内亚一个非常偏远的地区的成年人和儿童进行了评估，看看他们的反应是否与生活在不那么偏远的地区的人的反应有什么不同。参与者听一个描述一种特定情绪的故事，然后给他们看两到三张面部表情的图片。他们必须将面部表情与整个故事的主题进行匹配。

与来自不那么偏远的地区的人们进行对照，来自偏远的新几内亚南佛尔地区的人们能够以相同的速度识别出准确的面部表情。这项研究也发现恐惧和惊讶的情绪总是被识别错误。

G 选择新几内亚的原因是基于阿根廷、巴西、智利、日本和美国的人们对类似测试的早期反馈。埃克曼发现，在五个分散的地理位置上的参与者对于情绪都有着相似的面部表情。

他质疑自己的研究，并问道："如果生活在这五种文化里的人们都是看着同样的电影和电视节目长大的呢？难道他们一致同意的原因是他们是从同一个地方学来的这些表达方式的吗？还是因为他们有相似的背景和经历？比如，是从媒体或演员那里学到的？"

探索新几内亚的高地，在那里，古老的传统和生活方式是最重要的，在那里的调查应该能消除对他的发现的疑虑。新几内亚人几乎肯定不会和美国人看同样的电影长大。他的研究经受住了时间的考验，因为越来越多的现代方法也得出了同样的结论。

H 最后，某些情绪的表达也被普遍接受。其中包括愤怒、厌恶、快乐、悲伤和惊讶。特别值得注意的是，这些情绪都没有明确的社会成分，比如羞耻感或骄傲感。

关于轻蔑（具有社会成分）这一情绪的研究结果就不那么清楚了。有一些初步的证据表明，轻蔑和其他社会情绪的表达在不同的文化中是不同的。

Writing

Task 1

审　　题

地图显示 Ryemouth 村 1995 年至今的发展变化。

图表类型

地图

分析思路

（1）找不同：可从两图中的一个方向往其对角方向（如从东北方至西南方向）找两图的不同点，或者也可以根据图中的文字（如 farmland 和 golf course）来找不同点。如果根据文字内容不同来进行描述变化，可以按某一顺序来进行描述（如从上到下），例如可以先从左图位于上方的 farmland 描述到图片下方的 fishing port。

（2）找相同：找出所有不同处后，相同之处自然就清晰明了。如两图中的 cafe 和 hotel 没有发生变化。

参考写作结构

首　　　段：改述题目
综　述　段：总结两图中最明显的差异
主体段1/2：分段对比两张图片上方/下方的变化

参考范文[⊖]

The two maps illustrate the layout of a village named Ryemouth in 1995 and how it looks at present after upgrades that have taken place.

It is clear that the place has undergone extensive changes in that more residential buildings as well as public facilities have been established. However, this is at the expense of a large amount of open space and green land.

⊖ 范文中加色字为高分表达。

The most significant change occurs in the south of the village where a fishing port and a fish market near the sea have been demolished. In their place are now an array of apartments, opposite which are some restaurants. They replaced shops that once stood on the same spot. Nearby, a hotel and a cafe in the southeast corner have remained since 1995, with an addition of a car park beside the hotel. As for the northwestern part, the original housing area has been expanded southward along the main road leading to the seashore.

Another important difference between the layout in 1995 and today concerns the open area in the northeast. This area, which used to consist of massive farmland and a forest park, has been transformed into sites for playing golf and tennis respectively. The part that once was a forest park also contributed some space to the construction of the residential buildings nearby.

Overall: 7.5

 **Task 2**

审　题

有人认为减少通勤时间最好的方法是把市中心附近的公园和花园替换为上班族的公寓，而有的人不这么认为。讨论双方观点并给出自己的想法。

讨论对象

把市中心附近公园或花园替换为公寓楼是否是减少通勤时间最好的方法

写作观点选择

陈述双方观点后可赞同其中一方观点或双方观点，或是提出自己的新观点

写作论据准备

同意把市中心附近公园或花园替换为公寓楼

◇ 通勤时间减少 reduce commuting time
◇ 更好地利用土地资源 better use of land resources

不同意把市中心附近公园或花园替换为公寓楼

◇ 绿化面积变少，空气质量差 less green area, poor air quality
◇ 没有户外放松的空间 lack of outdoor places to relax

参考写作结构

首　段：转述题干信息 + 表明个人观点

主体段1：陈述观点1及其论据

主体段2：陈述观点2及其论据

末　　段：给出个人观点

参考范文

Long commuting time has become a serious concern among the public, especially those who live far away from city centres. While some believe that the best solution to this is to replace gardens and parks with residential buildings, I would argue that there are more effective measures to solve the problem.

Apparently, the travelling time from one's home to their workplace is determined by the distance and the traffic along the way. If one's home and workplace are both located in the city centre, it surely saves people from spending hours stuck in traffic during rush hours, since they can just walk or bike to their office. Therefore, having more apartments replace parks and gardens would seemingly prove an appropriate solution.

However, replacing recreation grounds with houses neglects the necessity of green space and the exorbitant housing price. Without public parks and gardens in the downtown, life can be monotonous for residents there; they would find little or no opportunity to get away from the hustle and bustle of city life, which can be detrimental to their well-being in the long run. Another problem is that not everyone can afford to buy or rent an apartment at the heart of a city's Central Business District, which means this solution is not feasible enough to be carried out.

In fact, in order to reduce the commuting time, there are better measures than building apartments in the city centres. One is to take advantage of the advanced telecommunication technologies by which those who live on the outskirts of the city can work from home. This will shed the number of hours wasted on commuting. Also, governments should improve the efficiency of public transport systems so that more commuters would be able to stop driving cars to work. Consequently, the traffic congestion **could be alleviated and commuting time shortened.**

In conclusion, having more apartments at the cost of fewer parks and gardens in urban centres is not a practical way to reduce travelling time; instead, alternative approaches ranging from **telecommuting** to **encouraging the use of public transport should be considered.**

Overall：7.5

○ 范文中加色字为高分表达。

Speaking

Part 1 | Number

What is your favourite number?

Unlucky for some yet lucky for me, my favourite number is 13 and it has stuck with me all my life. Interestingly, my house number includes 13, and so does my mobile number. So, even though the world may stay divided on 13, I believe it has been around me as a token from my guardian angel.

高分表达

◇ stick with 伴随

◇ stay divided on 对……有分歧

◇ token /'təʊkən/ *n.* 标志

◇ guardian angel 守护天使

Are you good at remembering phone numbers?

Unfortunately, I have always had an extremely hard time remembering phone numbers. Whenever I hear someone's phone number, it goes in one ear and out the other. It seems to me that I have the memory of a goldfish when I try to reel off telephone numbers. However, I have always admired people who can rattle them off with relative ease.

高分表达

◇ go in one ear and out the other 左耳 进右耳出

◇ have the memory of a goldfish 记忆力 不好

◇ reel off 一口气说

◇ rattle off 飞快说出

◇ with relative ease 相对轻松地

Do you usually use numbers?

I do. Numbers play an extremely important part in my everyday life. They are necessary when I make calculations or plan my spending budget. I mainly rely on my smartphone when I use numbers. It is exceptionally useful if I want to avoid cramming my brain with numerical data.

高分表达

- play an extremely important part 起到很重要的作用
- make calculations 计算
- plan one's spending budget 计划某人的支出预算
- rely on 依赖
- exceptionally /ɪkˈsepʃənəli/ *ad.* 格外地
- cram one's brain with 把……塞进头脑

Are you good at maths?

Maths has always given me a hard time. To be honest, even though I know that maths skills are increasingly important, I am not a maths person. I have no clue how to study it and when I try to, I always feel like a lost ball in the high weeds. However, being on bad terms with math made me realise how much I admire people who excel at it.

高分表达

- give someone a hard time 让某人吃苦头
- to be honest 说实话
- increasingly important 越来越重要
- a maths person 擅长数学的人
- have no clue 毫无头绪
- feel like a lost ball in the high weeds 感到不知所措
- be on bad terms with 和……关系不好
- excel at 擅长

Part 2

Describe a crowded place you went to.

You should say:

 when you went there

 who you went there with

 why you went there

and how you felt about it.

You will have to talk about the topic for one to two minutes. You have one minute to think about what you are going to say. You can make some notes to help you if you wish.

I made a promise to myself that one day I would visit the Museum of Modern Art in New York, which I finally did two years ago when I went to America.

My family decided to go on a trip to New York and as we are all passionate art lovers, the Museum of Modern Art was a must-see place. It is one of the largest, most influential and overcrowded museums. On the day we visited it, it was full to capacity with excited crowds thronging around to admire the splendor of the museum. The lively buzz of excitement created a convivial atmosphere prevailing every corner of the building.

My primary reason to visit this museum was amazing Salvador Dali and his work *The Persistence of Memory*. His surrealist paintings have always been a source of fascination for me because I believe that they are a powerful incarnation of his brilliant mind and imagination. People are flocking to his paintings to ponder his priceless artwork.

The splendor of the museum was mesmerising, and I felt enormously proud of myself and privileged to stand there with other visitors, soaking up every minute of my visit. Observing Dali's paintings opened doors to a world of fantasy where the harsh realities of everyday life do not exist. We all feasted our eyes on the paintings, and it was truly a joy to behold. Even though it was difficult to battle my way through other art lovers in the crowd, witnessing Dali's impressive work was such an invaluable experience that made me feel on top of the world.

高分表达

- ◇ passionate art lovers 充满激情的艺术爱好者
- ◇ must-see /'mʌst'siː/ a. 必看的
- ◇ influential /ˌɪnfluˈenʃl/ a. 有影响的
- ◇ throng /θrɒŋ/ v. 拥塞
- ◇ splendor /'splendə/ n. 光彩
- ◇ buzz of excitement 兴奋的喧闹声
- ◇ a convivial atmosphere 欢乐的气氛
- ◇ prevail /prɪˈveɪl/ v. 弥漫
- ◇ primary /'praɪməri/ a. 主要的
- ◇ surrealist paintings 超现实主义画作
- ◇ a source of fascination 令人着迷的事物
- ◇ powerful incarnation 强有力的化身

- ◇ flock /flɒk/ v. 聚集
- ◇ ponder /'pɒndə(r)/ v. 仔细思考
- ◇ priceless /'praɪsləs/ a. 无价的
- ◇ mesmerising /'mezməraɪzɪŋ/ a. 有吸引力的
- ◇ enormously /ɪˈnɔːməsli/ ad. 非常地
- ◇ privileged /'prɪvəlɪdʒd/ a. 幸运的
- ◇ soak up 吸收
- ◇ a world of fantasy 梦幻世界
- ◇ harsh /hɑː(r)ʃ/ a. 残酷的
- ◇ feast one's eyes 一饱眼福
- ◇ a joy to behold 十分悦目
- ◇ feel on top of the world 觉得棒极了

Part 3

Do people like to go to crowded places? Why?

In my opinion, people generally dislike crowded places because it is never easy to cope with battling your way through a crowd. Places swarming with people do not usually make an enjoyable experience. A feeling of frustration and anxiety may overwhelm people when they are packed like sardines. Furthermore, fighting through the crowds can be particularly stressful for claustrophobic people. On the other hand, sometimes crowded places are unavoidable if you want to enjoy a great concert or performance.

高分表达

◇ cope with 应对
◇ swarming with people 挤满了人
◇ feeling of frustration 懊恼的感觉
◇ anxiety /æŋˈzaɪəti/ n. 焦虑
◇ overwhelm /ˌəʊvəˈwelm/ v. 使不知所措
◇ be packed like sardines 挤得像沙丁鱼

◇ fight through 努力战胜
◇ claustrophobic /klɔːstrəˈfəʊbɪk/ a. 患幽闭恐怖症的
◇ unavoidable /ˌʌnəˈvɔɪdəb(ə)l/ a. 不可避免的

How can the problem of traffic congestion be solved?

From my standpoint, traffic congestion is an inescapable condition in large and growing metropolitan areas. It needs an effective and long-term solution which would ease frustration amongst traffic participants. One way to reduce traffic congestion is to build enough road capacity to handle people who travel at the same time. Moreover, existing road traffic laws should be enforced as it would prevent illegal parking or traffic jams in peak hours. This problem can also be addressed by adding more traffic lights or improving public transport, which would encourage more people to use it.

高分表达

◇ from one's standpoint 从某人的角度来看
◇ inescapable /ˌɪnɪˈskeɪpəbl/ a. 不可避免的
◇ growing metropolitan areas 日益增长的大城市
◇ ease frustration 缓解沮丧

◇ reduce traffic congestion 减少交通拥堵
◇ road capacity 道路通行能力
◇ enforce /ɪnˈfɔː(r)s/ v. 强制执行
◇ peak hours 高峰时间
◇ be addressed 被解决

Why do people like to live in big cities even though there are severe traffic jams?

The main reason why people choose to live in big cities despite severe traffic jams is that large urban areas are more dynamic, and they offer a variety of cultures. Also, metropolitan areas offer better career advancement, which means that people will easily find a position relevant to their education. Another sound reason is easier access to healthcare in an emergency. Furthermore, all amenities are usually within reach and people are extremely likely to find interesting places that appeal to them.

高分表达

◇ severe traffic jams 严重的交通堵塞

◇ dynamic /daɪˈnæmɪk/ a. 充满活力的

◇ career advancement 职业发展

◇ a position relevant to one's education
与某人的教育相关的职位

◇ sound reason 合理的原因

◇ easier access to 更容易获得

◇ within reach 伸手可及的

◇ appeal to 吸引

What public facilities does your city have?

My city offers excellent public facilities which ensure the well-being of all citizens. First of all, there are various excellent schools and universities where people can study for free and overcome social and economic barriers. Also, medical facilities ensure the development of modern medical solutions to different diseases, which has a significant impact on the quality of life. Moreover, our public transportation is efficient and reliable, providing us with an excellent connection between different regions of the country and forming a sustainable and healthy community.

高分表达

◇ ensure the well-being 确保安康

◇ overcome social and economic barriers
克服社会和经济障碍

◇ have a significant impact on 对……有
重大影响

◇ efficient and reliable 高效可靠的

◇ sustainable /səˈsteɪnəbl/ a. 可持续的

IELTS Listening Answer Sheet

Candidate Name

Candidate No.

Centre No.

Test Date

Day　　Month　　Year

Listening　Listening　Listening　Listening　Listening　Listening　Listening

Marker use only

1		✓ ✗
2		✓ ✗
3		✓ ✗
4		✓ ✗
5		✓ ✗
6		✓ ✗
7		✓ ✗
8		✓ ✗
9		✓ ✗
10		✓ ✗
11		✓ ✗
12		✓ ✗
13		✓ ✗
14		✓ ✗
15		✓ ✗
16		✓ ✗
17		✓ ✗
18		✓ ✗
19		✓ ✗
20		✓ ✗

Marker use only

21		✓ ✗
22		✓ ✗
23		✓ ✗
24		✓ ✗
25		✓ ✗
26		✓ ✗
27		✓ ✗
28		✓ ✗
29		✓ ✗
30		✓ ✗
31		✓ ✗
32		✓ ✗
33		✓ ✗
34		✓ ✗
35		✓ ✗
36		✓ ✗
37		✓ ✗
38		✓ ✗
39		✓ ✗
40		✓ ✗

Marker 2 Signature:

Marker 1 Signature:

Listening Total:

IELTS Reading Answer Sheet

Candidate Name

Candidate No.

Centre No.

Test Module ☐ Academic ☐ General Training

Test Date Day [ ] Month [ ] Year [ ]

Reading Reading Reading Reading Reading Reading Reading

Marker use only

1		1 ✓ ✗
2		2 ✓ ✗
3		3 ✓ ✗
4		4 ✓ ✗
5		5 ✓ ✗
6		6 ✓ ✗
7		7 ✓ ✗
8		8 ✓ ✗
9		9 ✓ ✗
10		10 ✓ ✗
11		11 ✓ ✗
12		12 ✓ ✗
13		13 ✓ ✗
14		14 ✓ ✗
15		15 ✓ ✗
16		16 ✓ ✗
17		17 ✓ ✗
18		18 ✓ ✗
19		19 ✓ ✗
20		20 ✓ ✗

Marker use only

21		21 ✓ ✗
22		22 ✓ ✗
23		23 ✓ ✗
24		24 ✓ ✗
25		25 ✓ ✗
26		26 ✓ ✗
27		27 ✓ ✗
28		28 ✓ ✗
29		29 ✓ ✗
30		30 ✓ ✗
31		31 ✓ ✗
32		32 ✓ ✗
33		33 ✓ ✗
34		34 ✓ ✗
35		35 ✓ ✗
36		36 ✓ ✗
37		37 ✓ ✗
38		38 ✓ ✗
39		39 ✓ ✗
40		40 ✓ ✗

Marker 2 Signature:

Marker 1 Signature:

Reading Total:

IELTS Writing Answer Sheet – TASK 1

Candidate Name

Candidate No.

Centre No.

Test Module ☐ Academic ☐ General Training

Test Date Day Month Year

If you need more space to write your answer, use an additional sheet and write in the space provided to indicate how many sheets you are using: Sheet of

Writing Task 1   Writing Task 1   Writing Task 1   Writing Task 1

Do not write below this line

Do not write in this area. Please continue your answer on the other side of this sheet.

247

IELTS Writing Answer Sheet – TASK 2

Candidate
Name

Candidate
No.

Centre
No.

Test
Module   ☐ Academic   ☐ General Training

Test Date

Day   Month   Year

If you need more space to write your answer, use an additional sheet and write in the space provided to indicate how many sheets you are using: Sheet   of

Writing Task 2   Writing Task 2   Writing Task 2   Writing Task 2

Do not write below this line

Do not write in this area. Please continue your answer on the other side of this sheet.